More Basic Chess Openings

Gábor Kállai

First published in 1997 by Gloucester Publishers plc, (formerly Everyman Publishers plc), Northburgh House, 10 Northburgh Street, London, EC1V 0AT

Reprinted 2003

British Library Cataloguing-in-Publication Data
A catalogue record for this book is available from the British Library.

ISBN 1 85744 206 7

To Marika, Oli, Beni and Lili

Distributed in North America by The Globe Pequot Press, P.O Box 480, 246 Goose Lane, Guilford, CT 06437-0480.

All other sales enquiries should be directed to Gloucester Publishers plc, Northburgh House, 10 Northburgh Street, London, EC1V 0AT
tel: 020 7253 7887 fax: 020 7379 4060
email: info@everymanchess.com
website: www.everymanchess.com

Advisor: János Szabolcsi
Translator: Zita Rajcsányi

Proofreading: Tim Wall and Alexander Meynell

Typeset by ChessSetter

Contents

Symbols

+	Check
±	Slight advantage to White
∓	Slight advantage to Black
±	Clear advantage to White
∓	Clear advantage to Black
+−	White wins
−+	Black wins
∞	Unclear position
??	Blunder
?	Weak move
?!	Dubious move
!?	Interesting move
!	Good move
!!	Outstanding move

Introduction

This is the second volume of a two-part series covering every chess opening.

It deals with the 'Closed Games', that is to say all openings which do not start with 1 e4.

If White prefers a long positional struggle, a strategic battle instead of a tactical one, often maintaining a slight advantage to the endgame then the 'Closed Games' are for him! On the other hand Black, if he is ready for active counterplay and is aware that his lack of one tempo is even less significant than in the blitzkrieg of Open Games... well, then he also has no reason to fear the Closed Games! Most often White opens with 1 d4 and follows up with 2 c4.

If Black decides to castle by developing his bishop via the f8-a3 diagonal then he can choose from the **Queen's Gambit, Queen's Indian, Bogo-Indian** or **Nimzo-Indian Defences**. If, however, he hopes to place his bishop on g7 then he has the **Grünfeld Indian, King's Indian, Modern Defence** and the Benoni at his disposal. For those who favour more offbeat setups, there are the **Dutch** and **Old Indian Defences** and various **Gambits**. If White wishes to avoid both 1 d4 and 1 e4, he can choose either the **English** (1 c4) or **Réti Opening** (1 ♘f3). Other first moves are seen only rarely but should still be studied from Black's perspective.

Queen's Gambit

1 d4 d5 2 c4

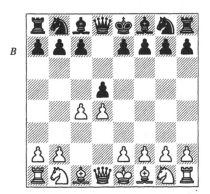

The move c2-c4 fits into the general rule of openings: first the pawns, then the knights. In this case after c2-c4 the knight will feel comfortable on c3. So whenever you see a chessboard with 1 d4 d5 on it remember that the c-pawn is an active character for both sides, and that a knight developed on c3 or c6 belongs behind the pawn!

In the diagram position Black has three good ways to answer: he can capture on c4 (**Queen's Gambit Accepted**), or protect his pawn on d5. This may be done by either ...e6 (**Classical Queen's Gambit**) or ...c6 (**Slav Defense**). Other variations are objectively weaker but by no means harmless! For these less common sub-variations see the section '**Albin and other lines**'.

Queen's Gambit Accepted

---

1 d4 d5 2 c4 dxc4

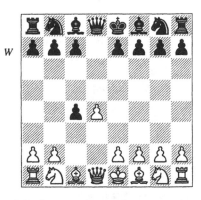

Black opts for a clear-cut situation in the centre and in the tensionless position that arises he plans to develop his pieces to their natural squares. A long-term prospect is to take on d4 after the pawn thrust ...c7-c5. Then White will then recapture with the pawn to maintain his initiative in a more or less even game.

3 ♘f3

A logical development, nipping ...e7-e5 in the bud. Other moves are:

a) 3 e3, when Black's best is 3...♘f6 4 ♗xc4 e6 5 ♘f3 c5 with transposition to the 3 ♘f3 lines.

b) 3 ♘c3 e5 4 d5 c6 5 e4 ♘f6 6 ♗g5 ♗b4 leads to sharp play, threatening 7...♕a5.

c) 3 e4!? e5 4 Nf3 Bb4+ 5 Bd2 Bxd2+ 6 Nbxd2 exd4 7 Bxc4 Nc6 8 0-0 Nf6 9 e5 Nd5 10 Nb3 0-0 11 Nbxd4 is even. 3 e4 can also be met by 3...Nf6 4 e5 Nd5 5 Bxc4 Nb6 6 Bb3 Nc6 7 Be3 Bf5 8 Nc3 e6 and after ...Be7 and ...0-0 Black completes his development.

3...Nf6

Less good is 3...c5: 4 d5 e6 5 Nc3 exd5 6 Qxd5 Qxd5 7 Nxd5 Bd6 8 e4 ±.

Now White has:

I. 4 Nc3
II. 4 e3

Another try is 4 Qa4+, when after 4...c6 5 Qxc4 Bf5 6 g3 e6 7 Bg2 Nbd7 8 0-0 Be7 9 Nc3 0-0, Black is fine. An instructive mistake is 10 Rd1? Bc2 11 Rd2 Nb6! and the queen goes. And on 10 Bg5 or 10 Bf4, 10...Ne4! holds.

I. 1 d4 d5 2 c4 dxc4 3 Nf3 Nf6 4 Nc3

White is aiming for complete control of the centre with 5 e4, and will then try to win his c-pawn back.

4...c6

This position can also be reached via the Slav Defence (1 d4 d5 2 c4 c6 3 Nf3 Nf6 4 Nc3 dxc4). Also interesting is 4...a6 5 e4 b5 6 e5 Nd5 7 a4 Nxc3 8 bxc3 Qd5! 9 g3 Bb7 10 Bg2 Qd7 11 Ba3 g6 12 0-0 Bg7 13 Re1 0-0 14

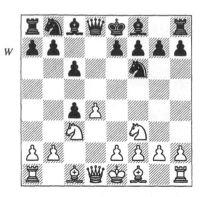

e6!? fxe6 15 Ne5 Qc8 16 Bh3 Bd5 with equal chances. But White has an edge after 4...c5 5 d5! e6 6 e4 exd5 7 e5! Nfd7 8 Qxd5 followed by Bxc4.

5 a4

An unclear pawn sacrifice is 5 e4 b5 6 e5 Nd5 7 a4 e6 8 axb5 Nxc3 9 bxc3 cxb5 10 Ng5 Bb7 11 Qh5 Qd7.

5...Bf5

Or 5...Bg4 6 Ne5 Bh5 7 Nxc4 e6 8 Bg5! Bb4 9 f3! ± and White threatens to start an offensive with g2-g4 and e2-e4.

6 e3

The game explodes after 6 Ne5: 6...e6 7 f3 Bb4 8 e4 Bxe4!? 9 fxe4 Nxe4 10 Bd2 Qxd4 11 Nxe4 Qxe4+ 12 Qe2 Bxd2+ 13 Kxd2 Qd5+ 14 Kc2 Na6 15 Nxc4 0-0-0 and the three pawns counterbalance the piece. If Black wants to sidestep these complications he can play 6...Nbd7 7 Nxc4 Qc7 8 g3! e5 9 dxe5 Nxe5 10 Bf4 Nfd7 11 Nxe5 Nxe5 12 Qd4 Bd6 13 Rd1, when White has the initiative.

6...e6 7 ♗xc4 ♗b4 8 0-0 0-0

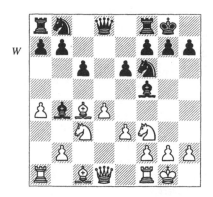

Plans and Counterplans:
On **9 ♕b3** Black has 9...♕b6 10 ♘h4 ♗g6 with ...a7-a5, ...♘bd7 and ...e7-e5 to follow, while on **9 ♘h4** ♗g6 and ...♘bd7, ...♕e7, ...a7-a5 and again ...e7-e5 is possible. Finally, on **9 ♕e2** ♘bd7 10 e4 ♗g6 11 ♗d3 ♗h5! 12 ♗f4 ♖e8 (threatening 13...e5) 13 e5 ♘d5 with a full-scale fight. Although White stands somewhat more freely the game is about even.

II. 1 d4 d5 2 c4 dxc4 3 ♘f3 ♘f6 4 e3

Now the pawn on c4 falls prey, as after 4...b5 5 a4 c6 6 axb5 cxb5 7 b3 cxb3 8 ♗xb5+ and 9 ♕xb3 the pawn would still be lost but under much worse circumstances.
   4...e6
   4...♗g4 5 ♗xc4 e6 (the threat was ♗xf7+ and ♘e5+) 6 h3 ♗h5 7 ♘c3 a6 (preparing 8...♘c6) 8 g4! ♗g6 9 ♘e5 ♘bd7 10 ♘xg6 hxg6 11 ♗f1 and 12 ♗g2 ±.

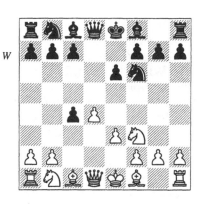

5 ♗xc4 c5 6 0-0 a6 7 a4
   Should White not parry ...b7-b5 and play 7 ♗d3, Black has a rosy position after 7...cxd4 (7...b5?! 8 a4!) 8 exd4 ♗e7 9 ♘c3 b5 10 a3 ♗b7 11 ♗g5 ♘bd7 followed by ...♘b6, ...♘bd5 and ...0-0. Another try is 7 ♕e2 b5 8 ♗b3 ♗b7 9 ♖d1 ♘bd7 10 ♘c3 ♕b6 11 d5 ♘xd5 12 ♗xd5 exd5 13 ♘xd5 ♗xd5 14 ♖xd5 ♗e7 15 e4 ♕b7 16 ♗g5 ♘b6 17 ♖ad1 f6 18 ♗f4 0-0 =.
   7...♘c6 8 ♕e2 cxd4 9 ♖d1 ♗e7 10 exd4 0-0 11 ♘c3

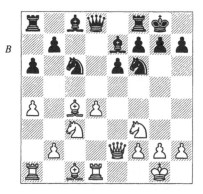

Black has to reckon with the threat of the advance d4-d5, and his light-squared bishop still needs to be developed.

On **11...♞b4** 12 ♞e5 ♞fd5 13 ♛g4 White has a pull, therefore Black should play **11...♞d5** 12 ♛e4 ♞cb4 13 ♞e5 ♛d6 (13...b6? 14 ♞c6! ♞xc6 15 ♞xd5 exd5 16 ♝xd5 wins a pawn), and follow up with 14...b6 and 15...♝b7. In this dynamically balanced position Black often defends with ...f7-f6 or even ...f7-f5 while White can envisage an attack along the open third rank (♜a1-a3-g3/h3).

Classical Queen's Gambit

1 d4 d5 2 c4 e6

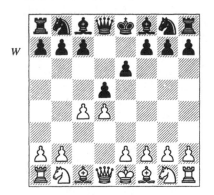

This variation, which is perhaps the most ancient form of the Queen's Gambit, is recommended to players who prefer long struggles and testing endgames. Black is preparing for ...c7-c5, which he can play immediately (see the Tarrasch Defence), or lay the groundwork for in a slower fashion. In this case, he first castles

after ...♞f6 and ...♝e7 and then plays for instance ...b7-b6 and ...♝b7 to complete his development. White can make use of this period of calm to put his pieces on their ideal squares: ♞c3, ♞f3, ♝g5, e3, ♜c1, ♝d3, 0-0, etc. It is typical of the whole line that White restrains his f1 bishop in order to recapture on c4 without any loss of tempi.

The following sections summarize the **Classical Queen's Gambit:**

I. Exchange Variation (cxd5 exd5 on the third move or later)
II. Tarrasch Defence (Black plays ...c7-c5)
III. Black plays ...♝b4 (3 ♞c3 ♞f6 4 ♞f3 ♝b4)
IV. ♝f4 Variation (3 ♞c3 ♞f6 4 ♞f3 ♝e7 5 ♝f4)
V. Tartakower Variation (3 ♞c3 ♞f6 4 ♞f3 ♝e7 5 ♝g5 0-0 6 e3 h6 7 ♝h4 b6)
VI. Orthodox Variation (3 ♞c3 ♞f6 4 ♞f3 ♝e7 5 ♝g5 0-0 6 e3 ♞bd7)
VII. Catalan Opening (White fianchettoes his bishop to g2).

I. Exchange Variation

Black has a variety of move-orders to choose from in the Classical Queen's Gambit: he can play either ...c7-c6 or ...e7-e6 first and he can then also select the order of ...♞f6 and ...♝e7. White, in turn, can capture on d5 at similar but not identical moments. First let us take a look at the ensuing pawn formation!

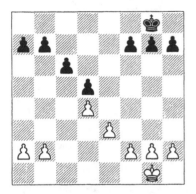

Normally the advance e3-e4 is unfavourable for White on account of the weakening of the pawn on d4. Therefore he usually seeks to initiate play on the queenside, launching a 'minority attack', that is he starts an offensive with his a- and b-pawns against the entire black queenside. First b2-b4, then a2-a4, then b4-b5. Then he takes on c6 and after the recapture White already has a target: the pawn on c6, ripe for attack along the open files. Black often tries to salvage himself with an obstructive ...a7-a5 and, after the exchange on b4, he goes ...b7-b5. If this should fail he can still generate counterplay in the centre and on the kingside, most often with the habitual ...♘f6-e4.

We shall examine the following move-orders:

A. 1 d4 d5 2 c4 e6 3 ♘c3 ♗e7
B. 1 d4 d5 2 c4 e6 3 ♘c3 c6 4 cxd5 exd5
C. 1 d4 d5 2 c4 e6 3 ♘c3 ♘f6 4 cxd5 exd5
D. 1 d4 d5 2 c4 e6 3 ♘c3 ♘f6 4 ♘f3 c6

A. 1 d4 d5 2 c4 e6 3 ♘c3 ♗e7

This move-order, in contrast to the more usual 3...♘f6, prevents 4 cxd5 exd5 5 ♗g5.

4 cxd5 exd5

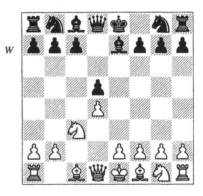

5 ♗f4

On 5 ♕c2 a solid set-up is ...♗f6, ...♘e7, ...g7-g6, ...♗f5 and ...0-0.

5...c6

The best response! It is useful to make the necessary moves first and then react flexibly to the opponent's plan.

6 e3

Warding off ...♗c8-f5 with 6 ♕c2 fails to 6...g6 7 e3 ♗f5 8 ♗d3 ♗xd3 9 ♕xd3, when Black has managed to get rid of his troublesome bishop.

6...♗f5 7 g4

7 ♕b3 ♕b6 = shows the benefits of ...c7-c6.

7...♗e6

In case of 7...♗g6 8 h4 h5 9 g5 White enjoys great spatial advantage (±).

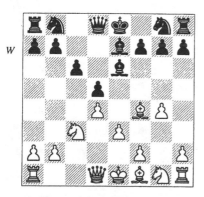

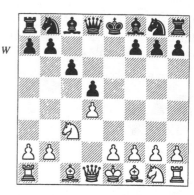

Against Black's harmonious piece play White has employed an aggressive strategy of g2-g4, with castling queenside to follow. Black should continue consistently with 8 h3 ♘f6 9 ♘f3 0-0 10 ♕c2 c5 11 0-0-0 ♘c6 =.

B. 1 d4 d5 2 c4 e6 3 ♘c3 c6 4 cxd5 exd5

5 ♗f4

On 5 ♕c2 the customary answer is 5...g6 6 ♗f4 ♗f5 7 ♕b3 ♕b6 =.

5...♗d6 6 ♗g3 ♘e7

Of course not 6...♗xg3? 7 hxg3 and White builds up pressure along the h-file.

7 e3 ♘f5 8 ♗xd6 ♘xd6 9 ♘ge2 0-0 10 ♘f4 ♗f5 =.

C. 1 d4 d5 2 c4 e6 3 ♘c3 ♘f6 4 cxd5 exd5

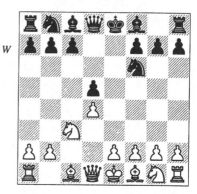

This is the ideal moment for White to capture on d5. The knight on g1 has not yet committed himself to f3 (often it stands better on e2), while Black has already played ...♘f6, allowing ♗g5.

5 ♗g5 c6

5...♘bd7 is a trap: 6 ♘xd5? ♘xd5! 7 ♗xd8 ♗b4+ winning a piece. But 6 e3 c6 7 ♕c2 ♗e7 is only a different move-order to the text.

6 ♕c2 ♗e7

6...g6 7 ♘f3 ♗g7 8 e3 ♗f5 9 ♗d3 ±.

7 e3 ♘bd7 8 ♗d3 0-0

A well-known releasing move is 8...♘h5: 9 ♗xe7 ♕xe7 10 ♘ge2 ♘b6 11 0-0-0 and White unleashes an attack with h2-h3 and g2-g4 (±).

9 ♘ge2

9 ♘f3 ♖e8 10 0-0 ♘f8 11 ♖ab1 a5 12 a3 ♘e4 13 ♗xe7 ♕xe7 and Black holds the whole position together.

9...♖e8

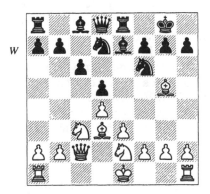

Plans and Counterplans:
White has to decide where to place his king:

a) 10 0-0-0 ♕a5 11 ♔b1 b5 12 ♘g3 h6 13 h4 ♘b6 with sufficient play for Black on the queenside.

b) 10 0-0 ♘f8 (10...♘e4 11 ♗f4!? f5? 12 ♘xd5 cxd5 13 ♗c7 +−) 11 f3!? (11 ♖ab1 ♗e6 12 b4 a6 13 ♘a4! ♘6d7 14 ♗xe7 ♕xe7 15 ♘c5 and White has a slight edge) 11...♘h5 12 ♗xe7 ♕xe7 13 e4 dxe4 14 fxe4 ♗e6, when Black can deal serious blows against the white centre with ...♖ad8, ...♘f6, ...♘g6 and ...c6-c5.

D. 1 d4 d5 2 c4 e6 3 ♘c3 ♘f6 4 ♘f3 c6

Attention! This is also the basic position of the Semi-Slav Defence!

5 cxd5

A popular way to avoid the sharp 'Botvinnik' variation (5 ♗g5 dxc4).

5...exd5

6 ♗g5

On 6 ♗f4 either 6...♗f5 or 6...♗e7 7 e3 ♘h5 is good.

6...h6!?

Or 6...♗f5 7 ♕b3!? ♕b6!? (or 7...♘bd7 8 e4!? dxe4 9 ♗c4! ∞) 8 ♗xf6 gxf6 and despite Black's ugly kingside pawn formation, the bishop pair keeps his chances alive =/∞.

7 ♗h4 ♗f5 8 ♕b3

Or 8 e3 ♗e7 intending ...♘bd7, ...0-0 and ...♘e4 with an easy game.

8...g5!

This is why ...h7-h6 was necessary. Of course 9 ♕xb7? is now an outright blunder: 9...gxh4 10 ♕xa8

♕b6 netting the queen (...♗d6, ...0-0 and ...♘bd7) while setting his sights on the b2-pawn.

9 ♗g3 ♕b6 10 e3 ♕xb3 11 axb3 ♘bd7 =.

II. Tarrasch Defence (Black plays ...c7-c5)

By playing ...c7-c5 Black immediately puts up a fight in the centre. In order to achieve active piece play and dynamic possibilities he is even prepared to accept an isolated pawn on d5.

Black has three different ways to carry out ...c7-c5:

A. 1 d4 d5 2 c4 e6 3 ♘c3 c5 – the **Tarrasch Defence** when on 4 cxd5 only the pawn can recapture (4...exd5).
B. Improved Tarrasch: 1 d4 d5 2 c4 e6 3 ♘c3 ♘f6 4 ♘f3 c5 when after 5 cxd5 Black can continue 5...♘xd5.
C. Dutch Variation: 1 d4 d5 2 c4 e6 3 ♘c3 ♘f6 4 ♗g5 c5?! where ...c7-c5?! is less than advisable.

A. 1 d4 d5 2 c4 e6 3 ♘c3 c5 (Tarrasch Defence)

4 cxd5

With his last move White has created a target: the pawn on d5. Definitely weaker is 4 ♘f3?! cxd4 5 ♘xd4 e5 6 ♘f3 d4 7 ♘d5 ♘c6 =, as the white pieces have been wandering around the board too much. Pieces that are tossed into

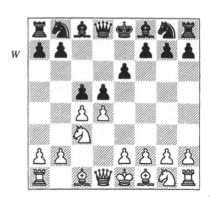

the centre too early are likely to be attacked and give the opponent extra tempi.

4...exd5

The Hennig-Schara Gambit offers Black an interesting game but White can still emerge on top with careful play: 4...cxd4?! 5 ♕xd4 ♘c6! 6 ♕d1 exd5 7 ♕xd5 ♗e6 (on 7...♗d7 8 ♘f3 intending the set-up e2-e3, a2-a3, ♕c2, ♗e2 and 0-0) 8 ♕xd8+ ♖xd8 9 e3 ♘b4 10 ♗b5+ ♚e7 11 ♚f1 followed by ♘f3, ♗d2 and White keeps his extra pawn while completing his development (±/±).

5 ♘f3

5 dxc5 is illogical in view of 5...d4!?, when things become very murky.

5...♘c6 6 g3

The other path is 6 e3 ♘f6 7 ♗e2 ♗e7 8 dxc5 ♗xc5 9 0-0 0-0 10 b3 a6!? (...a7-a6 is a useful move in this position, making room for the bishop on a7 and preventing the manoeuvre ♘c3-b5-d4) 11 ♗b2 ♕d6 and Black has strong prospects with ...♗e6, ...♖fd8, ...♖ac8 and ...♝a7-b8. 6 g3 is more consistent as after ♝g2 another piece applies pressure to the pawn on d5.

6...♞f6

On 6...c4 7 ♝g2 ♝b4 8 0-0 ♞ge7, 9 e4!? blows up the inflexible Black centre.

7 ♝g2 ♝e7

Or 7...♝e6 8 0-0, with b2-b3, ♝b2, d4xc5, ♖c1 and ♞a4 to follow, when White has a grip on the dark squares (d4, c5, b6 and e5).

8 0-0 0-0

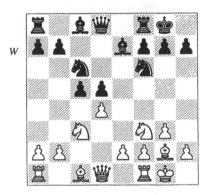

Plans and Counterplans:
White must activate his dark-squared bishop, but how? On **9 b3** ♞e4 10 ♝b2 ♝f6 11 ♞a4 ♖e8 12 ♖c1 b6 Black has an active game. White should therefore place his bishop on g5 (either right away or after 9 dxc5) to undermine the defence of the pawn on d5 : **9 ♝g5** cxd4 (9...♝e6 is not bad, only a bit passive) 10 ♞xd4 h6 11 ♝e3 ♖e8 with mutual chances. White may try to make room for his rook on d1 by moving his queen, but the

queen has no secure squares, for example, 12 ♕b3 ♞a5 or 12 ♕a4 ♝d7. Another attempt is capturing on c6 followed by ♖c1 and ♞a4 and penetration along the c-file. Black, in turn, can attack the pawn on e2 by means of ...♝f8 and ...♝g4, and occasionally the exchange sacrifice ...♖xe3 can be dangerous. On the other hand, after **9 dxc5** ♝xc5 10 ♝g5 Black has 10...d4 11 ♝xf6 ♕xf6 12 ♞d5 ♕d8 (12...♕d6!? 13 ♞d2 ♝e6 14 ♞f4 ♝b6 is also interesting) 13 ♞d2 ♖e8, when the pressure along the e-file, the bishop pair and the advanced black pawn set against the mobile knights and powerful light-squared bishop again make for a dynamically level position.

B. 1 d4 d5 2 c4 e6 3 ♞c3 ♞f6 4 ♞f3 c5 (Improved Tarrasch)

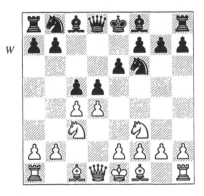

5 cxd5

White may also hold the centre with 5 e3 ♞c6 6 a3! (6 ♝e2? dxc4! 7 ♝xc4 a6 =) 6...a6! and now after 7 dxc5 ♝xc5 8 b4 Black must retreat to d6: 8...♗d6 9 cxd5 exd5 10 ♗b2 0-0 11 ♗e2 ♗e6 12 0-0 ♕e7 with a future ...♖ad8 and ...♗b8.

5...♘xd5!?

This is why they call it the 'improved' Tarrasch! Now White can choose between:

B1. 6 g3
B2. 6 e4 and
B3. 6 e3.

B1. 1 d4 d5 2 c4 e6 3 ♘c3 ♘f6 4 ♘f3 c5 5 cxd5 ♘xd5 6 g3

6...♘c6 7 ♗g2 ♗e7

7...cxd4!? comes into consideration: 8 ♘xd4 ♘xc3 9 bxc3 ♘xd4 10 ♕xd4 ♕xd4 11 cxd4 ♗d6 =, although White can try 8 ♘xd5!? ♕xd5 9 0-0, threatening 10 ♘xd4 ♕xd4? 11 ♗xc6+ +– as well as 10 ♗f4 and 11 ♘e5.

8 0-0 0-0 9 e4 ♘xc3 10 bxc3 b6!?

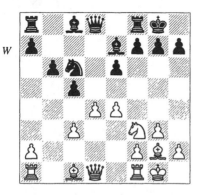

On the White 'questions' Black has the following answers:

a) **11 d5** exd5 12 exd5 ♘a5 13 ♕c2 ♘c4! 14 ♗f4 ♗d6 =.

b) **11 ♗e3** ♗b7 12 ♕e2 ♘a5 13 ♘e5 ♕c7 and Black brings in the rooks (...♖ac8 and ...♖fd8 =).

c) **11 ♗f4** cxd4 12 cxd4 ♗a6! 13 ♖e1 ♘b4 14 ♗f1 ♗xf1 15 ♖xf1 ♖c8 =.

B2. 1 d4 d5 2 c4 e6 3 ♘c3 ♘f6 4 ♘f3 c5 5 cxd5 ♘xd5 6 e4

6...♘xc3 7 bxc3 cxd4 8 cxd4

Plans and Counterplans:
White enjoys a spatial advantage but Black can operate with the possibility ...♗b4+. For instance:

a) **8...♗b4+** 9 ♗d2 ♗xd2+ 10 ♕xd2 0-0 11 ♗c4 ♘c6 12 0-0 b6 13 ♖ad1 ♗b7 14 ♖fe1 ♖c8 15 d5! (this is the only way to seize the initiative) 15...exd5 16 ♗xd5 ±.

b) **8...♘c6** 9 ♗c4 b5 10 ♗e2 (10 ♗xb5?? ♕a5+ –+) 10...♗b4+ 11 ♗d2 ♕a5 12 d5!? exd5 13 exd5 ♘e7 14 0-0 ♗xd2 15 ♘xd2 0-0 16 ♘b3 and the pawn on d5 is still giving Black a headache (±).

B3. 1 d4 d5 2 c4 e6 3 ♘c3 ♘f6 4 ♘f3 c5 5 cxd5 ♘xd5 6 e3

6...♘c6 7 ♗d3

Another common move is 7 ♗c4: 7...cxd4 8 exd4 ♗e7 9 0-0 0-0 10 ♖e1 and now either 10...♘xc3 11 bxc3 b6 or 10...♗f6 and 11...b6 leads to equality.

7...cxd4 8 exd4 ♗e7 9 0-0 0-0 10 ♖e1

Plans and Counterplans:

White tries to force ...g7-g6 by means of exerting pressure on h7. Then he goes for a kingside attack with ♗h6, ♕e2-e4-g4, ♘e4, ♘e5 or ♘g5. Black should always watch out for the exchange on d5. He will have to opt for an attack against the pawn on d4 and liquidation into a favourable endgame. For example, **10...♗f6 11 ♗e4** (11 a3 ♘xc3 12 bxc3 b6) 11...♘ce7 12 ♘e5 g6 13 ♗h6 ♗g7 14 ♔xg7 ♔xg7 15 ♕f3 ±, or **10...♕d6!?** 11 a3 ♖d8 12 ♕c2 h6! 13 ♘xd5 ♕xd5 14 ♗e3 ♗d7 =. On 10...♕d6!? it is wrong for White to play 11 ♘e4

♕c7 12 ♗g5? ♗xg5 13 ♘exg5 h6 14 ♘e4 ♕b6! as the pawns on b2 and d4 are hanging (∓).

Owing to different move-orders the diagram position can also be reached via the Panov Variation of the Caro-Kann Defence!

C. 1 d4 d5 2 c4 e6 3 ♘c3 ♘f6 4 ♗g5 c5?! (Dutch Variation)

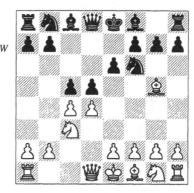

At this particular moment, action in the centre is uncalled for, due to the pin on the f6-knight.

5 cxd5 cxd4

If 5...exd5 6 ♗xf6! gxf6 7 e3 ± or 5...♕b6 6 ♗xf6 ♕xb2 7 ♖c1 gxf6 8 e3 cxd4 9 exd4 ♗b4 10 ♗b5+ ♗d7 11 ♗xd7+ ♘xd7 12 ♘ge2 ±.

6 ♕xd4 ♗e7

6...♘c6 7 ♗xf6 gxf6 8 ♕e4 ±.

7 e4 ♘c6 8 ♕d2 ♘xe4

8...♘d5? loses a piece in view of 9 exd5 ♗xg5 10 f4, and 8...exd5 9 ♗xf6 ♗xf6 10 exd5 gives a huge plus for White (±).

9 ♘xe4 exd5 10 ♗xe7 ♕xe7 11 ♕xd5 0-0

Or 11...f5 12 ♗b5 ♗d7 13 ♘ge2 fxe4 14 0-0 0-0-0 15 ♘g3 ±.

12 f3 ♘b4 13 ♕c4!

Luring the bishop to the e6-square.

13...♗e6 14 ♕c5 ♕xc5 15 ♘xc5 ♘c2+ 16 ♔d2 ♘xa1 17 ♘xe6 fxe6 18 ♗d3 and after **19 ♘e2**

The a1-knight falls and with two minor pieces against the rook White has a favourable game.

III. Black plays ...♗b4

1 d4 d5 2 c4 e6 3 ♘c3 ♘f6 4 ♘f3 ♗b4

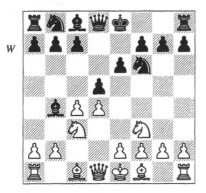

Black would gladly settle for a Nimzo-Indian here after 5 e3, but why would White want to shut his own dark-squared bishop out of the game? 5 ♗f4 is wrong in view of 5...dxc4! and a subsequent ...b7-b5 and ...♘d5, but 5 ♗g5 is logical. In the course of studying openings we can note that often the enemy pieces go 'in pairs'. For instance the knights on c3 and f6

both control the squares e4 and d5. Also the dark-squared bishops have a symmetrical task, namely pinning the knights from g5 and b4.

Should White fear the capture on c4 he can play 5 cxd5 exd5 at once (Ragozin Variation) or he can go 5 ♗g5 and let Black take the c-pawn (Vienna Variation).

A. 1 d4 d5 2 c4 e6 3 ♘c3 ♘f6 4 ♘f3 ♗b4 5 cxd5 (Ragozin Variation)

B. 1 d4 d5 2 c4 e6 3 ♘c3 ♘f6 4 ♘f3 ♗b4 5 ♗g5 (Vienna Variation).

White controls nothing but air after 5 ♕a4+ ♘c6 6 ♘e5 ♗d7 7 ♘xd7 (7 ♘xc6?! ♗xc3+ 8 bxc3 ♗xc6 9 ♕b3 dxc4 10 ♕xc4 ♘e4! and Black is on top in view of the threats ...♕h4 and ...♘d6. The latter stymies White's kingside by attacking g2) 7...♕xd7 8 e3 e5!? 9 dxe5 d4 with a pleasant initiative for Black.

A. 1 d4 d5 2 c4 e6 3 ♘c3 ♘f6 4 ♘f3 ♗b4 5 cxd5 (Ragozin Variation)

5...exd5 6 ♗g5 *(D)*
6...♘bd7

On 6...h6, 7 ♗h4 g5 8 ♗g3 ♘e4 is slightly suspect. Instead White should play 7 ♗xf6 ♕xf6 8 ♕b3 ♕d6 (8...c5 9 dxc5!?) 9 a3 ♗xc3+ 10 ♕xc3 0-0 11 ♖c1 c6 12 e3 ♗f5 13 ♗e2 with a queenside minority

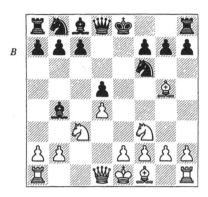

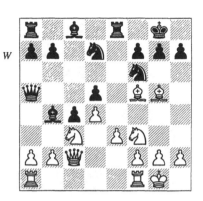

attack to follow (b2-b4, a2-a4 and b4-b5 ±).

7 e3 c5 8 ♗d3

The quiet 8 ♗e2 is interesting: 8...♛a5 9 0-0 0-0 10 dxc5 ♗xc3 11 bxc3 ♛xc5 12 ♖c1 and White's bishop pair and dominance over the dark squares is more significant than his shattered queenside (±). His next moves might be c3-c4, ♛d4 or ♘d4.

8...c4 9 ♗f5 ♛a5 10 ♛c2

10 0-0 ♗xc3 11 bxc3 ♘e4! (or 11...♛xc3 12 ♛b1 and besides 13 e4 White is also threatening 13 ♗xf6 ♘xf6 14 ♗xc8 ♖xc8 15 ♛xb7 ±) 12 ♛c2 ♘xg5 13 ♘xg5 g6 =.

10...0-0 11 0-0 ♖e8

To stop the blow 12 ♗xd7 ♘xd7 13 e4!

Plans and Counterplans:

Black will pose a question to the bishop on f5 with ...g7-g6: swap or retreat? Otherwise he intends to mobilize his queenside majority and perhaps take on c3 and then take aim at the c-pawn with ...♘b6-a4. White plans to push

e3-e4, because after opening up the centre he can take a closer look at the enemy monarch. Some examples that might give you a better 'feeling' for the position: 12 ♘d2!? (allowing f2-f3) 12...g6 13 ♗xd7 ♘xd7 14 f3 ♘b6 15 ♗f4 (15 e4? dxe4 and the bishop on g5 is threatened) 15...♗xc3 (15...♗f8 16 e4 ♗g7 17 ♗e3 ♗e6 =) 16 bxc3 ♛a4!? 17 ♛c1 ♗f5 ∞; or instead of 13 ♗xd7 White can play 13 ♗h3 ♗xc3 14 bxc3 ♘e4 15 ♘xe4 dxe4 16 ♗xd7 (16 ♗h6 ♘f6) 16...♗xd7 17 ♗f4 ♗c6 =.

B. 1 d4 d5 2 c4 e6 3 ♘c3 ♘f6 4 ♘f3 ♗b4 5 ♗g5 (Vienna Variation)

5...dxc4 *(D)*

6 e4

The only move, as after 6 ♛a4+ ♘c6 7 e4 ♗d7 or 6 e3 b5 7 a4 c6 Black is doing fine.

6...c5

6...b5 7 e5 h6 8 exf6 (8 ♗h4 g5 9 ♘xg5 ♘d5 10 ♘xf7! with great complications) 8...hxg5 9 fxg7 ♖g8

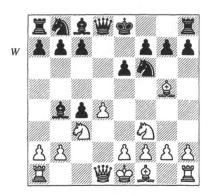

10 h4! g4 11 ♘e5 f5?! 12 ♕d2! with the threat of 13 ♕h6 and then 0-0-0.

7 ♗xc4

7 e5 stirs things up: 7...h6 8 ♗d2! cxd4 9 exf6 dxc3 10 bxc3 ♗f8 11 fxg7 ♗xg7 12 ♗xc4 and White has a pull (±). So on 7 e5 mandatory is 7...cxd4. Now both 8 ♘xd4 ♕a5 9 exf6 ♗xc3+ 10 bxc3 ♕xg5 and 8 exf6 gxf6 9 ♗h4 ♘c6 offer White nothing, so he should continue 8 ♕a4+ ♘c6 9 0-0-0, but even now Black has a variety of promising lines: 9...♗xc3 10 bxc3 h6 11 exf6 hxg5 12 fxg7 ♖g8 13 h4 ♕f6! ∞; 9...h6!? 10 ♘xd4 ♗xc3 11 ♘xc6 ♗d7! ∞; or the piece sacrifice 9...♗d7 10 ♘e4 ♗e7 11 exf6 gxf6 12 ♗h4 ♖c8 and Black has good chances.

7...cxd4

7...♕a5? 8 ♗xf6 ♗xc3+ 9 bxc3 ♕xc3+ 10 ♘d2 gxf6 11 dxc5 and 12 ♖c1 ±.

8 ♘xd4 ♗xc3+ 9 bxc3 ♕a5 10 ♗b5+!? (D)

The previously popular 10 ♗xf6 ♕xc3+ 11 ♔f1 gxf6 (11...♕xc4+?

12 ♔g1 threatening 13 ♖c1 +−) 12 ♖c1 ♕a5 is nowadays considered defensible for Black, therefore White has come up with the new weapon 10 ♗b5+.

Plans and Counterplans:
Black has to decide how to interpose:

a) 10...♗d7 11 ♗xf6 gxf6 (not 11...♕xc3+? 12 ♔f1 gxf6 13 ♖c1 and 14 ♖c8+ +−) 12 ♕b3 0-0 13 0-0 ♘c6 14 ♗xc6 ♗xc6 15 ♘xc6 bxc6 16 ♖ae1 and White will try to galvanize this rather flat position into action with e4-e5.

b) 10...♘bd7 11 ♗xf6 ♕xc3+ 12 ♔f1 gxf6 13 h4! ♔e7 14 ♖h3! ♕a5 15 ♖b1 ♖d8 16 ♕c1 and Black's sufferings are too much for a pawn. It is useful to know the motif of digging out the rook from the damaged kingside with h2-h4 and ♖h3.

IV. ♗f4 Variation

1 d4 d5 2 c4 e6 3 ♘c3 ♘f6 4 ♘f3 ♗e7 5 ♗f4

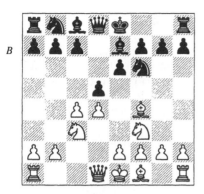

White presses strongly against the squares e5 and c7. He will often play the prophylactic move h2-h3 to provide the bishop on f4 with an emergency exit after a possible ...♘f6-h5.

5...0-0 6 e3 c5

Other moves are weaker:

a) 6...c6 7 ♖c1 ♘bd7 8 ♗d3 dxc4 9 ♗xc4 ♘d5 10 ♗g3 ♘xc3 11 bxc3 ±.

b) 6...♘bd7 7 cxd5 ♘xd5 8 ♘xd5 exd5 9 ♗d3 c6 10 0-0 ♘f6 11 ♕c2 a5 12 h3 ♗d6 13 ♗xd6 ♕xd6 14 ♘e5 ±.

c) 6...b6 7 ♖c1 c5 8 cxd5 exd5 9 ♗e2 ♗b7 10 0-0 ♘bd7 11 ♘e5 ±.

Obviously Black has to be careful as in an open position White is likely to have an edge due to the bishop on f4.

7 dxc5

Forced, otherwise Black would capture on d4 and c4. 7 cxd5 ♘xd5 8 ♘xd5 ♕xd5 9 dxc5 ♕xc5 is insufficient for an advantage.

7...♗xc5 8 ♕c2

Vacating the d1-square for the rook. The bishop on f1 bides its time to recapture on c4 from its home square. Worse is 8 cxd5 ♘xd5 9 ♘xd5 exd5 10 a3 ♘c6 11 ♗d3 ♗b6 12 0-0 ♗g4 =.

8...♘c6 9 a3 ♕a5

The queen impedes b2-b4 and at the same time steps out of the d-file.

10 0-0-0!?

This daring move is the latest theoretical issue. The almost compulsory line used to be 10 ♖d1 ♗e7 11 ♘d2 e5 12 ♘b3 ♕b6 13 ♗g5 d4 14 ♗xf6 ♗xf6 15 ♘d5 ♕d8 16 ♗d3 g6 17 exd4 ♘xd4 18 ♘xd4 exd4 19 ♘xf6+ ♕xf6 20 0-0 ♗g4!? =. But this is dangerous only in the case of an impatient or uninformed opponent. After 10 0-0-0!? the tempo changes. The immediate threat is g2-g4!

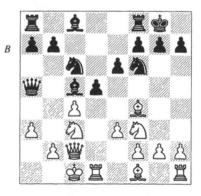

Plans and Counterplans:
White is taking chances with his plan as his king's position is anything but bomb-proof. However, there is no instant refutation because Black gets the worst of it after **10...dxc4** 11 ♗xc4 a6 12 ♘g5!

♗e7 13 h4 h6 14 g4 b5 15 ♘ce4 with a strong attack for White; or **10...♘e4?!** 11 ♘b5! a6 12 ♘c7 e5 13 ♖xd5! and White is on top. The best continuation is **10...♗e7** 11 g4!? dxc4 (11...♘xg4 is too rash in view of both 12 ♖g1 and 12 cxd5 ±) 12 ♗xc4 e5 (12...♘xg4 13 ♖g1 e5 14 ♗g5!?) 13 g5 exf4 14 gxf6 ♗xf6 15 ♘d5 ♘e7! 16 ♘xf6+ gxf6 17 ♖hg1+ ♔h8 18 ♕e4 ♘g6 19 ♕d4 ♕b6 and Black holds. An interesting alternative is **10...♗d7!?** 11 g4 ♖fc8 12 ♔b1 b5! 13 cxb5 (13 cxd5 b4 14 dxc6 ♗xc6) 13...♘e7 with a promising attack for the pawn.

V. 1 d4 d5 2 c4 e6 3 ♘c3 ♘f6 4 ♘f3 ♗e7 5 ♗g5 0-0 6 e3 h6 (Tartakower Variation)

This important move prepares for ...b7-b6 and ...♗b7 as 6...b6?! at once is wrong in view of 7 cxd5 ♘xd5 8 ♗xe7 ♕xe7 9 ♘xd5 exd5 10 ♖c1 ♗e6 11 ♗d3 c5? 12 dxc5 bxc5 13 ♕c2! and both c5 and h7 are under attack.

7 ♗h4

The swap 7 ♗xf6 is interesting: 7...♗xf6 8 ♖c1 c6 (8...b6?! 9 cxd5 exd5 10 ♗d3 ♗b7 11 0-0 ♕e7 12 ♖e1 c5 13 e4! ±) 9 ♗d3 ♘d7 10 0-0 dxc4 (on 10...♗e7 11 ♕e2, intending e3-e4 with an advantage in the centre) 11 ♗xc4 e5 12 h3 exd4 13 exd4! (It is not easy to select the moment at which a pawn recapture is needed, even if it creates an isolated pawn. Now it is

well justified as the pawn on d4 restrains the black pieces by controlling the squares c5 and e5) 13...♘b6 14 ♗b3 ♗f5 =. White has play on the e-file (♖e1, ♘e4, ♘e5) while Black would prefer swapping (...♖e8) or will advance his a-pawn and start harassing the bishop on b3 and thus the c4-square.

7...b6

On the simplifying 7...♘e4 8 ♗xe7 ♕xe7 9 cxd5! (White forces the exchange and creates a superior pawn-formation) 9...♘xc3 10 bxc3 exd5 11 ♕b3 ♖d8 12 c4! White stands somewhat better owing to his centre pawns on d4 and e3 (±). Black has to try for equality with the move ...c6-c5. But back to 7...b6, the basic position of the Tartakower!

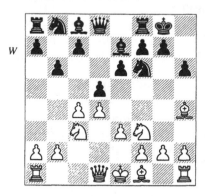

Plans and Counterplans:
Black opts for the obvious set-up ...♗b7, ...♘bd7 and ...c7-c5 sometimes combined with ...d5xc4 or ...♘e4. White can take on d5 or even f6 but he should wait until

the black bishop is already on b7, otherwise it gets good play on the open c8-h3 diagonal, e.g.: **8 ♗xf6?!** ♗xf6 9 cxd5 exd5 10 ♗e2 ♗e6 11 0-0 c5 =. Other lines are:

a) 8 cxd5 ♘xd5 9 ♗xe7 ♕xe7 10 ♘xd5 exd5 11 ♖c1 ♗e6! (or 11...♗b7 12 ♕a4 c5 13 ♕a3 ♖c8 14 ♗d3 a5 15 0-0 ♘a6 16 ♘e5! ±. The two typical moves for White in this position are ♕a3, pinning the c-pawn, and ♘e5!) 12 ♕a4 c5 13 ♕a3 ♖c8 14 ♗e2 ♕b7! = and in exchange for the pawn on c5, the b-pawn is hanging. Instead of 12 ♕a4 White should play 12 ♗d3 c5 13 dxc5 bxc5 14 0-0 ♘d7 15 e4 dxe4 16 ♗xe4 ♖ad8 17 ♗b1 ♘e5 18 ♕e2 ♘xf3+ 19 ♕xf3 and White's advantage is practically non-existent (=).

b) 8 ♕b3 ♗b7 9 ♗xf6 ♗xf6 10 cxd5 exd5 11 ♖d1 (the point of 8 ♕b3 is to allow ♖d1 and thereby stop ...c7-c5) 11...♖e8 and Black follows up with ...c7-c6 and ...♘d7-f8-e6.

c) 8 ♖c1 ♗b7 9 ♗xf6 (on 9 ♗d3 or 9 ♗e2, 9...dxc4 10 ♗xc4 ♘bd7 11 0-0 c5 and the game is level) 9...♗xf6 10 cxd5 exd5 11 b4 c6 12 ♗e2 ♕d6 and, after ...♘bd7 with ...a7-a5 to follow, the game is equal.

d) 8 ♗e2 (one of the most popular lines nowadays, White tries to spare the move ♖c1) 8...♗b7 9 ♗xf6 ♗xf6 10 cxd5 exd5 11 0-0 c6 (11...c5!? 12 dxc5 ♗xc3!? =) 12 b4 ♖e8 13 ♕b3 a5 14 b5 c5! 15 dxc5 bxc5 16 ♖ac1 ♗xc3! 17 ♕xc3 ♘d7

and Black is very active. His plan is ...♕b6 with the advance of one of the central pawns.

The resilience of the Tartakower is demonstrated by the fact that it is present in the repertoire of nearly every leading contemporary grandmaster, and is often played with both colours.

VI. 1 d4 d5 2 c4 e6 3 ♘c3 ♘f6 4 ♘f3 ♗e7 5 ♗g5 0-0 6 e3 ♘bd7 (Orthodox Variation)

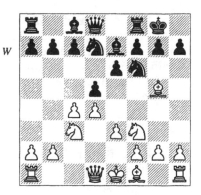

This ancient variation, which is also known as the Capablanca Variation, is reliable for Black, but complete equality is far from guaranteed if White plays correctly.

7 ♖c1

This keeps up the tension between c4 and d5 in order to recapture on c4 with the bishop in one move. Another try is 7 ♕c2 c5 8 cxd5 ♘xd5 9 ♗xe7 ♕xe7 10 ♘xd5 exd5 11 ♗d3 g6 12 dxc5 ♘xc5 13 0-0 and Black is slightly worse due to his isolated pawn.

7...c6

On 7...c5 8 cxd5 ♘xd5 9 ♗xe7 ♘xe7 10 ♗e2, followed by 0-0, ♕a4, ♖fd1 ±, while 7...b6 8 cxd5 exd5 9 ♗d3 ♗b7 10 0-0 and ♕e2, ♗a6, ♖fd1, ♘e5 is also better for White (±). But 7...a6!? deserves attention, preparing 8...dxc4 9 ♗xc4 b5 10 ♗b3 c5. Black need not worry about 8 c5 c6 9 ♗d3 e5! 10 dxe5 ♘e8, therefore White should play 8 cxd5 exd5 9 ♗d3 transposing to the Exchange Variation.

8 ♗d3 dxc4 9 ♗xc4 ♘d5

Alternatively, 9...b5 10 ♗d3 a6 11 e4 h6 12 ♗f4 ♗b7 13 e5 ♘d5 14 ♘xd5 cxd5 15 0-0 ± or 9...h6 10 ♗h4 ♘d5 11 ♗g3 followed by e4 ±.

10 ♗xe7 ♕xe7

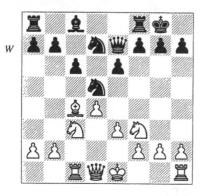

Plans and Counterplans:
Black is aiming for ...♘xc3 and ...e6-e5 which White can either allow or sidestep.

a) 11 0-0 ♘xc3 12 ♖xc3 (12 bxc3 b6 followed by ...c7-c5 and ...♗b7) 12...e5 13 dxe5 (13 ♕c2 exd4 14 exd4 ♘b6 15 ♖e1 ♕d8 16

♗b3 ♘d5 =) 13...♘xe5 14 ♘xe5 ♕xe5 15 f4, threatening not only e3-e4 but often f4-f5 and f5-f6 as well (±).

b) 11 ♘e4! (a beautiful move, avoiding the exchange of knights. Who else could have come up with an antidote to the Capablanca Variation but Alekhine?) and now:

b1) 11...♘5f6 12 ♘xf6+ ♕xf6 13 0-0 e5 14 d5 (14 e4 exd4 15 ♕xd4 ±) 14...e4 15 ♘d2 ♕g6 16 dxc6 bxc6 17 ♔h1, planning ♗e2 and ♘c4 ±.

b2) 11...e5 12 dxe5 ♘xe5 13 ♘xe5 ♕xe5 14 ♗xd5 cxd5 15 ♘c3 ♖d8 16 ♕d4 ±.

b3) 11...♕b4+ 12 ♕d2 ♕xd2+ 13 ♔xd2! This kind of queen exchange is favourable for White because he keeps his king in the centre for the forthcoming endgame while Black has an awful lot of weaknesses (e5, c5 and d6). White's next moves will be ♔e2, ♖ed1, a2-a3 and b2-b4.

VII. 1 d4 d5 2 c4 e6 3 ♘f3 ♘f6 4 g3 (Catalan Opening)

In tournament practice this diagram is often reached via the move-order 1 d4 ♘f6 2 c4 e6 3 g3 d5 4 ♘f3. White's set-up is quite predictable: ♗g2, 0-0, ♕c2, getting ready for e2-e4. But first it is Black's turn to show his hand. He can either capture c4 (**Open Catalan**) or develop while keeping the centre closed (**Closed Catalan**).

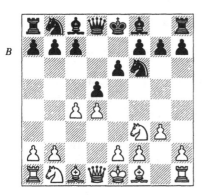

A. 1 d4 d5 2 c4 e6 3 ♘f3 ♘f6 4 g3 dxc4 5 ♗g2 (Open Catalan)

B. 1 d4 d5 2 c4 e6 3 ♘f3 ♘f6 4 g3 ♗e7 5 ♗g2 0-0 6 0-0 ♘bd7 (Closed Catalan)

A. 1 d4 d5 2 c4 e6 3 ♘f3 ♘f6 4 g3 dxc4 5 ♗g2 (Open Catalan)

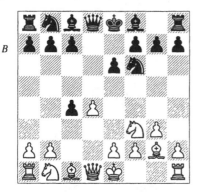

There is no hurry to win the pawn back. Besides, 5 ♕a4+ ♗d7 6 ♕xc4 ♗c6 7 ♗g2 ♗d5! 8 ♕d3 ♗e4 9 ♕d1 c5 10 ♘c3 ♗c6 11 0-0 cxd4 12 ♘xd4 ♗xg2 13 ♔xg2 a6 is dead equal.

5...♗e7

Black can also choose between a number of other interesting variations, all typical of the Catalan:

a) **5...b5** 6 ♘e5 ♘d5 7 a4 c6 8 0-0 ♗b7 (Black has secured his extra pawn so White transforms it into a positional sacrifice in return for a tremendous queenside initiative) 9 b3! cxb3 10 ♕xb3 a6 11 ♘c3 ♘d7 12 axb5 axb5 13 ♖xa8 ♗xa8 14 ♘xd5 exd5 15 e4! ♘xe5 16 dxe5 d4 17 e6! f6 18 e5! fxe5 19 ♗e4! and White is practically winning; the threat is ♕f3.

b) **5...♗d7** 6 ♘e5! ♗c6 7 ♘xc6 ♘xc6 8 e3 (not easy is 8 ♗xc6+ bxc6 9 ♕a4 ♕d5! ∞) 8...♕d7 9 0-0 ♖b8 10 ♕e2 b5 11 b3 cxb3 12 axb3, again with a good deal of compensation for the pawn (±).

c) **5...c5** 6 0-0 ♘c6 7 ♕a4 (also popular is 7 ♘e5 when 7...♘xd4?? loses to 8 e3! +−) 7...cxd4 8 ♘xd4 ♕xd4 9 ♗xc6+ ♗d7 10 ♖d1 ♕xd1+!? 11 ♕xd1 ♗xc6 12 ♘d2 h5. This queen sacrifice has been the topic of many lengthy discussions. Some say that rook, bishop and the initiative is worth a queen, while others claim that a queen is a queen after all. It is a fact that disputes of this kind usually end in a draw.

d) **5...♘c6** 6 ♕a4 ♗b4+ 7 ♗d2 ♘d5 8 ♗xb4 ♘xb4 9 0-0 ♖b8 10 ♘c3 a6 11 ♘e5 0-0 =.

e) **5...a6** 6 ♘e5 c5 7 ♗e3 ♘d5 8 dxc5 ♘d7 9 ♗d4 ♘xe5 10 ♗xe5 f6 11 ♗d4 ♗xc5! =.

6 0-0 0-0 7 ♕c2

On 7 ♘e5, the typical Catalan reply is 7...♘c6!? 8 ♗xc6 bxc6 9 ♘xc6 ♕e8 10 ♘xe7+ ♕xe7 11 ♕a4 e5 12 dxe5 ♕xe5 13 ♕xc4 ♗e6 14 ♕d3 ♘d5!?, when the position is unclear but about level.

7...a6

7...b5? 8 a4 c6 9 axb5 and 10 ♘g5! +−.

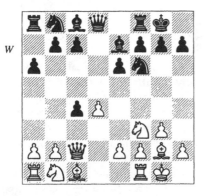

w

Plans and Counterplans:

Now White may capture on c4 immediately and allow Black to develop with ...b7-b5 and ...♗b7, or he can try to block Black's queenside with a2-a4. More specifically:

a) 8 ♕xc4 b5 9 ♕c2 ♗b7 10 ♗d2 (10 ♗g5 ♘bd7 11 ♘bd2 ♖c8 12 ♗xf6 ♘xf6 13 ♘b3 c5 14 dxc5 ♗d5 = or 10 ♗f4 ♘c6 11 ♖d1 ♘b4 12 ♕c1 ♖c8 =) 10...♗e4 11 ♕c1 ♘bd7 12 ♗a5 ♖c8 13 ♘c3 ♗a8 14 a4 and now on both 14...bxa4 15 ♘xa4 ♕e8! and 14...♖b8 15 axb5 axb5 16 b4 ♗d6, followed by ...♕e7 and ...e6-e5, Black maintains equality.

b) 8 a4 ♗d7 9 ♘e5 (9 ♕xc4 ♗c6 10 ♗g5 ♗d5 11 ♕d3 ♗e4 12 ♕e3 ♗c6 13 ♘c3 ♘bd7 14 ♕d3 ♗b4 =) 9...♗c6!? 10 ♘xc6 ♘xc6 11 ♗xc6 ♘xc6 12 ♕xc4 ♕d5 =.

B. 1 d4 d5 2 c4 e6 3 ♘f3 ♘f6 4 g3 ♗e7 5 ♗g2 0-0 6 0-0 ♘bd7
(Closed Catalan)

On 6...b6, White can play 7 ♘e5 ♗b7 8 ♘c3 with a ♗f4, ♕a4, ♖ac1, ♖fd1 'dream-set-up' to follow.

7 ♕c2

Another way to prepare for e2-e4 is b2-b3, ♗b2 followed by ♘c3 or ♘bd2.

7...c6

This position can also arise via the Slav Defence: 1 d4 d5 2 c4 c6 3 ♘f3 ♘f6 4 ♕c2 e6 5 g3 ♗e7 6 ♗g2 0-0 7 0-0 ♘bd7.

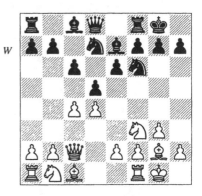

w

Plans and Counterplans:

White will execute e2-e4 after the preliminary b2-b3, ♗b2 and ♘bd2 or ♘c3. Black, after playing ...b7-b6 and ...♗b7, may opt for a swap on e4 but in this case he has to make sure that he can carry through the liberating ...c6-c5.

Instead of the exchange on e4 he can also go for ...c6-c5 right away, e.g. **8 b3** b6 **9 ℤd1 ♗b7 10 ♘c3 ℤc8 11 e4** dxe4 **12 ♘xe4** c5 or **8 ♘bd2** b6 **9 b3 ♗b7 10 e4 ℤc8 11 ♗b2** c5 **12 exd5** exd5 **13 dxc5** dxc4 **14 ♘xc4** b5 **15 ♘ce5 ℤxc5**. In the Catalan White is always slightly on top, but Black faces no immediate problems. However, there is one thing that Black has to keep in mind! He should never open the position in such a way that the bishop on g2 becomes dominant. White's task is to maintain his plus until the ending, when even a single tempo can be decisive.

Slav Defence

---

1 d4 d5 2 c4 c6

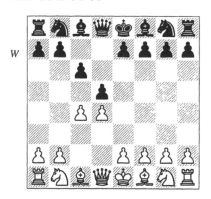

This section deals with lines in which Black opts for an early ...c7-c6. Of course, the positions with ...e7-e6 and ...c7-c6 can also be reached via the 2...e6 lines and other transpositions.

Let us see what we have under the heading 'Slav Defence':

I. 3 cxd5 cxd5 (Exchange Variation)
II. 3 ♘c3
III. 3 ♘f3 ♘f6 4 ♘c3 e6 5 e3 (Meran Variation)
IV. 3 ♘f3 ♘f6 4 ♘c3 e6 5 ♗g5 dxc4 (Botvinnik Variation)
V. 3 ♘f3 ♘f6 4 ♘c3 e6 5 ♗g5 ♘bd7 (Cambridge Springs Variation)

Sections IV and V differ from the Orthodox Queen's Gambit because in the latter Black plays 5...♗e7 in answer to 5 ♗g5. The variation 3 ♘f3 ♘f6 4 ♘c3 dxc4 has already been examined in the section on the Queen's Gambit Accepted.

I. 1 d4 d5 2 c4 c6 3 cxd5 cxd5
(Exchange Variation)

With the exchange on d5 White keeps his initial advantage of the first move, but in a completely symmetrical position. This seemingly colourless position used to be assessed as hopelessly drawish. Nowadays, however, so much theory has been created in the Exchange Variation that even Black has the chance to mix things up!

4 ♘f3

On 4 ♘c3 two suggestions: the watchful 4...♘f6 5 ♗f4 ♘c6 6 e3 a6 7 ♗d3 (7 ♘f3 ♗g4) 7...♗g4 8 f3 ♗h5 9 ♘ge2 e6 10 ♖c1 ♗g6 with ...♗e7 and ...0-0 =, and the sharp 4...e5!? 5 ♘f3 (5 dxe5 d4 6 ♘e4 ♕a5+ 7 ♗d2 ♕xe5 8 ♘g3 ♘f6 9 ♘f3 ♕d6 and a future ...♗e7, ...0-0, ...♘c6 with satisfactory play for Black) 5...e4 6 ♘e5 f6! 7 ♕a4+ ♘d7! 8 ♘xd7 (8 ♘g4 ♔f7 9 ♘e3 ♘b6 10 ♕b3 ♗e6 ∓) 8...♗xd7 9 ♕b3 ♗c6 =.

4...♘f6 5 ♘c3 ♘c6 6 ♗f4

More natural than 6 ♘e5, when after 6...e6 7 ♘xc6 bxc6 Black will achieve the equalizing ...c6-c5.

6...♗f5

Black gets a safe game but is a little worse after 6...e6 7 e3 ♗d6 8 ♗g3 (8 ♗d3!?), as it is hard to activate the bishop on c8. But 6...a6 is perfectly OK, e.g. 7 e3 ♗g4 8 ♗e2 ♗xf3 9 ♗xf3 e6 10 0-0 ♗d6 = or 7 ♖c1 ♘e4 8 e3 ♘xc3 9 bxc3 (9 ♖xc3? e5! 10 dxe5 ♗b4 ∓) 9...e6 =.

7 e3 e6

Plans and Counterplans:
White has several alternatives, but none of them present Black with serious problems:

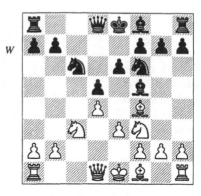

a) 8 ♘e5 ♘xe5 (it is better not to let White capture on c6 here) 9 ♗xe5 ♘d7 10 ♕b3 ♘xe5 11 dxe5 ♗e7 12 ♗b5+ (if 12 ♕xb7, 12...0-0 threatening 13...♖b8) 12...♔f8 and Black's bishop pair makes up for the temporary discomfort of his king.

b) 8 ♕b3 ♕b6 9 ♗b5 ♘h5 10 ♗g5 h6 11 ♗h4 g5 12 ♗g3 ♘xg3 13 hxg3 ♗g7 =.

c) 8 ♗d3 ♗xd3 9 ♕xd3 ♗e7! (9...♗d6 =) 10 0-0 0-0 11 ♖fc1 a6 12 ♗g5 ♘d7 and the knight begins its journey to c4 via d7 and b6. If White does not swap his dark-squared bishop, Black maintains control over the c5-square while White's c4 is less protected.

d) 8 ♗b5 (the best move, forcing Black to deviate from the 'mirror-game' to stop the threat of ♘e5) 8...♘d7!? 9 ♕a4 ♖c8 10 0-0 a6 (Black must clear the smoke on the queenside before castling in order to achieve counterplay against the white offensive) 11 ♗xc6 ♖xc6 12 ♖fc1 ♗e7 13 ♘e2 (13 ♘d1 b5 14 ♕b3 ♖c4 15 ♘d2

♕a5! and the rook on c4 is taboo since the white queen would get into trouble) 13...♕b6 14 ♖xc6 bxc6 15 ♖c1 ♗d3! 16 ♕d1 (16 ♖xc6 ♕xb2 17 ♖xc8+ ♗d8 18 ♘c1 ♗b5) 16...♗xe2 17 ♕xe2 0-0 =.

In the Exchange Variation, the open c-file more or less ensures that events are localized on the queenside. Even though White has the initial advantage, the player who gets his pieces to the key squares and achieves an advance of pawns will enjoy the better middlegame.

II. 3 ♘c3

After 3 ♘c3 Black cannot enjoy the luxury of immediately developing his bishop on f5, for example, 3...♘f6 4 e3 ♗f5?! 5 cxd5 cxd5 6 ♕b3 b6 (6...♕b6 7 ♘xd5) 7 ♗b5+ followed by 8 ♘xd5 winning a pawn, while if Black captures on c4 then 3...dxc4 4 e4 b5 5 a4 b4 6 ♘a2, winning back the pawn with a superior position (±). On 3 ♘c3, besides 3...♘f6, Black has two major sidelines:

A. 3...e5!? and
B. 3...e6, when White has the option of the 'Marshall Gambit' 4 e4.

A. 1 d4 d5 2 c4 c6 3 ♘c3 e5!?

4 dxe5
For 4 cxd5 cxd5 5 ♘f3 see the Exchange Variation. Both 4 ♘f3

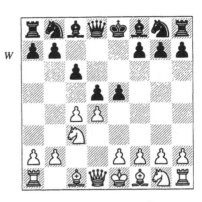

e4 and 4 e3 exd4 5 exd4 ♘f6 offer instant equality.

4...d4 5 ♘e4 ♕a5+ 6 ♗d2
This is more testing than 6 ♘d2 ♘d7 7 ♘f3 ♘xe5 8 ♘xd4 ♘xc4 9 e3 ♘xd2 10 ♗xd2 ♗b4 with equality.

6...♕xe5 7 ♘g3 ♘f6
7...c5 is interesting, making room for the knight on c6: 8 ♘f3 ♕c7 9 ♕c2 ♘c6 10 0-0-0 ♘f6 followed by the obvious 11...♗g4 and ...0-0-0 =.

8 ♘f3 ♕d6 9 ♕c2 ♗e7 10 0-0-0 0-0 11 e3!? dxe3 12 ♗c3 ♕c7
Or 12...♕f4 13 fxe3 ♕xe3+ 14 ♔b1 and White has the upper hand due to Black's underdevelopment and awkwardly placed queen.

13 fxe3 ♘a6 14 a3 ♗e6

Plans and Counterplans:
Now White can obtain the bishop pair with 15 ♘f5, but after the continuation 15...♖fd8 16 ♘xe7+ ♕xe7 Black has some counterplay on the light squares with ...♘c5-e4 or ...♗g4.

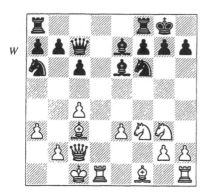

B. 1 d4 d5 2 c4 c6 3 ♘c3 e6

4 e4
The Marshall Gambit.
4...dxe4 5 ♘xe4 ♗b4+

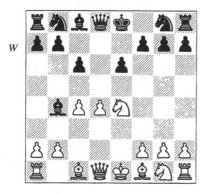

An early e2-e4 is nearly always met by ...♗b4 in these Slav positions.
6 ♗d2
Or 6 ♘c3 c5 7 a3 ♗a5 8 ♗e3 ♘f6 =.
6...♕xd4
Not 6...♗xd2+ 7 ♕xd2 ±.
7 ♗xb4 ♕xe4+ 8 ♗e2
8 ♘e2 is weaker: 8...♘a6 9 ♗f8 ♘e7 (9...♔xf8?? 10 ♕d8 mate!) 10

♗xg7 ♘b4 11 ♕d6 ♘d3+ 12 ♔d2 ♘f5.

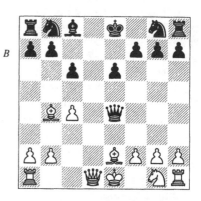

Plans and Counterplans:
Black needs to be extremely careful as White threatens a mating attack with ♕d6 or ♕d2 and 0-0-0. **8...♕xg2** is bad: 9 ♗f3 ♕g6 10 ♘e2 ♘a6 11 ♗a3 ♘e7 12 ♖g1 ♕f6 13 ♘c3 ♘f5 14 ♘e4 with a huge advantage for White. Besides a number of other interesting moves (8...♘a6, 8...c5, 8...♘e7) a well-trodden path is **8...♘d7**: 9 ♕d6 c5 10 ♗xc5 ♕xg2 11 ♗f3 ♕g5 12 ♗e3 ♕a5+ 13 b4 ♕e5 and Black's extra pawn is neutralized by the bishop pair and active play for White. The line 9 ♘f3 b6 10 ♘d2 ♕f4 11 ♗f3 ♘e5 12 ♗e4 ♗b7 is also unclear (=/∞).

1 d4 d5 2 c4 c6 3 ♘f3 ♘f6
Again Black should not capture on c4: 3...dxc4 4 e3 b5 5 a4 e6 6 b3! ♗b4+ 7 ♗d2 ♗xd2+ 8 ♘fxd2 a5 9 bxc4 b4 10 c5!? ± and White occupies important outposts with his pieces (c4, d6 and b3).

4 ♘c3

This is the accurate move-order as 4 e3 can be met by 4...♗f5 5 ♘c3 e6 6 ♗d3 ♗xd3 7 ♕xd3 ♘bd7 with ...♗e7 and ...0-0 to follow and Black has got rid of all the problems that usually come up with developing the bishop on c8 (=).

4...e6

4...♗f5?! 5 cxd5 cxd5 6 ♕b3! with a clear advantage for White. For 4...dxc4, see the section on the Queen's Gambit Accepted.

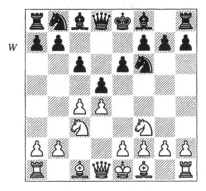

Now White has to watch his step because Black is already well enough developed to defend his extra pawn with ...b7-b5, ...a7-a6 and ...♗b7 following a possible capture on c4. 5 ♕b3 is worthy of attention, but after, for example, 5...dxc4 6 ♕xc4 b5! 7 ♕d3 ♘bd7 8 g3 ♗b7 9 ♗g2 a6 10 ♗g5 c5! gives Black easy equality. So what is left is offering the pawn with either **5 e3** (the Meran Variation – section III) or **5 ♗g5** (sections IV and V).

III. Meran Variation

1 d4 d5 2 c4 c6 3 ♘f3 ♘f6 4 ♘c3 e6 5 e3

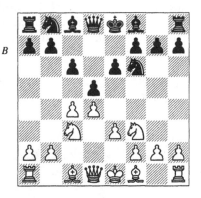

White is aiming for a slow expansion of his kingside and, after castling, he plans to achieve a central plus with e3-e4. This can be answered by Black with various moves:

- take on c4 and then prepare for ...c5 with ...b7-b5 and ...a7-a6
- take on c4 and play ...e6-e5
- play an immediate ...e6-e5

As to which plan is good and when we shall see in detail!

5...♘bd7

Practically the only sensible move after which, depending on White's plan, Black will develop his bishop from f8 to d6 or e7, or he can change the structure of the centre right away by means of ...d5xc4.

White's main continuations are:

A. 6 ♕c2 and
B. 6 ♗d3

6 b3 is also a possible move, when 6...♘e4!? 7 ♘xe4 (7 ♗d2 f5!) 7...dxe4 8 ♘d2 f5 9 ♗b2 ♗d6 followed by ...0-0, ...♕e7 and ...e6-e5 is satisfactory for Black.

A. 1 d4 d5 2 c4 c6 3 ♘f3 ♘f6 4 ♘c3 e6 5 e3 ♘bd7 6 ♕c2

6 ♕c2 fits well into three different plans: a set-up with b2-b3, ♗b2; an immediate e3-e4; or the latest fashion ♗e2 and 0-0.

6...♗d6
The exchange ...d5xc4 should be withheld until the bishop on f1 has moved. The bishop obviously stands more actively on d6 than on e7.

7 ♗e2
Alternatively:

a) 7 e4 dxe4 8 ♘xe4 ♘xe4 9 ♕xe4 e5!? 10 dxe5 0-0 11 exd6!? ♖e8 12 ♕xe8+ ♕xe8 13 ♗e3 ♘f6 14 0-0-0 ♗e6 15 ♗d3 b5! with mutual chances.

b) 7 b3 0-0 8 ♗e2 dxc4! 9 bxc4 e5 10 0-0 ♖e8 11 ♗b2 e4 (another idea is 11...exd4!?) 12 ♘d2 ♕e7 and Black's advanced e-pawn offers him equal chances.

7...0-0 8 0-0

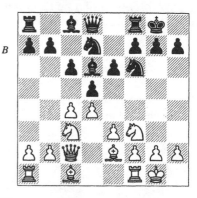

Plans and Counterplans:
Here Black can play **8...e5** right away, because after 9 cxd5 cxd5 10 dxe5 ♘xe5 11 ♘xe5 ♗xe5 his attacking prospects counterbalance his weak isolated pawn. A more restrained policy is **8...♖e8**, awaiting exchanges after e3-e4 and preparing the thrust ...e6-e5. Black may also capture on c4, for example **8...dxc4** 9 ♗xc4 a6 with 10...c5 to follow or, instead of 9...a6, 9...b5 10 ♗e2 ♗b7, when both ...a7-a6 followed by ...c6-c5 and ...♕c7 followed by ...e7-e5 are playable. White can either play e3-e4 or continue b2-b3, ♗b2, ♖fd1 or ♖ac1, h2-h3 and a2-a3, strengthening his position and staying put until Black commits himself. According to current theory, the position is equal.

B. 1 d4 d5 2 c4 c6 3 ♘f3 ♘f6 4 ♘c3 e6 5 e3 ♘bd7 6 ♗d3

6...dxc4

Black cannot allow White to play e3-e4 here: 6...♗d6?! 7 0-0 0-0 8 e4 dxc4 (8...dxe4 9 ♘xe4 ♘xe4 10 ♗xe4 with a strong attack: ♗c2 and ♕d3) 9 ♗xc4 e5 10 ♗g5 ♕e7 11 ♖e1 with a slightly better position for White.

7 ♗xc4 b5

This represents as important gain of space, and can be combined with either ...b5-b4 or the thrust ...c6-c5 after ...a7-a6.

8 ♗d3

The right move, because after 8...b4?, 9 ♘e4 hampers the move ...c6-c5. The other bishop retreats are inferior, for example, 8 ♗b3?! b4 9 ♘e2 ♗e7, ...0-0, ...♗b7 and ...c6-c5 =; or 8 ♗e2 ♗b7 9 0-0 ♗e7 10 e4 b4 11 e5 bxc3 12 exf6 ♘xf6 13 bxc3 0-0 14 ♖b1 ♕c7 =.

8...a6

Also satisfactory is 8...♗b7 9 e4 b4 10 ♘a4 c5 11 e5 ♘d5 12 ♘xc5 ♗xc5 13 dxc5 ♕a5 (it is important

to stop ♗b5) 14 0-0 ♘xc5 with equality.

9 e4

White is in a hurry as on 9 0-0, 9...c5 is even stronger.

9...c5

and now White can advance either of his central pawns:

B1. 10 d5 or
B2. 10 e5

B1. 1 d4 d5 2 c4 c6 3 ♘f3 ♘f6 4 ♘c3 e6 5 e3 ♘bd7 6 ♗d3 dxc4 7 ♗xc4 b5 8 ♗d3 a6 9 e4 c5 10 d5

10...c4

A good move, vacating the c5-square for the knight. On 10...e5 11 b3! and a later a2-a4 can be annoying for Black, and 10...exd5? is met by 11 e5 ±.

11 dxe6 fxe6

11...cxd3 is not good enough: 12 exd7+ ♕xd7 13 0-0 ♗b7 14 ♖e1 ♗e7 15 e5 ♘d5 16 ♘e4 ±.

12 ♗c2 ♕c7!

To stop e4-e5.

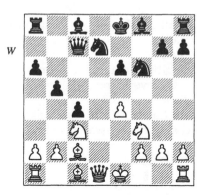

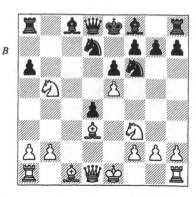

Plans and Counterplans:

White's plan involves the push e4-e5 to drive the knight away from f6, open the b1-h7 diagonal and vacate the e4-square. Black's aim is to stop this action. On **13 ♘g5**, a typical reply is 13...♘c5 and 14...h6, while on **13 0-0**, 13...♗c5 makes it more difficult for the f-pawn to move, e.g. 14 ♕e2 ♘e5! 15 ♘xe5 ♕xe5 16 ♗e3 ♗xe3 17 ♕xe3 0-0 18 ♖ad1 ♘g4 19 ♕g3 ♕xg3 20 hxg3 ♖a7! =.

B2. 1 d4 d5 2 c4 c6 3 ♘f3 ♘f6 4 ♘c3 e6 5 e3 ♘bd7 6 ♗d3 dxc4 7 ♗xc4 b5 8 ♗d3 a6 9 e4 c5 10 e5

10...cxd4
Not 10...♘g4? 11 ♗e4! ±.
11 ♘xb5! *(D)*
Everything is upside down! Black is forced to enter into fierce combat as on the quiet 11...♘g4, 12 ♕a4! is unpleasant. Therefore Black must capture something:
a) **11...♘xe5!?** 12 ♘xe5 axb5 13 ♗xb5+ (13 0-0 ♕d5 14 ♕e2 ♗a6 and Black is fine or 13 ♕f3

♗b4+ 14 ♔e2 ♖b8 15 ♕g3 ♕d6! with equal chances) 13...♗d7 14 ♘xd7 ♕a5+ 15 ♗d2 ♕xb5 16 ♘xf8 ♔xf8 17 a4!? ♕xb2 18 0-0 and Black's positional disadvantage is compensated by his extra pawn.

b) **11...axb5** 12 exf6 gxf6 (not 12...♕b6 13 fxg7 ♗xg7 14 ♕e2 0-0 15 0-0 ♘c5 16 ♗xh7+! ♔xh7 17 ♘g5+ ♔g6 18 ♕g4 with a dangerous attack) 13 0-0 (on 13 ♘xd4 ♕b6! Black has a superb game: 14 ♘xb5 ♗b7 followed by ...♖g8. Also 14 ♗xb5 ♗b4+ 15 ♔f1 e5 and 14 ♗e4 ♖a4! 15 ♗e3 ♗c5 are more attractive for Black) 13...♕b6 14 ♕e2 ♗a6 15 a4 ♘c5!? 16 axb5 ♗b7 where Black, besides attacking the pawn on g2, can also opt for a future ...e6-e5, while White pins his hopes on Black's insecure king position.

IV. 1 d4 d5 2 c4 c6 3 ♘f3 ♘f6 4 ♘c3 e6 5 ♗g5 dxc4 (Botvinnik Variation)

The Botvinnik Variation leads to possibly the most exciting position of the Queen's Gambit, in which both sides sacrifice material at an early stage. Black can also try the cunning 5...h6, as on 6 ♗h4 dxc4 7 e4 g5 8 ♗g3 b5 he has the upper hand. So 5...h6 should be met by 6 ♗xf6 ♕xf6 7 e3 ♘d7 8 ♗d3 dxc4 9 ♗xc4 ♗d6 10 0-0 ♕e7 11 ♘e4 ♗c7 12 ♖c1! 0-0 13 ♕c2 ♖d8 14 ♖fd1 a5 15 ♗b3 ♘f8 16 a3 ♗d7 17 ♘c5! ♖a7 18 e4! and White is on top in the centre.

6 e4

On 6 a4 the common move is 6...♗b4!: 7 e4 ♗xc3+ 8 bxc3 ♕a5 9 e5 ♘e4 10 ♗d2 ♕d5 with ...0-0, ...♘bd7 and ...f7-f5 to come (=).

6...b5 7 e5

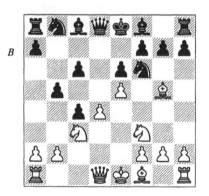

7...h6!

It is worth remembering that one can sometimes avoid the loss of a pinned piece by attacking the pinning piece!

8 ♗h4 g5 9 ♘xg5

Very consistent. On 9 ♗g3?!, 9...♘d5 10 h4 g4 11 ♘d2 h5 is tough going for White, while after 9 exf6 gxh4 10 ♘e5 ♕xf6 11 a4

Black can make a splendid sacrifice: 11...h3! 12 g3 c5! 13 ♗xh3 cxd4 14 ♘g4 ♕g7! 15 ♕f3 dxc3 16 ♕xa8 cxb2 17 ♖d1 ♗b4+ 18 ♔e2 c3! 19 ♕xb8 0-0 and Black's connected pawns outweigh the white rook. On 20 ♕xb5 c2 21 ♕xb4 ♗a6+ 22 ♔e3 ♖c8!! 23 ♖c1 h5 24 ♔d2 ♕g5+ 25 ♘e3 ♕d8+ Black is winning.

9...hxg5

On 9...♘d5 White can choose between the modest 10 ♘f3 ♕a5 11 ♖c1 ♗b4 12 ♕d2 followed by ♗e2, 0-0 and a2-a3 ±, and the whirlpool of complications that arise with 10 ♘xf7!? ♕xh4 11 ♘xh8 ♗b4 12 ♖c1 ♕e4+ 13 ♗e2 ♘f4 14 a3 ♘xg2+ 15 ♔f1 ♘e3+ 16 fxe3 ♕xh1+ 17 ♔f2 ♕xh2+ 18 ♔e1 ♗e7 19 ♔d2 and White invades on the kingside (±).

10 ♗xg5 ♘bd7 (D)

Much worse is 10...♗e7?! 11 exf6 ♗xf6 12 ♗xf6 ♕xf6 13 g3! ♗b7 14 ♗g2 with pressure along the long diagonal (±).

11 exf6

11 g3 often leads to the same thing, although Black can deviate with 11...♖g8 12 h4 ♖xg5 13 hxg5 ♘d5 14 g6! fxg6 15 ♕g4 (15 ♖h7!?) 15...♕e7 16 ♕xg6+ ♕f7 17 ♕xf7+ ♔xf7 18 ♗g2 ♘7b6 19 ♘e4 ± or 11...♕a5! 12 exf6 b4 13 ♘e4 ♗a6 and, due to Black's light-squared bishop, the bishop on f1 must develop to e2, when g2-g3 becomes a disadvantage: 14 ♗e2 0-0-0 15 0-0 ♕f5 16 ♕c2 ♘b6 17 ♖ad1 ♕h3 18 ♗h4 ♖xh4! 19

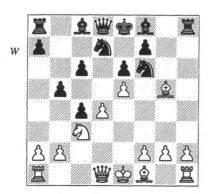

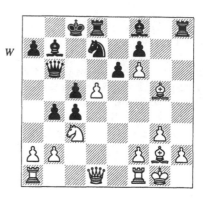

gxh4 ♗h6! and Black's attack looks scary.

11...♗b7

It is important that Black occupies the long diagonal in time, thus making ...c6-c5 possible. 11...♘xf6 is wrong in view of 12 ♕f3.

12 g3 ♕b6

12...c5 13 d5 ♘b6 is beautifully refuted by 14 dxe6! ♕xd1+ 15 ♖xd1 ♗xh1 16 e7 a6 17 h4! ♗h6 18 f4 b4 19 ♖d6! ♖b8 20 ♘d1 ♗xg5 21 fxg5 and the white pawn-chain smothers Black (+−). Instead of 13...♘b6, an interesting alternative is 13...♘e5!? 14 ♗g2 ♘d3+ 15 ♔f1 ♕d7 with unclear play.

13 ♗g2 c5

After 13...0-0-0 14 0-0 ♘e5 White's way to glory is a queen sacrifice: 15 ♗e3 c5 16 dxe5 ♖xd1 17 ♖fxd1 ♗xg2 18 ♔xg2 ♕c6 19 f3 b4 20 ♘e4 ♕b5 21 ♖d2, intending 22 ♖ad1, when the rooks penetrate along the d-file.

14 d5 0-0-0 15 0-0 b4

In tournament practice, dispute about the Botvinnik Variation begins here.

Plans and Counterplans:

a) 16 dxe6 ♗xg2 17 e7 ♗xf1 18 ♘d5 ♕b7 19 exd8♕+ ♔xd8 20 ♔xf1 ♖xh2 ∞.

b) 16 ♖b1 ♕a6 (16...bxc3? 17 bxc3 ♕a6 18 ♖xb7 followed by d5xe6 and e6-e7 ±) 17 dxe6 ♗xg2 18 e7 ♗a8! 19 exd8♕+ ♔xd8 and Black emerges with a great advantage.

c) 16 ♘a4 (the most dangerous continuation) 16...♕b5 and now not 17 dxe6 ♗xg2 18 ♔xg2 ♕c6+ 19 f3 ♕xe6 20 ♕c2 ♘e5 21 ♖ae1 ♖d4, when the game has opened up for Black, but 17 a3!, when by increasing his attack White gains access to the a-file. Finally both 17...♘b8 18 axb4 cxb4 19 ♗e3 and 17...exd5 18 axb4 cxb4 19 ♕d4!? lead to a double-edged game.

Even these few sample lines provide an insight into the whys and wherefores of the Botvinnik. White opts for an attack on the black king, but an early exchange of pieces is favourable for him as well, as he gets the better ending owing to his kingside majority. Black must even watch out for the occasional queen sacrifice (see 13...0-0-0 14 0-0 ♘e5 15 ♗e3 c5 16 dxe5!). Black directs his forces against the weak d4-pawn and, after gaining control of the centre, he slowly but surely advances the queenside pawns. Also after an exchange of the light-squared bishops, Black may be able to launch a kingside attack of his own.

Who is better? This is a rich area for improvements, and the theoretical assessment bounces back and forth between the two parties. So it is up to the reader to take the side that suits him better.

V. 1 d4 d5 2 c4 c6 3 ♘f3 ♘f6 4 ♘c3 e6 5 ♗g5 ♘bd7 (Cambridge Springs Defence)

Now Black is really threatening to take on c4!

6 e3 ♕a5

If White is circumspect he can cross Black's plan of ...♗b4 and ...♘e4 which is directed not only against the knight on c3 but also the bishop on g5. He can choose between:

A. 7 cxd5 and
B. 7 ♘d2.

A. 1 d4 d5 2 c4 c6 3 ♘f3 ♘f6 4 ♘c3 e6 5 ♗g5 ♘bd7 6 e3 ♕a5 7 cxd5

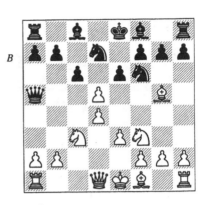

7...♘xd5

The best recapture. Others are:

a) 7...cxd5?! is ugly: 8 ♗d3 ♘e4 9 ♕c2 ♗b4 10 0-0 ♘xc3? 11 bxc3 ♗xc3 12 ♖ac1 ♗b4 13 ♕xc8+! +−.

b) 7...exd5 8 ♗d3 ♘e4 9 0-0 ♘xc3 10 bxc3 ♕xc3 11 e4! ± and in the open position Black's underdevelopment becomes apparent.

c) 7...♘e4 8 dxe6 fxe6 9 ♕a4 ♕xa4 10 ♘xa4 ♗b4+ 11 ♔e2 b5 12 ♘c5 ♘dxc5 13 dxc5 ♗xc5 14 ♖c1 with pressure on the black queenside (±).

8 ♕d2 ♘7b6

On 8...♗b4 White is well compensated for his pawn: 9 ♖c1 e5 10 a3! ♗xc3 11 bxc3 ♕xa3 12 e4 ♘c7 13 ♗d3 ±.

9 ♗d3

9 e4?? loses to 9...♘xc3 10 bxc3 ♘a4 11 ♖c1 ♘xc3! 12 ♖xc3? ♗b4 cashing in.

9...♘xc3 10 bxc3 ♘a4!

The pawn on c3 is indefensible as on 11 ♖c1, 11...♘xc3! 12 ♖xc3 ♗b4 is again winning.

11 0-0 ♕xc3 12 ♕e2 ♕b2

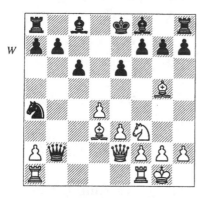

Here Black would gladly continue chasing the enemy queen and even force a draw by repetition. White has two possibilities to sidestep this: **13 ♗c2 ♕b5 14 ♕d1 ♘c3 15 ♕d2 ♘e2+ 16 ♔h1 ♗b4 17 a4** and **13 ♕d1 ♘c3 14 ♕e1 f6 15 ♗h4 ♘d5!?**, but he cannot easily make his advantage felt (=).

B. 1 d4 d5 2 c4 c6 3 ♘f3 ♘f6 4 ♘c3 e6 5 ♗g5 ♘bd7 6 e3 ♕a5 7 ♘d2

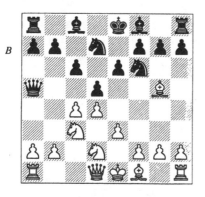

A multi-purpose move, unpinning the knight on c3 and taking control of the e4-square.

7...dxc4

Or 7...♗b4 8 ♕c2 0-0 9 a3 ♘e4 10 ♘cxe4 dxe4 11 ♗h4 and 0-0-0 with a small but tangible advantage (±).

8 ♗xf6

The g5-bishop was threatened!

8...♘xf6 9 ♘xc4 ♕c7 10 ♗e2 ♗e7 11 0-0 0-0 12 ♖c1 ♖d8 13 ♕c2 ♗d7 14 ♘e4 ♖ac8 15 a3 ♗e8

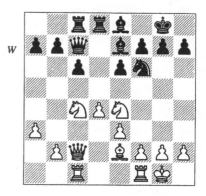

Plans and Counterplans:

White is solidly blocking Black's ...c6-c5 and ...e6-e5 moves and is therefore able to maintain a small advantage. Black will try to patiently survive White's queenside invasion (b2-b4, ♘c5, ♕b3 and a2-a4) and seek counterplay when the time is ripe. One unusual plan for Black is to put his knight on d5 and his queen to c7-b8-a8, so that when White goes b2-b4 and ♘e5, Black can start to attack the pawn on b4 with ...a7-a5.

Albin and other lines

1 d4 d5 2 c4 e5

If Black wants to disrupt White at an early stage he can choose between several rare lines on his second move. However, this strategy can only be successful if White is unprepared:

a) 2...♘f6? 3 cxd5! (forcing a piece to the d5-square in order to win time by kicking it around) 3...♘xd5 4 ♘f3 (premature is 4 e4 ♘f6 5 ♘c3 e5! 6 ♘f3 and Black is only a little worse ±) 4...♗f5 5 ♕b3 e6 6 ♘c3 ♘c6 7 e4 ♘xc3 8 exf5 ♘d5 9 a3 and now Black is clearly worse due to his weak b7-pawn (±).

b) 2...♗f5 3 cxd5 ♗xb1 (avoiding 3...♕xd5 4 ♘c3) 4 ♕a4+! ♕d7 5 ♕xd7+ ♘xd7 6 ♖xb1 ♘gf6 7 f3 ♘xd5 8 e4 and, with the bishop pair and a spatial plus, White has a clear pull (±).

c) 2...c5 3 cxd5 ♕xd5 4 ♘f3 cxd4 5 ♘c3 ♕a5 6 ♘xd4 ♘f6 7 ♘b3 ♕c7 8 g3 e5 9 ♗g2 ♘c6 10 0-0 with a significant advantage (±).

d) 2...♘c6 (the Chigorin Defence) 3 ♘c3 ♘f6 4 ♘f3 ♗g4 5 cxd5 ♘xd5 6 e4 ♘xc3 7 bxc3 e5 8 d5 ♘b8 9 ♕a4+ ♘d7 10 ♘xe5 ♕f6 11 ♗e2 ♕xe5 12 ♗xg4 ♕xc3+ 13 ♗d2 ♕xa1+ 14 ♔e2 ♕xh1 15 ♕xd7 mate. Should Black deviate with 3...dxc4, then 4 d5 ♘e5 5 f4! ♘g4 6 h3 ♘4h6 7 e4 secures White's advantage (±).

3 dxe5 d4 4 ♘f3

4 e3? is beautifully refuted by 4...♗b4+! 5 ♗d2 dxe3! 6 ♗xb4 exf2+ 7 ♔e2 fxg1♘+!

4...♘c6 5 g3

Also good is 5 a3!? and White can follow up with b2-b4 or e2-e3.

5...♗g4

Or 5...♗e6 6 ♘bd2 ♕d7 7 ♗g2 ♗h3 8 0-0 0-0-0 9 ♘b3 followed by ♕d3 and ♖d1 with a marked plus.

6 ♗g2 ♕d7 7 0-0 0-0-0 8 ♕b3!?

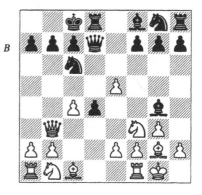

Plans and Counterplans:
Black opts for the familiar attack ...♗h3, ...h5-h4, ...♗xg2, ...h4xg3 and ...♕h3, but this is easily met by White's extra pawn and the pressure on the pawns on d4 and b7(!), for example **8...♗h3?** 9 e6! ♗xe6 (9...♕xe6 10 ♘g5! +−) 10 ♘e5! and now 10...♘xe5 11 ♕xb7 mate. Otherwise on 10...♕d6 11 ♘xc6 bxc6 12 ♕a4 Black can stop the clock.

On **8...♘ge7** 9 ♖d1 a similar trick is 9...♘g6? 10 ♘xd4! +−. Instead of 9...♘g6?, probably best is the reply 9...♕f5!? with the idea of ...♘e7-g6-e5. But White still gets the better of it after 10 ♘a3 followed by ♘c2. If White prefers to avoid the Albin he can play 1 d4 d5 2 ♘f3 and only on the third move c2-c4.

Queen's Pawn Opening

1 d4 d5 2 ♘f3

White holds his c-pawn back and, instead of an immediate central clash, first completes development behind his frontiers. The likely outcome is an equal game because Black is not hampered in organizing his army. What is more, after a usually successful ...c7-c5, Black can indeed act as 'White'!

Unnecessary is **2 e4?** dxe4 as on both 3 ♘c3 and 3 f3, 3...e5! is very effective, when Black is on top.

Other tries are:

2 ♗g5 h6! 3 ♗h4 c5 4 ♘c3 ♘c6 5 e3 (5 dxc5? ♕a5 6 ♕xd5 ♕b4! −+; this double attack is the reason why Black plays 2...h6) 5...♕a5 6 ♘f3 ♗g4 7 ♗e2 ♗xf3 8 ♗xf3 cxd4 9 exd4 e6 10 0-0 g5 11 ♗g3 ♗g7 ∓.

2 ♗f4 ♘f6 3 e3 e6 4 ♘d2 c5 5 c3 ♗d6 =.

On **2 ♘c3** ♘f6 3 ♗g5, 3...c5!? is again good, e.g. 4 ♗xf6 gxf6 5 e3 (5 e4 dxe4 6 dxc5 ♕a5 7 ♕h5 ♗g7, intending ...0-0 and ...f6-f5, favours Black) 5...cxd4 6 exd4 h5! 7 ♗e2 h4 8 ♗f3 e6 9 ♘ge2 ♗h6 10 0-0 ♘c6 11 ♖e1 ♗d7 12 ♘c1 ♔f8 = or 4 dxc5 d4! 5 ♗xf6 gxf6 6 ♘e4 ♕d5 7 ♕d3? ♗f5 8 ♘c3 ♕e5! 9 ♕b5+ ♗d7 10 ♕xb7 dxc3 and White is in grave danger (−+).

2...♘f6 3 e3

The alternatives are also harmless:

a) 3 ♗g5 ♘e4 4 ♗h4 (4 ♗f4 c5) 4...c5 5 e3 cxd4 6 exd4 ♕b6 7 ♕c1 g5! 8 ♘xg5 ♕h6! 9 ♕f4 f6 10 ♘h3 ♗xh3 11 ♕xh6 ♗xh6 12 gxh3 ♗c1! −+ or 5 c3 cxd4 6 cxd4 ♕b6 7 ♕b3 =.

b) 3 ♗f4 c5 4 e3 ♘c6 5 c3 ♕b6 6 ♕b3 c4!? 7 ♕xb6 (7 ♕c2 ♗f5! 8 ♕xf5? ♕xb2 9 ♗e2 e6! 10 ♕g5 ♕xa1 −+) 7...axb6 8 a3 b5 9 ♘e5 e6 10 ♘d2 b4! and Black is on top since he has achieved ...b5-b4, throwing a monkey wrench into the white queenside.

On **3 g3** the recurring set-up from the Réti Opening works again: 3...c6 4 ♗g2 ♗f5 5 0-0 e6 intending ...♘bd7, ...♗d6, ...h7-h6, ...0-0 and ...a7-a5 with comfortable play.

3...e6

Also good is the instant 3...c5 because 4 dxc5 is wrong in view of 4...e6 5 b4?! a5 6 c3 axb4 7 cxb4 b6!

4 ♗d3 c5 5 b3

Even less risky is 5 c3 ♘c6 6 ♘bd2 ♗d6 7 0-0 0-0 8 e4 (8 dxc5 ♗xc5 9 e4 e5 =) 8...cxd4 9 cxd4 dxe4 10 ♘xe4 ♗e7 =.

5...♘c6 6 ♗b2 ♗d6

This is better than the swap 6...cxd4 7 exd4, when White can play ♕e2, ♖e1 and ♘e5 to follow with an attack against the black king.

7 0-0 0-0

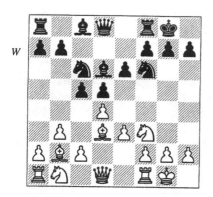

Plans and Counterplans:

White is planning to build up his centre with ♘e5 and f2-f4 while Black seeks counterplay on the queenside, possibly with ...♘b4. Here are some examples of how play could continue:

a) 8 ♘e5 ♕c7 9 f4 cxd4 10 exd4 ♘b4! 11 ♘c3 ♘xd3 12 ♕xd3 ♗d7! =.

b) 8 ♘bd2 ♕e7 9 ♘e5 cxd4 10 exd4 ♗a3 =.

c) 8 a3 b6 9 ♘e5 ♗b7 10 ♘d2 a6 11 f4 b5 12 dxc5 (the threat was ...c5-c4) 12...♗xc5 13 ♕f3 ♖c8 14 ♕g3 ♘xe5 15 ♗xe5 ♗d6 16 ♗d4 ♕e7 17 b4 g6 = and Black follows up with ...♘f6-e4.

Queen's Indian Defence

1 d4 ♘f6 2 c4 e6 3 ♘f3

Instead of 3 ♘f3, White can also play a Nimzo-Indian (3 ♘c3) or a Catalan Opening (3 g3), while on 3 ♘f3 Black has several possibilities: besides the Queen's Indian Defence he can choose the Queen's Gambit (3...d5), the Benoni Defence (3...c5 4 d5 exd5 5 cxd5) and the Bogo-Indian Defence (3...♗b4+).

White players need to be careful to select lines that keep them on familiar territory. If White, for example, prefers the Queen's Indian with 3 ♘f3, he cannot play the Benoni with f4 (1 d4 ♘f6 2 c4 c5 3 d5 e6 4 ♘c3 exd5 5 cxd5 d6 6 e4 g6 7 f4). Instead he has to opt for a line where the knight is quickly developed to f3. If he specifically prefers the Benoni with f4 he can reach this via 3 ♘c3 c5 4 d5 exd5 5 cxd5 d6 6 e4 g6 7 f4. But in this case he also has to be familiar with the Nimzo-Indian after 3 ♘c3 ♗b4. One should always try to select opening lines which are compatible with one another, if possible.

3...b6

The development of the bishop on c8 is a common problem for Black in the opening (Queen's Gambit, French Defence). Here Black creates the option of two diagonals for his bishop: on the a8-h1 diagonal he controls the main

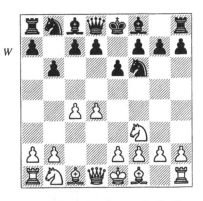

battlefield of the Queen's Indian, the squares e4 and d5, while on the a6-f1 diagonal he puts pressure on the c4-pawn, thereby disrupting White's development. The dark-squared bishop lies in wait: if White plays ♘c3 the bishop will grab the chance of pinning it with ...♗b4.

As we shall see, things are far from straightforward for Black. What is more, he will have to play very accurately to prevent White nursing his advantage into an endgame.

The most common lines are::

I. 4 e3
II. 4 a3 (Petrosian Variation)
III. 4 g3 (Classical Main Line)

The following are seen more rarely:

a) 4 ♗g5 ♗b7 5 e3 h6 6 ♗h4 ♗e7 7 ♗d3 ♘e4 8 ♗xe7 ♕xe7 9

♗c2 ♘g5 10 ♘bd2 0-0-0 with an equal position.

b) 4 ♗f4 ♗b7 5 e3 ♗e7 (now Black is threatening 6...♘h5, snaring the bishop on f4) 6 h3 c5!? 7 ♘c3 cxd4 8 exd4 0-0 9 ♗d3 d5 10 0-0 dxc4 11 ♗xc4 ♘c6 =.

c) 4 ♘c3 ♗b7 (4...♗b4 5 e3 transposes to the Nimzo-Indian) 5 ♗g5 h6 6 ♗h4 ♗b4 7 e3 g5 (also good is 7...♗xc3+ 8 bxc3 d6 followed by ...♘bd7 and ...♕e7, preserving the possibility of castling either side) 8 ♗g3 ♘e4 9 ♕c2 ♗xc3+ 10 bxc3 d6 11 ♗d3 f5 12 d5!? ♘c5! (12...♘d7 13 ♗xe4 fxe4 14 ♕xe4 ♕f6 ∞) 13 h4 g4 14 ♘d4 ♕f6 15 0-0 ♘ba6 with dynamic play, e.g. 16 ♘xe6 ♘xe6 17 ♗xf5!? (17 dxe6 0-0! 18 e7 ♖f7, followed by ...♖e8 and ...♘c5 ∓) 17...♘g7 18 ♗g6+ ♔d7 19 f3 ♖af8 20 fxg4 ♕e7 21 e4 ♘c5 ∞.

I. 1 d4 ♘f6 2 c4 e6 3 ♘f3 b6 4 e3

After ♗d3 White will now be ready to quickly castle kingside and complete his development with b2-b3, ♗b2 and ♘c3 or ♘bd2. This set-up is playable against almost any system of play by Black, and though it is not very ambitious, Black will still have to watch his step.

4...♗b7 5 ♗d3

On both 5 ♘c3 and 5 ♗e2, 5...d5 is good, reaching a Queen's Gambit in which White's bishop on c1 is locked in.

5...d5

Also possible is 5...c5 6 0-0 ♗e7 7 ♘c3 cxd4 8 exd4 d5! =.

6 0-0 ♗e7

Another healthy idea is 6...♗d6 7 b3 0-0 8 ♗b2 ♘bd7 9 ♘c3 a6 (against ♘b5) 10 ♖c1 ♕e7 with a future ...d5xc4 and ...c7-c5, or if the knight on c3 moves then ...♘e4.

7 b3 0-0 8 ♗b2 c5 9 ♘bd2

This knight will have the useful job of protecting his colleague from f3 after it jumps to e5. 9 ♘c3 cxd4 10 exd4 ♘c6 leads to equality.

9...cxd4 10 exd4 ♘c6 11 ♖c1 ♖c8 12 ♕e2 ♖e8 13 ♖fd1 *(D)*

Plans and Counterplans:
White may try ♘e5 or c4-c5 with a queenside expansion. The latter is usually prepared by a2-a3, threatening c4-c5 and b2-b4. So on a2-a3 Black must capture on c4. Black can also regroup with ...♗f8, ...g7-g6 and ...♗g7, then take on c4 with an attack against White's 'hanging centre'. Chances are about equal.

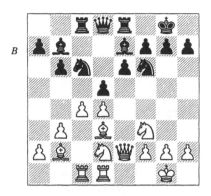

II. 1 d4 ♘f6 2 c4 e6 3 ♘f3 b6 4 a3 (Petrosian Variation)

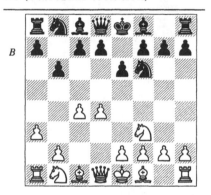

White's conception is ♘c3 followed by d4-d5 and e2-e4, when the centre is his! But here this strategy, typical of all 1 d4 openings, is preceded by the prophylactic a2-a3, directed against the pin with ♗b4. The two most common set-ups of Black are:

A. 4...♗a6 in connection with ...c7-c5 and

B. 4...♗b7, when measures are taken in the centre with ...d7-d5.

On the immediate **4...c5?!** White carries out his original intention: 5 d5! exd5 (5...♗a6 6 ♕c2 exd5 7 cxd5 ♗b7 8 e4 ♕e7 9 ♗d3 ♘xd5 10 0-0 ♘c7 11 ♗g5! f6 12 ♗f4 ♘e6 13 ♗g3 followed by 14 ♘c3 and ♘d5 with terrific play for the pawn) 6 cxd5 g6 7 ♘c3 ♗g7 8 e4 0-0 9 ♗d3 d6 10 h3! transposing into a Benoni position where Black's ...b7-b6 is worthless while White's extra move a2-a3 fits well into his plan of 0-0, ♖b1 and b2-b4 (±/±). In this line White's consistent harmonious play is apparent: he found the active d3-square for his bishop while preventing the pin ...♗g4 with h2-h3!

A. 1 d4 ♘f6 2 c4 e6 3 ♘f3 b6 4 a3 ♗a6

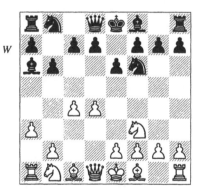

This move may seem odd at first sight but it is aimed at deflecting the queen from d1 in order to prevent a later d4-d5 in answer to ...c7-c5!

5 ♕c2

On 5 e3 or 5 ♘bd2 Black plays 5...d5! with a Queen's Gambit-like game in which White's bishop on c1 is stymied (=).

5...♗b7

5...d5?! is a major strategic blunder, as after 6 cxd5 exd5 7 ♘c3 White plays g2-g3, ♗g2 and 0-0, and puts pressure on the pawn on d5 with ♗g5, ♘e5 or ♘h4-f5. In this case White's queen is better on c2 while Black's bishop on a6 will sooner or later have to withdraw. 5...c5?! is also premature due to 6 d5.

6 ♘c3 c5!? 7 e4

The alternatives promise little for White:

a) 7 dxc5 bxc5 8 ♗g5 ♗e7 9 e3 d6 =.

b) 7 e3 cxd4 8 exd4 ♗e7 9 ♗d3 (9 ♗e2 0-0 and 10...d5 =) 9...♗xf3 10 gxf3 ♘c6 11 ♗e3 ♖c8 =.

7...cxd4 8 ♘xd4

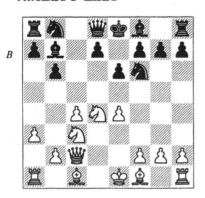

Plans and Counterplans:
Here Black often chooses a plain 'hedgehog' set-up, known from the English Opening or the Sicilian Defence: **8...d6** 9 ♗e2 ♗e7 10 0-0 0-0 11 ♗e3 a6 12 ♖fd1 ♕c7 13 f3 ♘bd7 with the interesting plan of ...♖ac8, ...♕b8 and ...♗d8-c7, after which the threat is ...d6-d5, when the pawn on h2 is hanging. In answer to this White plays ♔h1, ♗f1 and ♗g1 with spatial advantage and queenside initiative. The alternative **8...♗c5** 9 ♘b3 ♘c6 also deserves attention, when Black's idea is to take control of the dark squares with a future ...d7-d6, ...h7-h6 and ...e6-e5. The most fashionable move at the moment is **8...♘c6** 9 ♘xc6 ♗xc6 10 ♗f4 ♗c5!? (10...♘h5 11 ♗e3 ♕b8 12 0-0-0 ♗d6 13 g3 ±) 11 ♗e2 0-0 with balanced chances. For example, 12 ♖d1 a5! (a must against b2-b4) 13 ♗g3 ♕e7 14 e5 ♘e8 15 0-0 f5! = or 12 e5? ♘h5! 13 ♗xh5 ♕h4, when it is White who has cause to be apprehensive.

B. 1 d4 ♘f6 2 c4 e6 3 ♘f3 b6 4 a3 ♗b7 5 ♘c3 d5

A natural way to parry White's possible expansion with d4-d5 and e2-e4. Another way is 5...g6 6 d5 exd5 7 cxd5 ♗g7, when after ...0-0 and ...c7-c6 Black exploits the weaknesses of the white outposts.

6 cxd5

After 6 ♗g5 ♗e7 7 cxd5 ♘xd5 8 ♗xe7 ♘xe7 9 e3 ♘d7 Black equalizes easily with ...c7-c5. Now Black, depending on his style, can choose between two ways of recapturing: **6...exd5** with a slightly rigid centre (section B1) or the flexible **6...♘xd5** (section B2).

B1. 1 d4 ♘f6 2 c4 e6 3 ♘f3 b6 4 a3 ♗b7 5 ♘c3 d5 6 cxd5 exd5

7 g3!
White's target is the pawn on d5. Less effective are 7 ♗g5 ♗e7 8 e3 0-0 9 ♗d3 ♘bd7 10 0-0 c5 = and 7 ♗f4 ♗e7 (7...♗d6!?) 8 e3 0-0 9 ♗e2 c5 = .

7...♗e7
On 7...♗d6 possible is 8 ♗g5 and if 8...h6 9 ♗xf6 ♕xf6 10 ♘b5 ±.

8 ♕a4+!
A far-sighted move as after a future ...c7-c5 the queen's place is on a4.

8...c6
8...♕d7? is bad due to 9 ♕xd7+ ♘bxd7 10 ♘b5 while 8...♘bd7? is met by 9 ♘e5 with a large hole on c6.

9 ♗g2 0-0 10 0-0

Plans and Counterplans:
Black has to refrain from ...c7-c5 since after ♗f4, ♖fd1, ♖ac1 and ♘e5 White has strong pressure against the pawn on d5. Thus Black's correct plan is ...♘bd7, ...♖e8 and perhaps a queenside march with ...a7-a5 and ...b7-b5. White, in turn, opts for ♗f4, ♖ad1, ♘e5 and prepares to advance in the centre with e2-e4. Tournament praxis suggests that White stands slightly better (±).

B2. 1 d4 ♘f6 2 c4 e6 3 ♘f3 b6 4 a3 ♗b7 5 ♘c3 d5 6 cxd5 ♘xd5

7 e3
Other continuations are:
a) 7 ♕c2 ♘xc3 8 ♕xc3 (or 8 bxc3 ♗e7 9 e3 0-0 followed by ...c7-c5, ...♘c6 and ...♕c7) 8...♘d7 9 ♗g5!? ♗e7 10 ♗xe7 ♔xe7! 11 g3 ♘f6 12 ♗g2 ♕d6 13 0-0 ♖hc8 and after 14...c5 Black is OK.
b) 7 ♗d2 ♗e7 8 ♕c2 ♘d7 9 e4 ♘xc3 10 ♗xc3 0-0 11 ♖d1 ♕c8 12 ♗d3 ♖d8 13 0-0 c5 = .
c) 7 e4 ♘xc3 8 bxc3 ♗xe4 9 ♘e5 ♕h4! (the sole defence against ♗b5+, ♕g4 and ♕h5) 10 g3 ♕f6 11 ♗b5+ c6 12 f3 ♗d5 13 ♗e2 b5 and Black's acceptance of the tricky pawn sacrifice has proved to be worth its salt (∓).

7...♗e7
7...c5?! is premature on account of 8 ♗b5+! messing up Black's harmony: 8...♘c6 9 ♗d3 cxd4 10 exd4 and c6 is shown to be a truly bad square for the bishop: White

is already threatening 11 ♘e5. In the Queen's Indian after ...d7-d5 Black always has to be prepared for ♕a4+ and ♗b5+.

8 ♗b5+ c6 9 ♗d3 ♘xc3

9...0-0 at once is also possible: 10 e4 ♘xc3 11 bxc3 c5.

10 bxc3 c5 11 0-0 ♘c6

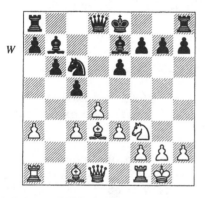

Plans and Counterplans:
White can play **12 e4** when after 12...0-0 13 ♗b2 cxd4 14 cxd4 ♗f6, 15 e5 is forced, after which White's dynamic centre has become rigid (=). White can also prepare e3-e4 with **12 ♗b2** 0-0 13 ♕e2 ♖c8 14 ♖ad1, but Black can play 14...cxd4 15 cxd4 ♗f6 16 e4 ♘a5 or 15 exd4 ♗d6 16 c4 ♘a5 17 ♘e5 ♗xe5 18 dxe5 ♕c7 ∞.

III. Classical Main Line

---

1 d4 ♘f6 2 c4 e6 3 ♘f3 b6 4 g3

In the 1 d4 openings the white light-squared bishop is usually well placed on g2, and this is particularly so in the Queen's Indian where it opposes its counterpart

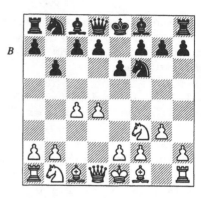

on b7. In case of a set-up with ♗g2 and ...♗b7 White is often able to advance d4-d5, and if Black captures this, the knight on f3 goes to h4 or e1, followed by cxd5. On 4 g3 Black can continue with

A. 4...♗b7 (Classical set-up) or
B. 4...♗a6 (Nimzowitsch's idea)

A. 1 d4 ♘f6 2 c4 e6 3 ♘f3 b6 4 g3 ♗b7 (Classical set-up)

5 ♗g2 ♗e7
Alternatively:

a) 5...c5?! would only help White after 6 d5! exd5 7 ♘h4 g6 8 ♘c3 ♗g7 9 0-0 0-0 10 ♗g5! ±. White, if permitted, always answers Black's move ...c7-c5 with d4-d5!

b) 5...♗b4+ 6 ♗d2 leads to a Bogo-Indian after 6...a5 7 0-0 0-0 8 ♗f4 (the threat is c4-c5, trapping the bishop) 8...♗e7 9 ♘c3 ♘e4 10 ♘a4!? d6 11 ♘d2 ♘xd2 12 ♗xb7 ♖a7 13 ♕xd2 ♖xb7 14 e4, followed by ♘c3, and the rooks occupy the central files with a clear spatial advantage for White (±).

6 0-0 0-0 7 ♘c3

7 d5!? is an exciting pawn sacrifice: 7...exd5 8 ♘h4 c6 9 cxd5 and now 9...♘xd5 10 ♘f5 ♘c7 11 ♘c3 d5!? 12 e4!?, with a complex struggle, or 9...cxd5 10 ♘c3 ♘a6 11 ♘f5 ♘c7 12 ♗f4 ♗c5 13 ♖c1 ♗c6 14 ♘a4 g6 15 ♘xc5 bxc5 16 ♗xc7 ♕xc7 17 ♘e7+ ♔g7 18 ♘xd5 ♗xd5 19 ♗xd5 ♖ab8 = and Black follows up with ...♕e5, ...d7-d6 and ...♖fe8.

After the text-move White is again threatening 8 d5. Blocking this with 7...d5 fails to 8 ♘e5!, e.g. 8...♘bd7? 9 cxd5 exd5 10 ♕a4! with some nasty threats against c6 and d5 (+−). Or 8...♘a6!? 9 ♗f4 c5 10 ♖c1 and Black has some serious difficulties. White will play 11 cxd5 exd5 12 ♕a4 followed by 13 ♖fd1.

7...♘e4

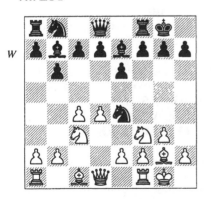

Black stops 8 d5 on positional grounds: his threat is 8...♘xc3, when White's queenside pawns are a wreck while Black easily develops with ...♘a6-c5.

White must protect his knight on c3 with either

A1. 8 ♗d2 or
A2. 8 ♕c2.

8 ♘xe4 ♗xe4 is equal, e.g. 9 ♗f4 c5 10 dxc5 bxc5 11 ♕d2 d5 or 9 ♘e1 ♗xg2 10 ♘xg2 d5 11 ♕a4 ♕e8 =.

A1. 1 d4 ♘f6 2 c4 e6 3 ♘f3 b6 4 g3 ♗b7 5 ♗g2 ♗e7 6 0-0 0-0 7 ♘c3 ♘e4 8 ♗d2

8...♗f6

By attacking the knight on c3 Black further delays d4-d5. Other tries are:

a) 8...♘xc3? 9 ♗xc3 ♗e4 10 d5! ♗f6 11 ♘d4! ±.

b) 8...d6?! 9 d5! ♘xc3 10 ♗xc3 e5 11 e4 and after ♘f3-e1-d3 White can opt for both f2-f4 and b2-b4 and c4-c5. In these closed centre type of games the bishop on b7 stands very poorly.

c) 8...d5 9 cxd5 exd5 10 ♖c1 ♘d7 11 ♕b3 ♘df6 ∞.

d) 8...f5!? 9 d5 ♗f6 10 ♖c1 ♘a6!? ∞.

9 ♖c1 c5!?

After 9...♘xd2 10 ♕xd2 d6 11 d5 the move ...c7-c5 is no longer possible.

10 d5 exd5 11 cxd5 ♘xd2 12 ♘xd2!?

White tries to occupy the e4-square with his knight, envisaging a kingside attack (f2-f4 and g2-g4).

12...d6 13 ♘de4

13 e4? is wrong on account of ...♘d7 and ...♕e7 as e4-e5 is permanently blocked and the d4-square would thus be weakened for nothing.

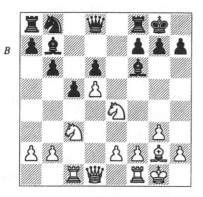

Plans and Counterplans:
In years gone by Black exclusively played **13...♗e7** here, when after the continuation 14 f4 ♘d7 15 g4! a6 16 a4 ♖e8 17 g5! White has a forceful initiative. Besides the pawn-roller h2-h4-h5-h6 White also has ♕d1-d3-g3/h3, ♗g2-h3, ♔h1 and ♖g1 plans at his disposal and Black is doomed to passive defence.

A recent invention is the more active **13...♗e5!** 14 ♕d2 ♗a6! (disallowing 15 f4 ♗d4+ 16 e3) 15 ♔h1 ♕e7 16 f4 ♗d4 17 ♖fe1 g6 18 e3 ♗g7, followed by 19...♘d7, when Black has managed to keep his dark-squared bishop alive and therefore has no cause for concern.

A2. 1 d4 ♘f6 2 c4 e6 3 ♘f3 b6 4 g3 ♗b7 5 ♗g2 ♗e7 6 0-0 0-0 7 ♘c3 ♘e4 8 ♕c2

8...♘xc3
If 8...f5 then 9 ♘e5, while on 8...d5, 9 cxd5 followed by ♗f4 and ♖ac1 is strong (±).

9 ♕xc3
9 bxc3 f5 10 d5 ♘a6 ∞.

9...c5
Other choices are:

a) 9...d6?! 10 ♕c2! (threatening 11 ♘g5! with the simultaneous threats of capturing on b7 and mate on h7!) 10...f5 11 ♘e1 ♗xg2 12 ♘xg2 with 13 e4 to follow ±.

b) 9...♗e4 10 ♗f4 and ♖ac1, ♖fd1 and ♘e1 ±.

c) 9...f5 10 b3 ♗f6 11 ♗b2 d6 12 ♖ad1 a5 13 ♘e1 ♗xg2 14 ♘xg2 ♘c6 15 ♕f3 ♕d7 16 e4!? ∞.

10 ♖d1
10 b3 cxd4 11 ♘xd4 ♗xg2 12 ♔xg2 ♗f6 13 ♗b2 ♘c6 =.

10...d6
10...♗f6 11 ♕d3!, again threatening 12 ♘g5.

11 b3
Also interesting is 11 ♗f4 ♘c6 12 ♕d2 ♘xd4 13 ♘xd4 ♗xg2 14 ♘xe6 fxe6 15 ♔xg2 with a tiny pull for White.

11...♗f6 12 ♗b2

Plans and Counterplans:
Black needs to play precisely here. **12...♘c6** 13 ♕d2 ♘xd4 14 ♘xd4 ♗xg2 15 ♘xe6 fxe6 16 ♔xg2 is slightly better for White, while on both **12...♕e7** and **12...♕c7** White

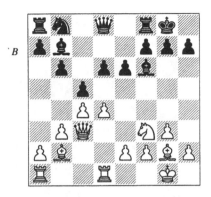

has 13 ♕c2 and 14 e4. Most accurate seems to be **12...♘d7** and now: 13 ♕d2 ♕e7 14 dxc5 ♗xb2 15 ♕xb2 dxc5 =; or 13 ♖d2!? ♕e7 14 ♖ad1 ♖fd8 15 ♕c2 ♖ac8 (Black has 16...d5 up his sleeve) 16 e4 cxd4 17 ♘xd4 a6 with balanced chances.

B. 1 d4 ♘f6 2 c4 e6 3 ♘f3 b6 4 g3 ♗a6!? (Nimzowitsch's idea)

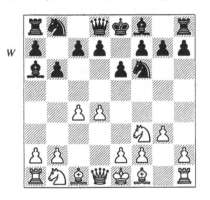

Aron Nimzowitsch – the 'inventor' of the Nimzo-Indian – first played this move in 1934. The point, just as it is in the Queen's Indian with a2-a3, is to disturb White's normal development.

5 b3

The pawn on c4 must be protected because 5 ♗g2? is met by 5...♗xc4 6 ♘e5 ♗d5 ∓. If the queen defends c4 then Black can aim for ...c7-c5:

a) 5 ♕c2 c5 6 ♗g2 ♗b7 7 dxc5 ♗xc5! = with a hedgehog set-up to follow: ...♗e7, ...d7-d6, ...a7-a6, ...0-0, ...♘bd7 and ...♕c7, when Black has counter-chances on the c-file. This is why 7...♗xc5 is better than 7...bxc5.

b) 5 ♕b3 ♘c6!? (threatening 6...♘a5) 6 ♘bd2 ♘a5 7 ♕a4 ♗b7 8 ♗g2 c5 9 0-0 ♗c6 10 ♕c2 cxd4 is equal.

c) 5 ♕a4 c5 6 ♗g2 ♗b7 7 0-0 (7 dxc5 ♗xc5 8 0-0 0-0 9 ♘c3 ♗e7 10 ♗f4 ♘a6 11 ♖ad1 ♘c5 12 ♕c2 ♕c8 13 ♘b5 ♘ce4) 7...cxd4 8 ♘xd4 ♗xg2 9 ♔xg2 ♕c7 10 ♘c3 ♗e7 with the idea of continuing ...0-0, ...a7-a6, ...♕b7, ...♖fc8, ...d7-d6 and ...♘bd7.

d) 5 ♘bd2 ♗b7 6 ♗g2 c5 7 e4 cxd4 (7...♘xe4? 8 ♘e5 ♘c3 9 ♗xb7 ♘xd1 10 ♗xa8 ±) 8 e5 ♘e4 9 ♘xe4 ♗xe4 =, or Black can play in the style of the Queen's Gambit, counting on the unfortunate placement of the knight on d2: 5...d5 6 ♗g2 ♗e7 7 0-0 0-0 with equality.

5...♗b4+!?

Forcing ♗d2 to disrupt the ideal set-up of ♗b2, ♘c3. Also interesting is 5...d5 6 ♗g2 dxc4 7 ♘e5 ♗b4+ 8 ♔f1 (8 ♗d2 cxb3! 9

axb3 &xd2+ 10 ₩xd2 ᐃd5 ∞) and
after 8...ᐃfd7, 8...c6 or 8...&d6
Black creates a material and positional imbalance. A more peaceful approach for White is 6 cxd5
exd5 7 &g2 c5 8 0-0 ᐃc6 9 &b2
Ⅱc8 10 ᐃc3 with good play against
Black's 'hanging pawn-centre'
with Ⅱc1, d4xc5, ᐃa4. Also playable is the strange-looking 5...b5,
when 6 cxb5 &xb5 7 &g2 &b4+ 8
&d2 a5 9 0-0 0-0 10 a3 &e7 11
ᐃc3 &a6 12 ₩c2 d5 13 Ⅱfc1 ᐃbd7
14 e4 is good for White ±.

6 &d2

6 ᐃbd2 would lose comically to
6...&c3 7 Ⅱb1 &b7 8 &b2 ᐃe4 9
Ⅱg1 ₩f6! 10 &c1 ᐃc6! 11 e3 ᐃb4
−+.

6...&e7

6...&xd2+?! solves White's problems: 7 ₩xd2 d5 8 cxd5 exd5 9
&g2 and after ᐃc3, 0-0, ᐃe5 and
Ⅱfd1 everything is in order.

7 &g2

For a short period it was fashionable to develop the bishop to
d3, but this is not seen very often
these days due to 7 ᐃc3 0-0 8 e4
&b7 9 &d3 d5 10 cxd5 exd5 11 e5
ᐃe4 with ...c7-c5 ∞, or instead of
8...&b7, 8...d5!? at once: 9 cxd5
&xf1 10 &xf1 exd5 11 e5 ᐃe4 ∞.

7...c6

Black would like to play ...d7-
d5 and in case of cxd5, answers
cxd5. After 7...d5 8 cxd5 exd5 9
0-0 0-0 10 ᐃc3 &b7 11 Ⅱc1 followed by &f4 and ᐃe5 White has
an easy plus. Instead of 8...exd5,
8...ᐃxd5 deserves attention with

the idea of ...0-0, ...ᐃd7 and ...c7-
c5.

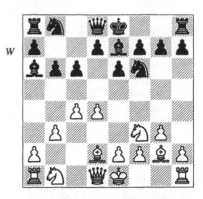

Plans and Counterplans:

White has no resources to stop
...d7-d5 but he can prepare to
meet it. Indeed, he should play
actively as after the straightforward **8 0-0** d5 9 ₩c2 (9 cxd5?!
cxd5: in this position, resembling
the Exchange Slav, Black's a6-
bishop is more active than its
counterpart at g2) 9...0-0 10 Ⅱd1
ᐃbd7 followed by 11...c5 and ...Ⅱc8
Black consolidates easily. So a different arrangement of pieces is
appropriate: **8 &c3!?** (vacating
the d2-square for the knight)
8...d5 and now:

a) 9 ᐃbd2 ᐃbd7 10 0-0 0-0 11
Ⅱe1 c5 12 e4 dxc4!? (12...dxe4 13
ᐃxe4 &b7 is also playable) 13 bxc4
cxd4 14 ᐃxd4 ᐃe5 15 ᐃxe6 fxe6
16 &xe5 &c5 17 Ⅱf1 ₩d3 and
Black has superb compensation
for the pawn,

b) 9 ᐃe5!? ᐃfd7 (there is another thing to remember: this is
the only method to dislodge an

unpleasant knight from e5 if the c6-square is weak!) 10 ♘xd7 ♘xd7 11 ♘d2 0-0 12 0-0 ♖c8 (an interesting alternative idea is 12...♘f6 13 e4 b5!?) 13 e4 and White has a reasonable game but Black is not without chances either. Here are a few of the many possible reactions: 13...dxe4 and ...b7-b5 or 13...dxc4 and again ...b7-b5 or 13...b5 at once, when White can sacrifice his c4-pawn with 14 ♖e1 only to get it back later with ♗f1. Also possible is 13...c5 14 exd5 exd5 15 dxc5 dxc4 16 c6!? cxb3 17 ♖e1 ♗b5 18 axb3 ♗xc6 19 ♗xc6 ♖xc6 20 ♖xa7 ♗f6 (20...♖xc3 21 ♘b1!) 21 ♘c4!?, when Black is still defending but the ending is drawish.

There is still no clear assessment of this most fashionable Queen's Indian line. It can be recommended for both sides!

Bogo-Indian Defence

1 d4 ♘f6 2 c4 e6 3 ♘f3 ♗b4+

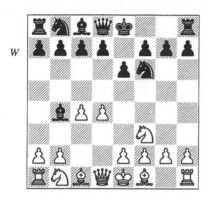

After this check White faces something of a dilemma: he can transpose to the **Nimzo-Indian** with 4 ♘c3 or play 4 ♘bd2. But in the former case, why not play 3 ♘c3 if you are happy with a Nimzo-Indian, and in the latter the bishop on c1 gets stuck, while the knight is not ideally placed on d2 either. The most natural move is 4 ♗d2 with a somewhat freer game for White, but Black still has some interesting strategical resources. For those who play the **Nimzo-Indian** with Black and on 3 ♘f3 do not like the **Queen's Indian**, the **Bogo-Indian** can be a good alternative.

This section is divided into:

I. 4 ♘bd2 and
II. 4 ♗d2.

I. 1 d4 ♘f6 2 c4 e6 3 ♘f3 ♗b4+ 4 ♘bd2

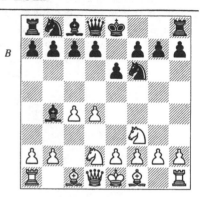

White aims for 5 a3, intending to play e2-e4 if the bishop retreats. Black can of course swap on d2 but this costs him the bishop pair. This may all sound straightforward enough, but in reality the situation is more difficult.

4...d5

It is logical to switch to a Queen's Gambit-like position in which the knight on b1 obviously belongs on c3 rather than d2. Both 4...0-0?! 5 a3 ♗e7 6 e4 ± and 4...c5 5 a3 ♗xd2+ 6 ♕xd2 cxd4 7 ♘xd4, when White develops via e2-e3, b2-b4 and ♗b2 while maintaining his bishop pair (±), are weaker. A more flexible answer is 4...b6!? 5 a3 ♗xd2+ 6 ♗xd2 ♗b7 7 ♗g5!? d6 8 e3 ♘bd7 9 ♗d3 and now Black can set about the bishop on g5: 9...h6 10 ♗h4 g5!? 11 ♗g3 h5 12 h3 ♘e4 and Black equalizes with ...f7-f5, ...♕f6 and ...0-0-0.

5 ♕a4+

After 5 e3 0-0 6 a3 ♗e7 7 b4 (7 ♗d3 c5! =) 7...a5 8 b5 c5! 9 bxc6 bxc6 =, Black has the moves ...c7-c5, ...♗a6, ...♘bd7 and ...♘e4 in hand.

5...♘c6 6 a3 ♗xd2+

6...♗e7 comes into consideration: 7 e3 0-0 8 ♕c2 a5 9 b3 ♖e8 and Black can try to organize his pieces with the following manoeuvre: ...♗f8, ...g7-g6, ...♗g7, ...♗d7, ...♘e7 and ...c7-c6. This regrouping manoeuvre is essential as in positions resembling the Queen's Gambit the knight is out of place on c6.

7 ♗xd2 ♘e4 8 ♖d1 0-0 9 e3

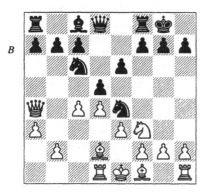

Plans and Counterplans:
It is obviously disadvantageous for Black to give up his active central pieces for the suffocated bishop on d2 with **9...♘xd2** 10

♖xd2 (±), but **9...♘e7** followed by ...b7-b6 and ...♗b7 is more logical. Another idea is **9...♗d7,** when after ...f7-f6 and ...♗e8 the bishop springs to life. Meanwhile White opts for ♕c2 and b2-b4, e.g. 9...♗d7 10 ♕c2 a5!? (to stop b2-b4) 11 ♗d3 f5 12 0-0 ♗e8 with double-edged play. After **9...♕f6!?** 10 ♗d3 ♕g6 11 0-0 ♘c5!? the game develops a tactical character. After 12 ♕xc6! ♘xd3 13 ♕xc7 ♘xb2 the battle really flares up.

II. 1 d4 ♘f6 2 c4 e6 3 ♘f3 ♗b4+ 4 ♗d2

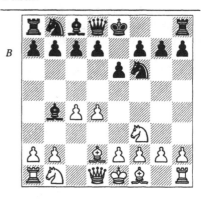

There are two common continuations:

A. 4...♕e7 and
B. 4...c5.

It is worth taking a look at some other lines:

a) **4...♗xd2+** 5 ♕xd2 (the general rule is to recapture on d2 with the queen in order to save the knight on b1 for the c3-square.

The only exception to this arises in the section on 4...♕e7) 5...0-0 6 g3 d6 (6...d5 7 ♗g2 c6 8 ♕c2 ♘bd7 9 ♘bd2 and after e2-e4 White is slightly better) 7 ♗g2 ♕e7 8 0-0 e5 9 ♘c3 c6 10 e4 ♖e8 11 ♘h4!? ±.

b) 4...a5 5 g3 (5 ♗xb4 axb4 is bad, as the pawn on b4, along with the open a-file, bears down on the white queenside. But 5 ♘c3 and e2-e3, ♗d3 and 0-0 is perfectly playable) 5...d5 6 ♕c2 ♘c6 7 a3 ♗e7 8 ♗g2 dxc4 9 ♕xc4 ♕d5 10 ♕d3 ♕e4 11 ♕xe4 ♘xe4 12 ♗f4 is slightly better for White.

c) 4...♗e7!? Seemingly Black has lost a tempo but in fact he has only provoked ♗d2 to take the b2-square away from the bishop. After 5 g3 d5 6 ♗g2 0-0 7 0-0 c6 8 ♕c2 b6, Black, as in the Closed Catalan, can play ...♗b7, ...♘bd7 and ...c6-c5.

A. 1 d4 ♘f6 2 c4 e6 3 ♘f3 ♗b4+ 4 ♗d2 ♕e7

5 g3
From the above comments it should be evident that White's strongest plan is to fianchetto the bishop to g2.
    5...♘c6 6 ♗g2 ♗xd2+ 7 ♘bxd2
This is the exceptional situation when 7 ♕xd2? is worse in view of 7...♘e4! 8 ♕c2 ♕b4+ 9 ♘c3 (9 ♘bd2? ♘xd2 wins a pawn) 9...♘xc3 10 ♕xc3 ♕xc3+ 11 bxc3 with a terrible pawn structure in the forthcoming endgame.

7...d6 8 0-0 a5 9 e4 e5 10 d5 ♘b8 11 ♘e1

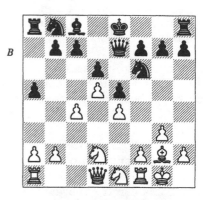

Plans and Counterplans:
After ♘e1-d3 White can play for f2-f4 or b2-b3, a2-a3, b2-b4 and c4-c5. In the latter case it is vital to know that if instead of b2-b3 White starts up with a2-a3, Black plays ...a5-a4! and White's queenside action is stopped for ever, while Black gains access to the squares b3 and c5.

In general, Black's may opt for the calm plan of ...0-0, ...b7-b6 and ...♘a6-c5 or he can set something under way immediately with 11...h5!? Now White best reacts with the blockading move 12 h4 and again follows up with ♘d3, b2-b3, a2-a3 and b3-b4. Overall it is White who can dictate the play (±).

B. 1 d4 ♘f6 2 c4 e6 3 ♘f3 ♗b4+ 4 ♗d2 c5!?

This open-minded move has made the 'Bogo' popular again.

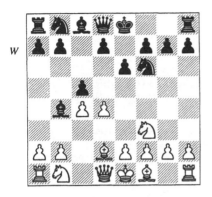

5 &xb4

Or 5 g3 ♕b6! and now 6 dxc5? is bad, as after 6...&xc5 both b2 and f2 are hanging. 5 a3 is met simply by 5...&xd2+ 6 ♕xd2 cxd4 7 ♘xd4 b6 followed by ...&b7, ...0-0 and ...a7-a6, ...d7-d6 or ...d7-d5 =.

5...cxb4 6 g3

Or 6 a3 bxa3 7 ♖xa3 0-0 and Black's idea is ...♘c6, ...d7-d6 and ...e6-e5 or ...b7-b6, ...&b7, ...d7-d6, ...♘c6, ...a7-a5 and ...♘b4. On 6 e3 0-0 again the plan of ...♘c6, ...d7-d6 and ...e6-e5 is good, when if White invades with d4-d5, the black knight returns to the centre via b8-d7-c5.

6...0-0 7 &g2 d6

7...d5 can be met by 8 ♘bd2 and 0-0, ♕b3 (♕a4), ♖ac1 and

c4xd5! In this case Black will have the worse of the endgame due to his doubled b-pawns.

8 0-0

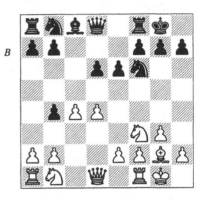

Plans and Counterplans:

Black does best with **8...♖e8**, waiting for White to commit himself. On 9 ♘bd2, Black can play 9...a5!? 10 e4 e5 11 a3 ♘a6!? to maintain the pressure on the dark squares (b4, c5, e5). 9 a3 ♘c6 10 ♘bd2 a5 11 e4 bxa3 12 ♖xa3 e5 13 d5 ♘b4 also leads to equality, while 10 d5 exd5 11 exd5 ♘e7 is unclear. Neither can White claim an advantage after 9 ♕d3!? ♘c6 10 ♘bd2 e5 11 e4 &g4! 12 d5 &xf3! 13 ♘xf3 ♘b8 14 a3 ♘a6 (=).

Nimzo-Indian Defence

1 d4 ♘f6 2 c4 e6 3 ♘c3 ♗b4

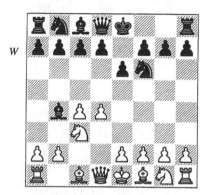

Black takes the opportunity to pin the knight on c3 and thus thwart White's plan of e4 and d5. Compared to the calm positional game of a **Queen's Indian**, the **Nimzo-Indian** is characterized by sharp strategical play. White often allows, or even provokes, Black to capture the knight on c3 in order to obtain the bishop pair and strengthen his centre. Of course there is always a price to pay for such an advantage: in this case the doubled c-pawns will be difficult to mobilize. Black may play ...0-0, ...c7-c5, ...d7-d5, ...b7-b6 and ...♘e4 depending on which of the following plans White chooses:

I. 4 g3
II. 4 f3
III. 4 a3 (Sämisch Variation)

IV. 4 ♕c2 (Capablanca Variation)
V. 4 e3 (Rubinstein Variation).

A few other lines of lesser importance are:

a) 4 ♗d2 0-0 5 ♕c2 d5 6 e3 ♘bd7 followed by 7...c5 and Black equalizes.

b) 4 ♕b3 c5 5 dxc5 ♘c6 6 ♘f3 ♘e4! 7 ♗d2 ♘xd2 8 ♘xd2 0-0 =. 4 ♕b3 is definitely worse than 4 ♕c2, as after a2-a3 the b-pawn is obstructed.

c) 4 ♗g5 h6 5 ♗h4 c5 6 d5 d6 (or 6...b5!? 7 dxe6 fxe6 8 cxb5 d5 ∞) 7 e3 ♗xc3 8 bxc3 e5 with a complicated position in which, after ...♕e7 and ...♘bd7 Black is ready to get going with ...g7-g5 and ...h7-h5, while White develops via f2-f3, ♗d3, ♕c2 and ♘e2 and awaits ...g7-g5, after which he intends to open the position for his bishops with h2-h4. In this line the moral is that Black should wait until White's centre becomes inflexible before capturing on c3.

d) 4 ♘f3 usually transposes to other lines, for example, after ...d5 to the Ragozin Defence (Queen's Gambit) or after 4...c5 5 e3 to the Rubinstein Variation. After 4...c5 White can also vary with 5 d5 ♗xc3+ 6 bxc3 d6 7 e3 e5 8 ♕c2 ♕e7 9 ♗e2 0-0 10 ♘d2 e4 with equality.

I. 1 d4 ♘f6 2 c4 e6 3 ♘c3 ♗b4 4 g3

4...c5!?

The most common 'Nimzo' plan: swapping the c-pawn for the d4-pawn and then either building a hedgehog position or playing ...d7-d5.

5 ♘f3
5 d5? is a mistake on account of 5...♘e4 6 ♕d3 ♕f6. White has to be extremely accurate because the bishop on b4 is a dangerous piece.

5...cxd4 6 ♘xd4 0-0 7 ♗g2 d5

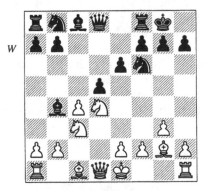

Plans and Counterplans:
If White continues **8 0-0** then after 8...dxc4 9 ♕a4 ♘a6 Black is fine, while **8 ♕b3 ♗xc3+ 9 bxc3** (9 ♕xc3 e5 and 10...d4) 9...dxc4 10 ♕xc4 e5 11 ♘b5 (11 ♘c2 ♗e6 12 ♕b5 ♗d5 =) 11...a6 12 ♘a3 ♗e6 is also equal. White's most consistent plan – just as it is in the Catalan Opening – is to take on d5: **8 cxd5 ♘xd5 9 ♗d2 ♗xc3**

(9...♘xc3 10 bxc3 ♗e7 is a risky continuation due to 11 ♖b1 with strong pressure on the queenside) 10 bxc3 e5 11 ♘b5 ♘c6 12 c4 ♘b6 13 c5 ♘c4 14 ♕c2 a6! 15 ♕xc4 ♗e6 16 ♕c2 axb5 ∞.

II. 1 d4 ♘f6 2 c4 e6 3 ♘c3 ♗b4 4 f3

4...d5

The sharp cotinuation 4...c5 5 d5 ♘h5 6 ♘h3 ♕h4+ 7 ♘f2 ♕xc4 is considered good for White nowadays: 8 e4 ♗xc3+ 9 bxc3 ♕xc3+ 10 ♗d2 ♕d4 11 ♕c1 exd5 12 ♗c3 ♕a4 13 ♕g5 d4 14 ♕xc5! ♕c6 15 ♕xd4 0-0 16 ♖b1! and White is much better due to the threat of 17 ♖b5. 4...d5 is justified by the fact that White's f2-f3 does not fit well into a Queen's Gambit type of position.

5 a3

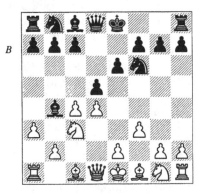

This is practically the only move if White still wants to play e2-e4. If White plays more passively then Black can simply play

...c7-c5, ...0-0 and ...♘c6 with a comfortable game.

Plans and Counterplans:
If Black tries to hang on to his bishop then after **5...♗e7** 6 e4 he somehow has to find a way to combat White's powerful centre. For example, 6...dxe4 7 fxe4 e5 8 d5 ♗c5 9 ♘f3 ♘g4 10 ♘a4 ♗f2+ 11 ♔e2, threatening 12 h3. It is better to withhold actions with 6...0-0 7 cxd5 exd5 8 e5 ♘e8 9 f4 c5 followed by ...c5xd4, ...♘c6 and ...♘e8-c7-e6 ∞, and 6...c5 7 cxd5 exd5 8 e5 ♘fd7 9 ♘xd5 cxd4 10 ♘xe7 ♕xe7 11 f4 f6 is also unclear.

The simple **5...♗xc3+!** 6 bxc3 c5 7 cxd5 ♘xd5 seems to be more consistent, after which Black's activity counterbalances White's bishop pair and central plus:

a) 8 ♕d2 cxd4 9 cxd4 ♘c6 10 e4 ♘b6 11 ♗b5 0-0 12 ♘e2 ♗d7 13 0-0 ♘e5! with good play along the c-file and especially on the foothold at c4.

b) 8 dxc5 ♕a5 9 e4 ♘f6 10 ♗e3!? 0-0 (White would gladly welcome 10...♕xc3+ 11 ♔f2, as the black queen can then be pushed around or exchanged) 11 ♕b3 ♘fd7 12 a4 ♕c7 (12...♘xc5? 13 ♕b4! ±) 13 ♕a3 ♘c6 14 ♘h3 ♘a5 15 ♗e2 b6!? 16 cxb6 axb6 =, and with 17...♗a6 Black swaps bishops and proceeds with ...♘a5-b7-c5 attacking the pawn on a4, with full compensation for the pawn.

III. 1 d4 ♘f6 2 c4 e6 3 ♘c3 ♗b4 4 a3 (Sämisch Variation)

4...♗xc3+ 5 bxc3 c5!?
With this move Black blockades White's doubled pawns, enables the queen to go to a5 and prepares for a queenside expansion via ...b7-b6 and ...♗b7.

6 e3
6 f3 d5 7 cxd5 ♘xd5 leads to section II. The trick 6 e4?! (not 6...♘xe4? 7 ♕g4!) would backfire after 6...♕a5 7 e5 ♘e4 8 ♗d2 ♘c6 ∓.

6...0-0 7 ♗d3 ♘c6
7...b6 is weaker due to 8 ♘e2 (the knight belongs here as on f3 it would block the f-pawn) 8...♗b7 9 0-0 d5!? 10 cxd5 ± and White has got rid of his rigid doubled pawns. After 7...♘c6 Black will still play ...b7-b6, but now with the idea of taking a closer look at the pawn on c4 with ...♗a6.

8 ♘e2

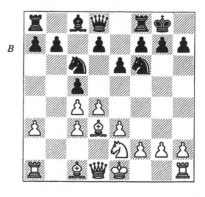

Plans and Counterplans:
Black has two different plans here. The first is to blockade the dark squares in the centre, thus limiting the strength of White's bishop pair with **8...e5!?** 9 0-0 (9 d5 e4! 10 ♗c2 ♘e5 ∓) 9...d6 10 e4 h6!? (grabbing the pawn on d4 is dangerous due to the annoying pin, ♗g5) 11 d5 ♘e7 and Black develops via ...♘g6, ...b7-b6 and ...♗d7. The other, even more ambitious plan is directed against the pawn on c4: **8...b6** 9 e4 ♘e8 (an excellent prophylactic move, preparing not only for 10 e5 d6 but also against the march of the f-pawn) 10 0-0 ♗a6 11 f4 f5! 12 ♘g3 g6 13 ♗e3 and now not 13...♘d6 14 exf5 ♘xc4 15 ♗xc4 ♗xc4 16 fxg6 ♗xf1 17 ♕h5 ♕e7 18 ♖xf1 with a pull for White, but 13...cxd4 14 cxd4 d5! 15 cxd5 ♗xd3 16 ♕xd3 fxe4 17 ♕xe4 ♕xd5 with equal chances.

IV. 1 d4 ♘f6 2 c4 e6 3 ♘c3 ♗b4 4 ♕c2 (Capablanca Variation)

Now after a2-a3 White will force Black to capture on c3 and then recapture with the queen. Black has three different strategies:

A. 4...0-0 followed by ...b7-b6,
B. 4...d5 with a Queen's Gambit style middlegame,
C. 4...c5, a typical Nimzo.

4...b6?! is bad in view of 5 e4! bxc3+ 6 bxc3 ♗b7 7 ♗d3 d6 8 f4

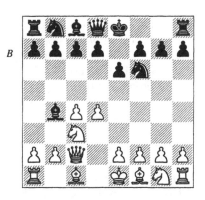

±, while on **4...d6** White can play 5 ♗g5!? ♘bd7 6 e3 c5 7 dxc5 dxc5 (7...♘xc5 8 ♘e2 and 0-0-0 ±) 8 0-0-0 ♗xc3 9 ♕xc3 ♕e7 10 ♗d3 b6 and now White has the option of an unusual manoeuvre: 11 f3 intending ♘g1-h3-f2 and ♗e4 ±.

Finally, **4...♘c6** 5 ♘f3 d6 6 a3 ♗xc3+ 7 ♕xc3 ♕e7 8 g3 e5 9 d5 ♘b8 10 ♗g2 0-0 11 0-0 h6 12 b4 is also slightly better for White (±) as Black must spend time dealing with White's plan of ♗b2 and c4-c5.

A. 1 d4 ♘f6 2 c4 e6 3 ♘c3 ♗b4 4 ♕c2 0-0

---

5 a3 ♗xc3+ 6 ♕xc3 b6
6...♘e4 is premature: 7 ♕c2 f5 8 g3 b6 9 ♗g2 ♗b7 10 ♘f3 ± with threats of ♘d2 and ♘g5, while White may also continue with 0-0, b2-b4, ♗b2, ♘e1 and f2-f3. However, 6...b5!? is a clever pawn sacrifice: 7 cxb5 c6!? and 8 bxc6?! ♘xc6 is bad as Black is much too active – he threatens ...♘e4 and ...♕a5+ as well as ...♗a6 or ...♗b7

and ...罝c8. So instead of 8 bxc6?!
White should play 8 奡g5! cxb5 9
e3 奡b7 10 包f3 h6 11 奡xf6 豐xf6
12 奡e2 罝c8 13 豐d3 a6 14 0-0 with
a small edge (±) and the possibility of undermining the black
pawns with a3-a4.

7 奡g5!?

After 7 包f3 奡b7 8 e3 d6 9 奡e2
包bd7 10 0-0 包e4 11 豐c2 f5 12 b4
Black can choose between ...包df6,
...罝f8-f6-g6, ...豐f6 and ...a7-a5, all
of which offer equal chances. 7
奡g5!? maintains the possibility of
controlling the e4 square, thus
parrying Black's usual plan of
...奡b7, ...d7-d6, ...包bd7 and ...包e4.

7...奡b7

After 7...c5 8 dxc5 bxc5 9 e3 d6
10 奡d3 包bd7 11 包e2 White's
bishops are quite effective in the
more open position (±).

8 e3

Or 8 f3 h6 9 奡h4 d5 10 e3
包bd7 11 cxd5 包xd5 12 奡xd8
包xc3 13 奡h4 包d5 14 奡f2 f5 =.

**8...h6 9 奡h4 d6 10 f3!? 包bd7
11 奡d3 c5 12 包e2 罝c8**

Plans and Counterplans:
Black is aiming for a total elimi-
nation of the centre with ...d7-d5
and ...奡a6, while White must
wait for the position to open up,
after which his bishops will gain
strength. Instead of 13 豐d2 cxd4
14 exd4 奡a6 15 罝c1 d5 =, White
should try 13 豐b3!? cxd4 (13...d5
14 cxd5 奡xd5 15 豐d1 and ±
merely because of the bishop
pair) 14 exd4 d5 15 0-0 dxc4 16

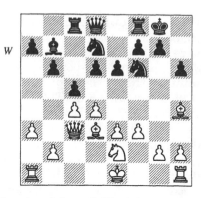

奡xc4 and though Black has no concrete weaknesses he has trouble
finding an active plan.

**B. 1 d4 包f6 2 c4 e6 3 包c3 奡b4 4
豐c2 d5**

5 cxd5

Something must be done about
the pawn on c4 as Black was
threatening 5...dxc4 6 e3 b5 ∓.
White's other possibility is 5 a3
奡xc3+ 6 豐xc3 包e4 7 豐c2 c5 8
dxc5 包c6 9 cxd5 exd5 10 包f3 奡f5
11 b4 0-0 (not 11...包g3? 12 豐b2
包xh1 13 豐xg7 罝f8 14 奡h6) 12
奡b2 b6 13 b5 bxc5 14 bxc6. Now
after 14...豐a5+ 15 包d2 罝ab8 16
c7! 豐xc7 17 包xe4 奡xe4 18 豐d2
罝b3 19 f3 奡g6 20 罝c1 Black has
insufficient compensation for the
piece, but the official best novelty
of the second half of 1993 has improved this whole line for Black:
14...罝b8! 15 包d2 d4 16 包xe4
奡xe4 17 豐d2 (17 豐xe4 豐a5+ 18
当d1 罝xb2 19 豐d3 c4 −+) 17...豐b6
18 c7 (18 奡c1 c4 19 c7 罝b7 20 f3
奡g6 21 e4 d3 and now it is best

for White to give back the piece on d3) 18...♕xb2 19 ♕xb2 ♖xb2 20 ♖c1 ♖c8 21 ♖xc5 ♖b1+ 22 ♔d2 ♖b2+ with a draw by perpetual on b1 and b2.

5...♕xd5!?

5...exd5, which resembles the Exchange Variation in the Queen's Gambit, is a little better for White: 6 ♗g5 h6 7 ♗xf6 ♕xf6 8 a3 ♗xc3+ 9 ♕xc3 0-0 10 e3 c6 11 ♘f3, and after ♗e2, 0-0 White can try for a minority attack with b2-b4, a2-a4 and b4-b5.

6 ♘f3 ♕f5!?

This is another fresh idea. The old 6...c5 7 ♗d2 ♗xc3 8 ♗xc3 cxd4 9 ♘xd4 ♘c6 10 e3 ♘xd4 11 ♗xd4 ♗d7 12 ♕c5 is slightly favourable for White.

7 ♕xf5

7 ♕b3 c5 8 a3 ♗a5 9 e3 ♘c6 =(∞).

7...exf5

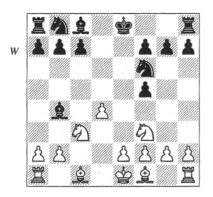

Plans and Counterplans:
White would love to make use of Black's doubled pawn and liquidate into a better ending by simply exchanging pieces, but Black

has a specific plan: after ...c7-c6, ...♘bd7-b6, ...♗d6 and ...♗e6 he will infiltrate on the light squares in the centre (c4, d5, e4), perhaps combined with ...a7-a5-a4. For example, 8 ♗d2 c6 9 e3 ♘bd7 10 ♗d3 ♘b6 11 ♘e2 ♗d6! 12 0-0 ♘e4 13 ♗a5 0-0 14 ♖fc1 ♖e8 15 ♘d2 ♘xd2 16 ♗xd2 a5! 17 a3 ♗e6 =.

C. 1 d4 ♘f6 2 c4 e6 3 ♘c3 ♗b4 4 ♕c2 c5

After the queen has deserted the d1-square Black need not be afraid of a d4-d5 thrust, so ...c7-c5, with the idea of an exchange on d4, is very logical at this juncture.

5 dxc5

This is more testing than 5 ♘f3 cxd4 6 ♘xd4 ♘c6 7 e3 d5 = or 5 e3 ♘c6 6 ♘f3 cxd4 7 exd4 d5 =.

5...0-0

Other tries are:

a) 5...♘a6 6 a3 ♗xc3+ 7 ♕xc3 ♘xc5 8 b4 ♘ce4 9 ♕c2 (9 ♕d4 d5 10 c5 b6) 9...d5 10 f3 ♘d6 11 c5 ♘f5 12 e3 ♕c7! with a messy game.

b) 5...♕c7 6 a3 ♗xc5 7 b4 ♗e7 8 ♘b5 ♕c6 9 ♘f3 d6 10 ♘fd4 ♕d7 11 e4 and White has won a sackful of tempi by kicking the black queen around (±).

c) 5...♗xc5, intending a hedgehog set-up with ...♕c7, ...♗e7, ...d7-d6, ...a7-a6, ...b7-b6, ...♗b7, ...♘bd7 and ...0-0. However this can be impeded by the new 6 ♘f3 ♕c7 7 g3! a6 8 ♗f4! d6 9 ♗g2

♘bd7 10 0-0 0-0 11 ♖ad1 h6 12 a3, threatening 13 b4 followed by c4-c5. Black did not get to retreat to e7 with his bishop and now the pawn on d6 is in trouble. Instead of 7...a6, the immediate 7...♗e7 is bad due to 8 ♘b5 or 8 ♗f4.

6 a3

Or 6 ♘f3 ♘a6!? 7 g3 ♘xc5 8 ♗g2 ♘ce4 ∞.

6...♗xc5 7 ♘f3

Plans and Counterplans:
Black intends to develop either via ...b7-b6 and ...♗b7 or by ...d7-d5:

a) 7...b6 8 ♗f4 ♗b7 9 ♖d1! (by attacking the d6-square, Black's ...♗e7 and ...d7-d6 plan is hindered) 9...♘c6 10 e3 ♖c8 11 ♗e2 with 0-0 to follow, when White is on top due to pressure along the d-file (±).

b) 7...d5 8 cxd5 (for 8 ♗f4 ♘c6 9 e3, see the Orthodox Queen's Gambit with ♗f4) 8...exd5 9 ♗g5 ♗e6 10 e3 h6 11 ♗h4 ♘c6 12 ♖d1 ♗e7 13 ♗e2 ♖c8 and White's advantage – Black's isolated d-pawn – is really only theoretical.

c) Black can also start with 7...♘c6 and if 8 ♗f4 then 8...d5 leading to the aforementioned Queen's Gambit, while on 8 ♗g5 Black plays 8...b6! (not 8...♘d4 9 ♘xd4 ♗xd4 10 e3 ♕a5 11 exd4 ♕xg5 12 ♕d2! ♕xd2+ 13 ♔xd2 with a better ending for White) 9 ♖d1 ♗b7 10 e4 ♗e7 11 ♗e2 ♖c8 12 0-0 ♕c7 13 ♘b5 ♕b8 14 ♗xf6 ♗xf6 15 ♖xd7 ♘e5 16 ♖xb7 (16 ♘xe5? ♗xe5 17 h3? ♗c6 −+) 16...♕xb7 17 ♘d6 ♕c7 18 ♘xc8 ♘xf3+ 19 ♗xf3 ♖xc8 leading to a drawish game due to the opposite-coloured bishops.

So, in conclusion, 7...♘c6 is best, and on 8 ♗f4, 8...d5 or on 8 ♗g5, 8...b6.

V. 1 d4 ♘f6 2 c4 e6 3 ♘c3 ♗b4 4 e3 (Rubinstein Variation)

This seemingly modest system requires thorough preparation. White plans to develop his kingside pieces as soon as possible via ♗d3, ♘e2 or ♘f3, or perhaps ♘e2 and a2-a3 right away.

4...0-0

It is good tactics to wait until White has unveiled his intentions and then react suitably. However, the normal Nimzo-Indian moves are not bad either. Here are some sample lines:

a) 4...c5!? 5 ♗d3 (5 ♘e2 cxd4 6 exd4 d5 7 c5 ♘e4 8 ♗d2 ♘xd2 9 ♕xd2 a5 10 a3 ♗xc3 11 ♘xc3 a4 is equal) 5...♘c6 6 ♘f3 ♗xc3+ 7 bxc3 d6 8 e4 e5 and, by the time

White has freed his dark-squared bishop, Black has succeeded in clogging up its light-squared colleague. For example, 9 d5 ♘e7 10 ♘h4 h6 11 f4 ♘g6! 12 ♘xg6 fxg6 13 fxe5 dxe5 14 ♗e3 b6 =.

b) 4...♘c6 5 ♗d3 e5!? 6 ♘e2 (6 d5 ♗xc3+ 7 bxc3 ♘e7 followed by ...d7-d6 and ...♘d7 =) 6...d5 7 cxd5 ♘xd5 8 e4 ♘b6 9 d5 ♘e7 10 a3 ♗d6 with a chaotic game in which Black's plan is ...0-0 and ...c7-c6. If White then captures the pawn, then ...bxc6 and ...♗e6 is possible.

c) 4...b6 is perhaps the least favourable line for Black as now White can exploit the situation of bishop b4. 5 ♘ge2 ♗a6!? (5...♗b7 6 a3 ♗e7 7 d5 0-0 8 e4 ±) 6 a3 ♗e7 (6...♗xc3+ 7 ♘xc3 d5 8 b3 ±) 7 ♘f4 d5 8 cxd5 ♗xf1 9 ♔xf1 exd5 10 ♕f3 d6 11 g4 ±.

5 ♗d3

Or 5 ♘e2 d5 6 a3 ♗e7 7 cxd5 exd5 8 g3 c6 9 ♗g2 a5 and with ...♘a6-c7, ...♘e8-d6 and ...f7-f5 Black puts pressure on the central light squares (c4, e4 and e6).

5...d5

Black's idea is ...c7-c5, followed by ...d5xc4 and ...c5xd4.

Now White's main possibilities are:

A. 6 a3
B. 6 ♘e2 and
C. 6 ♘f3.

A. 1 d4 ♘f6 2 c4 e6 3 ♘c3 ♗b4 4 e3 0-0 5 ♗d3 d5 6 a3

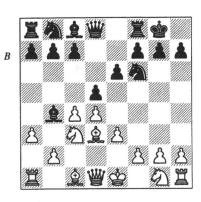

B

6...♗xc3+

Also possible are 6...♗e7 7 cxd5 exd5 8 b4 b6 and then ...c7-c5 and 6...dxc4!?, when 7 ♗xh7+ ♘xh7 8 axb4 e5 9 ♘ge2 (9 dxe5 ♕g5) 9...♘c6 10 b5 exd4 11 exd4 ♘b4 12 0-0 ♗f5 leads to a double-edged position while if instead of 7 ♗xh7+ White plays 7 ♗xc4 ♗d6 8 ♘f3 ♘c6, Black equalizes with ...e6-e5. Although these variations are not bad, if the knight on g1 has not yet gone to e2, it makes more sense to meet a2-a3 with ...♗xc3 to shatter the white queenside.

7 bxc3 dxc4

The immediate 7...c5 can be answered by 8 cxd5 exd5 9 ♘e2, when the position of the black pawn on d5 is slightly unfortunate for Black. He should therefore avoid this with the move order 7...dxc4.

8 ♗xc4 c5

Plans and Counterplans:
White is still some way from completing his development, and this

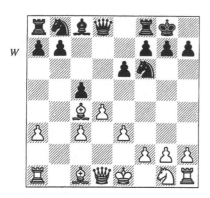

allows Black to equalize with ...e6-e5, for example 9 ♘e2 ♘c6 10 0-0 ♕e7 11 ♗a2 ♖d8 with 12...e5 to follow =.

B. 1 d4 ♘f6 2 c4 e6 3 ♘c3 ♗b4 4 e3 0-0 5 ♗d3 d5 6 ♘e2

6...c5
6...dxc4 comes into consideration: 7 ♗xc4 e5! and on 8 dxe5? ♕xd1+ 9 ♔xd1 ♘g4 ∓.
　7 cxd5
　Alternatively:
　a) 7 a3 cxd4! 8 axb4 dxc3 9 ♘xc3 (9 bxc3 ♘c6 10 cxd5 ♘xd5 11 e4 ♘b6 and ...e6-e5, ...♗e6 is already ∓!) 9...♘c6 10 b5 ♘b4 11 0-0 ♘xd3 12 ♕xd3 b6 with an equal position.
　b) 7 0-0 cxd4 8 exd4 dxc4 9 ♗xc4 ♘c6 10 a3 ♗e7 with the idea of ...b7-b6, ...♗b7, ...♖c8 and ...♘a5.
　7...cxd4
　7...exd5? 8 a3! ±.
　8 exd4 ♘xd5
　Also possible is 8...♕xd5 9 0-0 ♕h5.

9 0-0 ♘c6

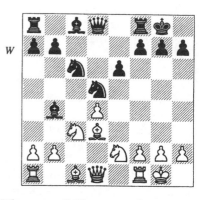

Plans and Counterplans:
White intends first to weaken Black's kingside and then attack it. Black must play patiently, planning exchanges and counting on the weakness of White's isolated d-pawn in the ending. For example, **10 ♕c2** h6 11 a3 ♗e7 12 ♖d1 ♗f6 13 ♗c4 ♘ce7 14 ♕e4 ♖e8 15 ♘f4 ♘xc3 16 bxc3 ♘f5 = or **10 ♗c2** ♖e8 11 ♕d3 g6 12 ♖d1 ♗f8 13 ♕f3 ♗g7 14 ♘e4 h6! with the manoeuvre ...♘e7-f5.

C. 1 d4 ♘f6 2 c4 e6 3 ♘c3 ♗b4 4 e3 0-0 5 ♗d3 d5 6 ♘f3

6...c5
6...b6 leads to a position that resembles the Queen's Indian: 7 0-0 ♗b7 8 cxd5 exd5 9 a3 ♗d6 10 b4 a6 and Black has ...♘bd7 and ...♘e4.
　7 0-0
　Or 7 a3 ♗xc3+ 8 bxc3 dxc4 9 ♗xc4 ♕a5 10 ♗b2 cxd4 11 exd4 b6 and 12...♗a6 =.

After 7 0-0 Black has two squares for his b8-knight: d7 (after 7...dxc4) and c6.

C1. 7...dxc4 and
C2. 7...♘c6.

C1. 1 d4 ♘f6 2 c4 e6 3 ♘c3 ♗b4 4 e3 0-0 5 ♗d3 d5 6 ♘f3 c5 7 0-0 dxc4

If Black wants to play ...♘bd7 then he should first stop c4xd5: 7...♘bd7?! 8 cxd5 exd5 9 a3 ♗a5 10 b4! cxb4 11 ♘b5 bxa3? 12 ♗xa3 ♖e8 13 ♘d6 ♖e6 14 ♘g5 ±.

8 ♗xc4 cxd4
Also possible is the immediate 8...♘bd7, although after 9 ♕e2 b6 10 a3 cxd4 11 axb4 dxc3 12 bxc3 ♕c7 13 ♗b2 ♗b7 14 ♗a6 White is slightly better.

9 exd4
White has to accept the isolated pawn in order to control the central c5 and e5 squares, and also to clear the way for his c1-bishop. 9 ♘xd4? can be met by 9...♕c7 10 ♕e2 a6!, threatening ...♗xc3, ...b7-b5, ...♗b7 and ...♘bd7, etc.

9...b6
It is necessary to carry out ...b7-b6 and ...♗b7 in order to blockade the pawn on d4.

10 ♗g5 ♗b7

Plans and Counterplans:
White has several options here:
  a) **11 ♘e5** h6 12 ♗h4 ♗e7 13 ♖e1 ♘bd7 14 ♘xf7 ♖xf7 15 ♗xe6 ♘f8 ∞.

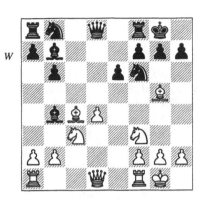

  b) **11 ♕e2** ♘bd7 12 ♘e5 ♗xc3 13 bxc3 ♕c7 14 ♘xd7 ♘xd7 and it is purely a matter of taste whether one prefers the bishop pair or the better pawn structure.

  c) **11 ♖e1** ♗xc3 12 bxc3 ♘bd7 13 ♗d3 ♕c7 14 ♖c1 ♕d6 15 ♗h4 ♖fc8!? 16 ♗g3 ♕a3 with an unclear position.

To put it briefly, Black often answers White's initiative with a queenside counterplay by ...♘bd7, ...♗xc3, ...♕c7. It is worth knowing that the diagram position can also be reached from the Caro-Kann Defence: 1 e4 c6 2 d4 d5 3 exd5 cxd5 4 c4 ♘f6 5 ♘c3 e6 6 ♘f3 ♗b4 7 ♗d3 dxc4 8 ♗xc4 0-0 9 0-0 b6 10 ♗g5 ♗b7.

C2. 1 d4 ♘f6 2 c4 e6 3 ♘c3 ♗b4 4 e3 0-0 5 ♗d3 d5 6 ♘f3 c5 7 0-0 ♘c6

8 a3
On 8 cxd5 exd5 9 a3 ♗xc3 10 bxc3 c4!? 11 ♗c2, 11...♗g4 is an ugly pin.

8...dxc4

8...♗xc3 keeps the centre closed, e.g. 9 bxc3 ♕c7 (9...dxc4 10 ♗xc4 ♕c7 11 ♗a2 e5!? 12 h3! e4 – 12...♖d8? 13 ♘g5 – 13 ♘h2 b6 and Black's idea is ...♖d8 and ...♘e5-d3) 10 cxd5 exd5 11 a4 ♖e8 12 ♗a3 c4 13 ♗c2 ♘e4 =.

9 ♗xc4 cxd4 10 exd4

A strange kind of endgame results after 10 axb4 dxc3 11 ♕xd8 (11 bxc3 ♕c7 12 ♕b3 b6 followed by ...♗b7 and ...a7-a5 =) 11...♖xd8 12 bxc3, for example 12...♘e4 13 b5 ♘e7 14 ♗b2 ♔f8 ±.

10...♗e7

In the line 10...♗xc3 11 bxc3 the knight would stand better on d7 instead of c6 since Black will need to seek play along the c-file.

11 ♕d3!? b6 12 ♗g5 ♗b7 13 ♖fe1

Plans and Counterplans:
White will now try to increase the pressure on Black's kingside

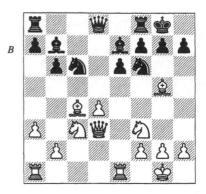

with ♖ad1, ♗c4-a2-b1 and ♘e5. **13...♘d5** is met by 14 ♗xd5! exd5 (14...♗xg5 15 ♗e4 g6 16 d5! ±) 15 ♗xe7 ♘xe7, as after 16 ♘g5 ♘g6 17 h4! White has some advantage (±). But Black has the improvement **13...h6!** and on 14 ♗h4, 14...♘a5 15 ♗a2 ♗xf3 16 ♕xf3 ♕xd4, as now 17 b4 is prohibited because the bishop on h4 is hanging! And on 14 ♗e3 ♗d6 Black has the opportunity to regroup with ...♘e7-d5.

White avoids the main lines

Naturally White has a wide selection of moves after **1 d4 ♘f6** but there are two lines that Black should carefully prepare for.

I. 1 d4 ♘f6 2 ♗g5

In this opening, the Trompowsky Attack, White opts for an exchange on f6, or at least to constantly threaten this capture.

2...c5!?

This is simpler than 2...♘e4 3 ♗h4 c5 4 f3 g5 5 fxe4 gxh4 6 e3 ♗h6 7 ♔f2!? and White has a natural plan of development by continuing ♘f3, ♘c3 or ♘b1-d2-c4 and c3.

3 d5

Or 3 ♗xf6 gxf6 4 d5 ♕b6 5 ♕c1 f5 6 g3 ♗g7 7 c3 d6, and Black continues by means of ...e6 and ...♘d7-f6.

3...♘e4 4 ♗h4 ♕b6 5 ♕c1 g5 6 ♗g3 ♕h6!!

This astounding move ties up the pawn on h2 so that 7...♘xg3 is now a threat, when only the f-pawn can recapture. Hence White has to play

7 ♗e5 f6 8 ♗xb8 ♖xb8 =

On 9 ♕e3, Black can play 9...g4! as 10 ♕xe4?? loses to 10...♕c1 mate!

II. 1 d4 ♘f6 2 ♘f3

This move-order often transposes to main lines after c2-c4, but White can also try to sidestep the Nimzo-and Queen's Indian.

2...e6 3 ♗g5 c5!

The thrust d4-d5 is now impossible, since White has not played c2-c4, so Black has time for an exchange on d4. 3...c5 also makes possible a future ...♕b6 which would attack the pawn on b2.

4 e3 h6!?

The immediate 4...♕b6!? is unclear: 5 ♘bd2!? ♕xb2 6 ♗d3 d5 7 c4, while 4...b6? is weak, as after 5 d5! exd5 6 ♘c3 ♗b7 7 ♘xd5 ♗xd5 8 ♗xf6 ♕xf6 9 ♕xd5 White stands better.

5 ♗h4 b6 6 c3

Not now 6 d5? g5! 7 ♗g3 exd5.

6...♗e7 7 ♘bd2 ♗b7 8 ♗d3

White's plan is 0-0, e3-e4 and ♕e2.

8...cxd4! 9 exd4

Or 9 cxd4 d5 =.

9...♘h5!

Now after both 10 ♗g3 ♘xg3 11 hxg3 d6 followed by ...♘d7 and ...a7-a6 and 10 ♗xe7 ♕xe7 (threatening 11...♘f4) Black has equalized.

Grünfeld Defence

1 d4 ♘f6 2 c4 g6 3 ♘c3 d5

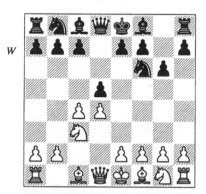

The Grünfeld is maybe the most dynamic answer to 1 d4, and it has become very popular in recent years. Black's position is flexible, powerful, and rich in possibilities, but against this White usually enjoys an advantage in the centre.

Black's plans are invariably based on the strength of the bishop on g7 and the centre-blasting move ...c7-c5, but the execution of this depends on White's set-up.

Note that it is important that Black plays ...d7-d5 only after 3 ♘c3 has been played, as this way after 4 cxd5 ♘xd5 5 e4 the d5-knight need not wander around losing tempi, but can simply be exchanged on c3. For example 1 d4 ♘f6 2 c4 g6 3 ♘f3 d5? is wrong due to 4 cxd5 ♘xd5 5 e4 ♘b6 6

h3! (to stop ...♗c8-g4, undermining the d4-pawn) 6...♗g7 7 ♘c3 followed by ♗e2, 0-0, ♗e3 with a clear spatial plus for White. Therefore on 3 ♘f3 correct is 3...♗g7 and if 4 ♘c3, only now comes 4...d5. Against systems with g2-g3 the Grünfeld is also good, even if the knight is not yet on c3, as ♗g2 and the thrust e2-e4 do not really go together.

This section is divided as follows:

I. 1 d4 ♘f6 2 c4 g6 3 ♘c3 d5 4 ♘f3 ♗g7 5 e3 (Solid, but a little passive)

II. 1 d4 ♘f6 2 c4 g6 3 ♘c3 d5 4 ♗f4

III. White plays ♗g5

IV. 1 d4 ♘f6 2 c4 g6 3 ♘c3 d5 4 ♘f3 ♗g7 5 ♕b3 (Russian System)

V. 1 d4 ♘f6 2 c4 g6 3 ♘c3 d5 4 cxd5 ♘xd5 5 e4 ♘xc3 6 bxc3 (Classical Main Line)

VI. Grünfeld against fianchetto set-ups.

I. 1 d4 ♘f6 2 c4 g6 3 ♘c3 d5 4 ♘f3 ♗g7 5 e3 (Solid, but a little passive)

Of course this line is not bad, only a little lukewarm. White refuses to undertake both the occupation of the centre and the development

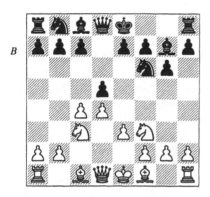

of the bishop on c1. Hence Black can play for ...c7-c5 without being disturbed.

5...0-0 6 ♗e2

Other choices are:

a) 6 ♗d3?! c5 7 0-0 (7 dxc5 dxc4 8 ♗xc4 ♕a5 with ...♕xc5 to follow) 7...cxd4 8 exd4 ♘c6 9 h3 b6 10 ♗g5 dxc4 11 ♗xc4 ♗b7 with ...♖c8, ...♘a5 in sight (∓).

b) 6 ♕b3 e6! 7 ♗e2 b6 and Black has a set plan: ...♗b7, ...♘bd7 and ...c7-c5.

c) 6 b4 b6!? 7 ♕b3 c5! 8 bxc5 bxc5 9 cxd5 ♘a6!? 10 ♗e2 ♖b8 11 ♕a4 ♘b4 12 0-0 ♘fxd5 =.

d) 6 cxd5 ♘xd5 7 ♗c4 ♘xc3 8 bxc3 c5 9 0-0 ♕c7 10 ♗e2 b6 11 a4 ♘c6 12 ♘d2 ♖d8 13 ♘c4! ♗a6! 14 ♘a3 ♗b7 and with ...♘c6-a5 and ...e6-e5 Black seizes the initiative.

e) 6 ♗d2 c5!? 7 dxc5 ♘a6 8 cxd5 ♘xc5 9 ♗c4 a6 10 a4 ♗f5 (interesting is 10...b6!? with the idea of ...♗b7, ...♖c8, ...♕d6, ...♖fd8 and perhaps ...♘e4) 11 0-0 ♖c8 12 ♕e2 ♘fe4 13 ♘d4 ♘xd2 14 ♕xd2 ♘e4 15 ♘xe4 ♗xe4 =.

6...c5

Black can instead prop up his centre with 6...c6, transposing into the Schlechter Defence. (This position can also be reached via the Slav Defence: 1 d4 d5 2 c4 c6 3 ♘c3 ♘f6 4 e3 g6 5 ♘f3 ♗g7 6 ♗e2 0-0.) White is slightly better after 7 0-0 ♗g4 8 cxd5 cxd5 9 ♕b3. In the Grünfeld Black does better to play the active ...c7-c5 than the inflexible ...c7-c6.

7 0-0

After the continuation 7 dxc5 ♕a5 8 cxd5 ♘xd5 9 ♕xd5 ♗xc3+ 10 ♗d2 ♖d8 11 ♕xd8+ (11 ♗xc3+ ♕xc3!) 11...♕xd8 12 ♗xc3 ♕c7 13 b4 a5 White has to fight for equality.

7...cxd4 8 exd4

After 8 ♘xd4 dxc4 9 ♗xc4 a6 Black threatens to take over in the centre with ...e6-e5.

8...♘c6

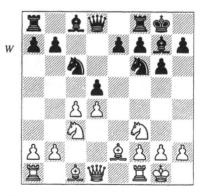

Plans and Counterplans:
Black will develop with ...b7-b6 and ...♗b7, followed by ...♖c8, ...d5xc4 and ...♘a5 or ...♘c6-b4-d5 with good play on the light

squares (c4, d5 and e4). White must either force an early d5xc4 to gain control of the centre or close the centre with c4-c5. For example, **9 ♗g5 ♗e6!?** 10 cxd5 ♗xd5 11 ♘xd5 ♕xd5 12 ♕a4 ♘e4 ∞, **9 ♗f4 ♗g4** 10 c5 ♘e4 = or **9 ♗e3 ♗g4** (9...dxc4 10 d5!? ♘a5 11 b4!) 10 c5 ♘e4 11 ♕a4 e5! is unclear. **9 h3** is met by 9...b6 and ...♗b7, while **9 ♘e5!?** dxc4 10 ♘xc6 bxc6 11 ♗xc4 ♘d5 is equal.

II. 1 d4 ♘f6 2 c4 g6 3 ♘c3 d5 4 ♗f4

The merits of White's plan are numerous: now e2-e3 no longer shuts in the bishop on c1 and the c1 square is vacated for the rook with pressure along the c-file and particularly on c7. Of course Black need not panic, he has central blows in hand, with his best chance again being ...c7-c5.

4...♗g7 5 e3

On 5 ♖c1 possible is 5...♘h5!? 6 ♗g5 (6 ♗d2 c5 =) 6...h6 7 ♗h4 c5 8 ♘xd5 ♘c6! ∓. White can instead try to postpone e2-e3 with 5 ♘f3 0-0 (another move is 5...c5!? 6 dxc5 ♕a5 7 cxd5 ♘xd5 8 ♕xd5 ♗xc3+ 9 ♗d2 ♗e6! 10 ♕xb7 ♗xd2+ 11 ♘xd2 0-0 because if White takes the rook on a8 then Black can play ...♖d8 followed by ...♗d5 trapping the queen) 6 ♖c1 dxc4 7 e4 and now Black undermines White's centre with 7...♗g4! 8 ♗xc4 ♗xf3 9 gxf3 (9 ♕xf3 ♘h5!?) 9...♘h5 10 ♗e3 e6 11 ♘e2 ♕f6 and Black has equalized due to his play against the doubled f-pawns and the f4-square.

5...0-0

The basic Grünfeld idea can also be played at once: 5...c5!?, e.g. 6 dxc5 ♕a5 7 ♖c1 (7 ♕a4+ ♕xa4 8 ♘xa4 ♘e4 9 f3 ♗d7 10 fxe4 ♗xa4 11 cxd5 ♗xb2 12 ♖b1 ♗c3+ 13 ♔f2 ♘d7 =) 7...♘e4 8 cxd5 ♘xc3 9 ♕d2 ♕xa2 10 bxc3 and now both 10...♕xd2+ 11 ♔xd2 ♘d7 12 ♗b5 0-0 13 ♗xd7 ♗xd7 14 e4 f5 15 e5 ♖fc8!? and 10...♕a5! 11 ♗c4 ♘d7 offer Black equal prospects. Finally, 6 ♘f3 cxd4 7 exd4 ♘c6 gives Black a comfortable game (after ...b7-b6, ...d5xc4 and ...♘a5, etc.).

6 ♘f3

Alternatively 6 cxd5 ♘xd5 7 ♘xd5 ♕xd5 8 ♗xc7 ♘a6!? 9 ♗xa6 (9 ♗g3 ♗f5 threatening ...♘b4, ...♕a5+, ...♖ac8-c2, etc.) 9...♕xg2 10 ♕f3 ♕xf3 11 ♘xf3 bxa6 leads to an unclear ending, while 6 ♕b3 dxc4 7 ♗xc4 c5 8 dxc5 ♕a5 and 6 ♖c1 c5 7 dxc5 ♗e6!? both promise equal chances.

6...c5 7 dxc5!?

Otherwise Black would capture on d4 and c4 and then comfortably develop his queenside.

7...♕a5

Also satisfactory is 7...♘e4: 8 ♖c1 (8 ♗e5 ♗xe5 9 ♘xe5 ♘xc3 10 bxc3 ♕a5 11 ♕d4 f6 12 ♘f3 ♘c6 =) 8...♘xc3 9 bxc3 dxc4 10 ♕xd8 ♖xd8 11 ♗xc4 ♘d7 =.

8 ♖c1 dxc4 9 ♗xc4 ♘c6 10 0-0 ♕xc5

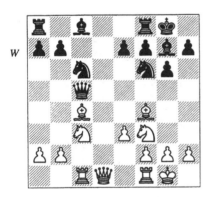

Plans and Counterplans:
White can launch an immediate attack by means of **11 ♘b5**, threatening both ♘c7 and ♗xf7+. Now 11...♕h5 12 ♘c7 ♖b8 13 h3 ♗d7!? is correct, with mutual chances. The alternative **11 ♗b3 ♕a5** (11...♕h5!?) 12 h3 ♗f5 13 ♕e2 ♘e4 14 ♘d5 e5!? is also unclear, e.g.:

a) 15 ♗h2 ♗e6 followed by ...♖fd8, and if necessary, White's threats of ♖xc6, ♘e7+, ♘xc6 can be parried by ...♔h8.

b) 15 ♗g5 ♘xg5 16 ♘xg5 ♕d8!? with active play in view of a future ...e5-e4.

c) 15 ♖xc6!? (the most exciting move) 15...bxc6 16 ♘e7+ ♔h8 17 ♘xc6 ♕b6 18 ♘cxe5 ♗e6! also leads to a balanced game between White's two extra pawns and Black's exchange advantage.

III. White plays ♗g5

---

1 d4 ♘f6 2 c4 g6 3 ♘c3 d5 4 ♘f3

4 ♗g5 at once is also possible. This move order prevents 4...♘e4 5 ♗h4 ♘xc3 6 bxc3 dxc4 7 e3 b5?, as after 8 a4 c6 9 axb5 cxb5 10 ♕f3! the rook on a8 is indefensible. However, Black can capitalize on the position of his bishop on f8: 4...♘e4 5 ♗h4 ♘xc3 6 bxc3 c5 7 cxd5 ♕xd5 8 e3 cxd4 9 ♕xd4 ♕xd4 10 cxd4 e6 11 ♗d3 ♗e7! with comfortable play for Black: ...♘c6, ...0-0 and ...♗d7 or ...b7-b6 and ...♗b7 =.

4...♗g7 5 ♗g5

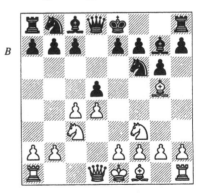

By threatening ♗xf6 White tries to encourage his opponent to defend the pawn on d5 or play

...d5xc4. After either of these options he could successfully carry out his plan: 5...c6 6 e3 (6 ♗xf6 ♗xf6 7 cxd5 cxd5 8 ♕b3 ±) 6...0-0 7 ♗d3 ♗e6 8 cxd5 ♘xd5 9 0-0 and Black is without counterplay, or 5...dxc4 6 e4 c5 7 ♗xc4 cxd4 8 ♕xd4 ♕xd4 9 ♘xd4 ♘xe4!? 10 ♘xe4 ♗xd4 11 0-0-0 with a dangerous initiative for the pawn.

5...♘e4!

This is one of the most common 'Grünfeld' moves, based on the typical principle of this opening that a threat should be answered with a counter-threat.

6 ♗h4

6 ♘xe4 dxe4 is out of the question but there are still a number of sidelines:

a) 6 cxd5 ♘xg5 7 ♘xg5 e6 (7...c6 is an interesting, but not quite sound, sacrifice: 8 ♕b3 e6 9 dxc6 ♘xc6 10 ♘f3 ♗xd4 11 0-0-0 and White is better. Things are more complicated after 8 dxc6?! ♘xc6 9 e3 0-0 10 ♘f3 e5!?) 8 ♕d2 (8 ♘f3 exd5 9 e3 0-0 10 b4 c6 followed by ...♗e6 and ...♘d7, ...f7-f5 or ...a7-a5!? with a level position) 8...exd5 9 ♕e3+ ♔f8 10 ♕f4 ♗f6 11 h4 h6 12 ♘f3 ♗e6 with a tough fight in which Black plans to mobilize his queen (...♕a5) after ...♘d7, ...c7-c6 and ...♔g7 or offer an exchange with ...♕b8, hoping for an ending with the bishop pair. Meanwhile White will try to make a profit from the insecure position of the black king via 0-0-0 and e2-e4.

b) 6 ♗f4 ♘xc3 7 bxc3 c5 8 e3 0-0 9 cxd5 cxd4 10 cxd4 ♕xd5 11 ♗e2 ♘c6 12 0-0 ♗f5 13 ♕a4 ♕a5!? 14 ♕b3 ♕b4! and in the forthcoming endgame Black's queenside majority and healthy pieces just about outweigh White's d4-pawn.

6...c5

This is more accurate than 6...♘xc3 7 bxc3 dxc4 8 e3 ♗e6 (8...b5 9 a4 c6 10 ♗e2 and ♘d2, ♗f3 with a good initiative for the pawn) 9 ♕b1!? and now White threatens to increase the pressure with ♘g5, e3-e4, ♕b4 and a2-a4.

7 cxd5 ♘xc3 8 bxc3 ♕xd5 9 e3 ♘c6 10 ♗e2 cxd4 11 cxd4 0-0

11...♕a5+ 12 ♕d2 ♗e6 13 ♖b1!? ±.

12 0-0 e5 13 dxe5 ♕a5!

13...♕xd1? 14 ♖fxd1 ♘xe5 15 ♘d4! ±.

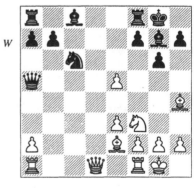

Plans and Counterplans:
White tries to delay Black's queenside development but in vain, for example: **14 ♗f6 ♗xf6 15 exf6 ♕f5**

16 ♘d4 ♕xf6 17 ♘xc6 ♕xc6 18
♗f3 ♕a6 19 ♕b3 ♖b8 20 ♗d5
♗e6! or **14 ♕b3** ♘xe5 15 ♘d4
♘c6 16 ♖ad1 (16 ♘xc6 bxc6 17
♖ac1 ♗e6 18 ♗c4 ♖ab8) 16...♘xd4
17 exd4 ♗d7! 18 ♕xb7 ♗a4 19
♖b1 ♗xd4 20 ♗c4 ♖ae8 21 ♗e7
♗c6! =.

IV. Russian System

**1 d4 ♘f6 2 c4 g6 3 ♘c3 d5 4
♘f3**
If White wishes to play ♕b3 it
is better to first strengthen the
centre with ♘f3. On the immediate 4 ♕b3 Black equalizes with
4...dxc4 5 ♕xc4 ♗e6! 6 ♕b5+
♗d7 7 ♕xb7 ♗c6 8 ♕b3 ♕xd4 9
♘f3 ♕b6.

4...♗g7 5 ♕b3

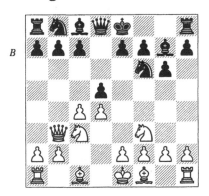

White wants to get hold of the
centre by retaining the knight
pair on c3 and f6. Although Black
now momentarily hands the central squares over to White, he will
later have several successful ways
to attack them.

5...dxc4
It is logical to lure the queen to
a vulnerable square. 5...c6 6 cxd5
cxd5 leads to an 'Exchange Slav'
in which the bishop on g7 is badly
placed in view of the closed centre.

6 ♕xc4 0-0 7 e4
On 7 e3 Black can play ...b7-b6,
...♗b7, ...♘bd7 and ...c7-c5, but after 7 e4 the plain 7...b6? is incorrect owing to 8 e5 ♘fd7 (8...♗a6 9
exf6 ♗xc4 10 fxg7 ♔xg7 11 ♗xc4
±; the three pieces overpower the
queen) 9 ♕d5 c6 10 ♕e4 ♗b7 11
h4! with a forceful attack. Let us
see an example of each of Black's
three main choices:

**A. 7...♘a6
B. 7...♗g4** and
C. 7...a6.

**A. 1 d4 ♘f6 2 c4 g6 3 ♘c3 d5 4
♘f3 ♗g7 5 ♕b3 dxc4 6 ♕xc4 0-0
7 e4 ♘a6**

Black opts for ...c7-c5.
8 ♗e2
Or 8 e5 ♘d7 9 e6 ♘b6 10 exf7+
♔h8 11 ♕b3 c5 12 ♗xa6 cxd4! with
a clear advantage for Black.
**8...c5 9 d5 e6 10 0-0 exd5 11
exd5 ♗f5 12 ♗f4**
Now Black will always have to
watch out for the d5-pawn. Play
might continue **12...♖e8** (alternatively 12...♘e8 13 ♘b5! ♗xb2 14
♖ad1! ±) 13 ♖ad1 ♘e4 14 ♘b5
♗d7 or **12...♕b6** 13 ♗e5 ♖fe8 14
b3 ♕b4 with an open fight.

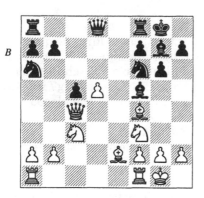

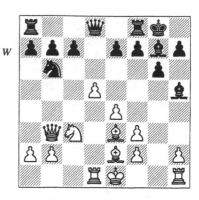

B. 1 d4 ♘f6 2 c4 g6 3 ♘c3 d5 4 ♘f3 ♗g7 5 ♕b3 dxc4 6 ♕xc4 0-0 7 e4 ♗g4

Black prepares for the manoeuvre ...♘d7-b6.

8 ♗e3

8 ♘e5 ♗e6 9 d5 ♗c8 10 ♗e2 e6 11 ♗f4 exd5 12 exd5 ♘e8, possibly followed by ...♘d6-f5.

8...♘fd7 9 ♕b3

Or 9 ♖d1 ♘c6 10 ♗e2 ♘b6 11 ♕c5 ♕d6 12 e5 ♕xc5 13 dxc5 ♘c8 14 h3 ♗xf3 15 ♗xf3 ♗xe5 16 ♗xc6 bxc6 ∞.

9...♘b6 10 ♖d1 ♘c6 11 d5 ♘e5 12 ♗e2 ♘xf3+ 13 gxf3 ♗h5

13...♗h3 14 ♖g1 and the bishop on h3 is out of play.

Plans and Counterplans:
After f3-f4 and the swap of bishops White starts rolling forward with his h-pawn or picking on the knight on b6 with a2-a4-a5. Black can open things up with ...♕c8 and ...c7-c6 or ...f7-f5, exploiting the position of the white king. Chances are even.

C. 1 d4 ♘f6 2 c4 g6 3 ♘c3 d5 4 ♘f3 ♗g7 5 ♕b3 dxc4 6 ♕xc4 0-0 7 e4 a6

8 ♕b3

In fact ...b7-b5 is unstoppable due to 8 a4 b5! 9 ♕b3 c5 10 dxc5 ♗e6!

8...b5

Also worth considering is 8...c5!? 9 dxc5 ♘bd7.

9 e5

Or 9 ♗e2 c5 10 dxc5 ♘bd7 11 e5 (11 c6?! ♘c5 12 ♕c2 b4!) 11...♘xc5 12 ♕b4 ♘fd7 ∞.

9...♘fd7

The old 9...♘g4 has seen better days: 10 h3 ♘h6 11 ♗d3 ♗b7 (11...♘f5 12 ♗e4 ♖a7 13 g4!) 12 ♗xh6! ♗xh6 13 ♗e4! and after either 13...♗xe4 14 ♘xe4, or 13...c6 14 0-0 e6 15 ♘a4! Black is unable to equalize due to his backward c-pawn.

10 ♗e3

10 e6?! is weaker: 10...fxe6 11 ♕xe6+ ♔h8 12 ♕e4 ♘b6 13 ♗e2 ♗f5 14 ♕h4 ♘c6 15 ♗h6 e5! and Black is better developed. After

10 h4 ♘b6 11 h5 ♘c6 12 ♗e3 ♘a5, Black has counterplay with 13...♘ac4.

10...♘b6 11 a4

Or 11 ♖d1 ♗b7 12 ♗e2 ♘c6 and again Black aims for ...♘a5-c4.

11...♗e6 12 ♕d1

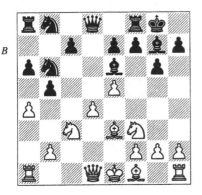

Plans and Counterplans:
White wishes to castle and keep the black c-pawn repressed. Black can either explode with **12...c5!?** 13 axb5 cxd4 14 ♕xd4 axb5 15 ♖xa8 ♘xa8 16 ♗xb5 ♘c7 17 ♗a4 ♘ba6 18 ♕h4 ♕b8!, or he can play on the light squares: **12...b4** 13 ♘e4 ♗d5 14 ♗d3 ♘c4 15 ♗c1 ♘a5. In both cases the outcome is a lively game with chances for both sides.

V. Classical Main Line

---

1 d4 ♘f6 2 c4 g6 3 ♘c3 d5 4 cxd5 ♘xd5 5 e4 ♘xc3

Black must capture on c3 as otherwise White could seize the centre with h2-h3!, ♘f3, ♗e2, ♗e3 and 0-0, when Black has no real counterplay. What is more, he even has problems developing his queenside pieces.

6 bxc3 ♗g7

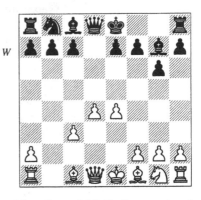

The Grünfeld Defence stands or falls on this position. White has occupied the centre, but his opponent is preparing an attack with ...c7-c5 and ...♘c6. After the exchange of knights on c3, White will aim at the somewhat weakened black kingside and Black will seek counterplay on the queenside and along the c-file. Black's plan is more or less obvious but White, being the first player, can pick the squares for his pieces.

Besides two classical continuations we shall also discuss the newest line in detail:

A. 7 ♘f3 c5 8 ♖b1 0-0 9 ♗e2 (Modern Main Line).
B. 7 ♗c4 0-0 8 ♘e2 c5 9 0-0 ♘c6 10 ♗e3 (Old Main Line)
C. 7 ♗b5+, an interesting check which is the latest try to mix up Black.

Black need not be afraid of White preventing ...c7-c5 with 7 ♗a3 as after 7...♘d7 8 ♘f3 c5 it is White who has to be careful: 9 ♗e2?! cxd4 10 cxd4?? ♕a5+ and the bishop on a3 falls. The set-up 7 ♗e3 c5 8 ♕d2 is much more natural, when White is able to continue with d4-d5. Here Black should play 8...♕a5, when 9 ♖c1 cxd4 10 cxd4 ♕xd2+ 11 ♔xd2 0-0 12 ♘f3 ♘c6 13 ♗b5 f5! is equal. And on 9 ♖b1 not 9...cxd4?! 10 cxd4 ♕xd2+ 11 ♔xd2, when with ♘f3, ♗d3, ♖hc1 White's pieces are ideally placed, but instead 9...b6!? (liberating the bishop on c8) 10 ♗b5+ ♗d7 11 ♗e2 0-0 12 ♖c1 ♖d8! 13 ♘f3 (13 d5 ♕a4! 14 c4 ♘a6 with ...♘b4! to follow) 13...♗b5! =.

A. Modern Main Line

1 d4 ♘f6 2 c4 g6 3 ♘c3 d5 4 cxd5 ♘xd5 5 e4 ♘xc3 6 bxc3 ♗g7 7 ♘f3 c5

On the passive 7...0-0 followed by ...b7-b6 and ...♗b7 White easily gets on top with the typical attack 8 ♗e3 and ♕d2, ♗d3, ♗h6, h2-h4-h5.

8 ♖b1

The text move is the correct way to start action because now after 8...♘c6 White can answer 9 d5. A less promising alternative is 8 ♗e3 ♕a5 9 ♕d2 0-0 10 ♖c1 (threatening d4-d5 and then c2-c4) 10...cxd4 11 cxd4 ♕xd2+ and now on either recapture (♘xd2 or

♔xd2) Black reaches equality with ...♘c6 and ...♖d8. Besides ...♗g4 Black also has ...f7-f5 to upset the white centre (d4, e4, ♘f3)!

8...0-0

8...♘c6? is a major blunder in view of 9 d5 ♗xc3+ 10 ♗d2 ♗xd2+ 11 ♕xd2 ♘d4 (11...♘a5 12 ♗b5+! ±) 12 ♘xd4 cxd4 13 ♕xd4 ♕a5+ 14 ♕d2 ♕xd2+ 15 ♔xd2 with an oppressive ending for Black: the white monarch goes to d4, the rooks to the c-file and after f2-f4 and e4-e5 Black is tied hand and foot.

9 ♗e2 cxd4

Black has several other possibilities:

a) 9...♕a5 10 0-0 ♕xa2 (or 10...♕xc3 11 ♗d2 ♕a3 12 ♕c2 ∞) 11 ♗g5 cxd4 12 cxd4 ♖e8 13 d5 with compensation for the pawn.

b) 9...b6 10 0-0 ♗b7 11 ♕d3 ♗a6 12 ♕e3 ♕c8!? =.

c) 9...♘c6 10 d5 ♘e5 (alternatively 10...♗xc3+ 11 ♗d2 ♗xd2+ 12 ♕xd2 with an attack via h2-h4-h5) 11 ♘xe5 ♗xe5 12 ♕d2 and White's aim is f2-f4 while Black will blast out with ...b7-b6 and ...e7-e6.

10 cxd4 ♕a5+ 11 ♗d2

11 ♕d2 leads to a typical position, similar to those we have already seen: 11...♕xd2+ 12 ♗xd2 b6 13 d5 ♘a6 14 ♗b5 ♗b7 15 0-0 ♘c5 16 ♖fe1 ♖fc8 17 ♗b4 ♖c7 18 a4 f5! with an unclear game. As a reminder: Black has again chosen the right time to confront his opponent with ...f7-f5!

11...♕xa2 12 0-0

Or 12 d5 e6 13 ♗b4 ♖d8 14 ♗e7 ♖e8 15 d6 ♘c6 16 ♗b5 ♗d7 17 0-0 a6 18 ♗xc6 ♗xc6 19 d7 ♖xe7 20 d8♕+ ♖xd8 21 ♕xd8 ♖e8 with the better chances for Black (∓).

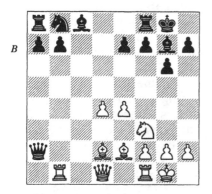

Plans and Counterplans:
Black can try to complete his development by ...b7-b6 and ...♗b7 and then bring the queen home via e6. White, following d4-d5, will exchange the light-coloured bishops and try to exploit the initiative given by his spatial advantage. The black bishop is more effective on the other diagonal: 12...♗g4! 13 ♗g5!? h6! 14 ♗e3 (or: 14 ♗xe7!? ♖e8 15 ♖xb7 ♘c6 16 ♗c5 ♖xe4 17 ♗d3 ♖xd4! 18 ♗xd4 ♘xd4 with sufficient counterplay for the exchange; or 14 ♗h4 g5 15 ♗g3 ♘c6 16 d5 ♖ad8 17 ♖xb7 f5! 18 ♕e1 ♗xf3 19 ♗xf3 ♘d4 =) 14...b6 15 ♖a1 ♕b2 (not 15...♕e6 16 h3 ♗xf3 17 ♗xf3 threatening e4-e5) 16 ♕d3 (16 ♖b1 ♕a2 =) 16...♕b4 17 h3 ♗xf3 18 ♗xf3 e5!? 19 d5 (19 dxe5? ♘c6!) 19...♘d7,

when chances are about equal. In this line it is important that the black queen does not retreat to e6 so that Black has the option of obstructing the bishop on f3 with ...e7-e5.

B. Old Main Line

1 d4 ♘f6 2 c4 g6 3 ♘c3 d5 4 cxd5 ♘xd5 5 e4 ♘xc3 6 bxc3 ♗g7 7 ♗c4 c5

Should Black neglect to play ...c7-c5, White seizes the initiative with ♘e2, ♗e3, ♕d2 followed by ♗h6 and h4.

8 ♘e2 ♘c6 9 ♗e3

After 9 d5?! ♘e5 10 ♗b5+ ♗d7 11 ♗xd7+ ♕xd7 White's light squares (c4, d3) are weak.

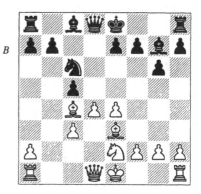

9...0-0 10 0-0

10 ♖c1 leads to fantastic complications: 10...cxd4 11 cxd4 ♕a5+ 12 ♔f1!? ♗d7!? 13 h4 ♖fc8 14 h5 ♘d8!, when Black can play on the queenside with the plan ...♗a4, ...♖c7, ...♖ac8 and ...b7-b5 whereas White plays f2-f3 or f2-f4 followed

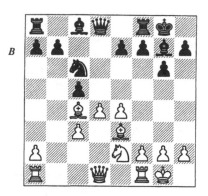

by ♔f2 and either opts for an attack or awaits an endgame with a spatial advantage.

At this point the play is divided into two acts – depending on how Black wishes to attack the white centre. Black can either play ...♕c7 and ...♖d8 (Section B1) or ...♗g4, ...c5xd4 and ...♘a5 (Section B2).

B1. 10...♕c7

11 ♖c1

The strongest move, protecting the bishop on c4 and 'talking' Black out of ever opening the c-file. Weaker is the continuation 11 ♗f4 ♕a5 12 d5 ♘e5 13 ♗b3 c4! 14 ♗c2 e6! and the white centre is no more.

11...♖d8 12 ♕d2

Also playable are:

a) 12 ♗f4 ♕d7 (12...e5? 13 ♗g5 ♖e8 14 d5 ±) 13 d5 ♘a5 14 ♗d3 b6 15 c4 e5 16 ♗d2 ♘b7 17 a4 ♘d6 ∞.

b) 12 f4 e6 followed by a plan worthy of attention: ...♘a5 and ...f7-f5!

12...a6!?

12...♘e5? is incorrect: 13 ♗b3 ♘g4 14 ♗f4 e5 15 ♗g3 ♗h6 16 ♗xe5! ♕xe5 17 ♕xh6! ♕xe4 18 ♗xf7+ with a splendid attack for White.

13 ♗h6

Also playable is 13 f4 b5 14 ♗d3 f5! ∞, but not 13 a4? ♗d7 14 ♕a2 ♗e8 15 ♕a3 b5! ∓.

13...♗h8

The game is level. White obtains nothing after 14 a4?! ♗d7, when Black is threatening 15...♘a5. A better idea is 14 ♕e3 b5 15 ♗b3 ♘a5 16 dxc5 ♗b7 with mutual chances. Instead of 13...♗h8, also possible is 13...b5!? 14 ♗xg7 ♔xg7 15 ♗b3 (15 ♗d3 ♕d7 16 d5 c4! and 17...e6) 15...♘a5 =.

B2. 10...♗g4

Black provokes f2-f3 in order to weaken the a7-g1 diagonal, which comes in very handy in some lines.

11 f3 ♘a5

To the c4 square!

12 ♗d3

These days there is little interest in 12 ♗xf7+ ♖xf7 13 fxg4 ♖xf1+ 14 ♔xf1. Although White is a pawn up Black has several effective counter-plans:

a) 14...♕d6 15 e5 ♕d5 threatening ...♕e4, ...♘c4, ...♖f8, etc.

b) 14...cxd4 15 cxd4 e5!? 16 d5 ♘c4 17 ♗f2 ♕f6 18 ♔g1 ♖f8 19 ♕e1 ♗h6 again with sufficient initiative for the pawn.

Or 12 ♗d5 ♗d7 with the threat of 13...e6.

12...cxd4 13 cxd4 ♗e6

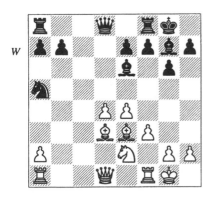

Plans and Counterplans:
White opts for d4-d5 but to carry this out he must sacrifice something!

a) 14 d5!? ♗xa1 15 ♕xa1 f6! For the time being the bishop on e6 is not hanging on account of its unprotected d3 colleague. Now 16 ♖b1 ♗f7 17 ♗h6 ♖e8 18 ♗b5 ♕d6 19 ♗xe8 ♗xe8 is equal, or 16 ♗h6 ♗d7!? 17 ♗xf8 ♕b6+! (now the weakness of the move f2-f3 becomes apparent) 18 ♘d4 ♖xf8 19 ♖b1 ♕d6 20 ♕c3 ♕e5! and Black is slightly better. Instead of 18 ♕d4, 18 ♘d4 followed by exchanges leads to an equal endgame. It is highly advisable for Black to give the exchange back as demonstrated above, otherwise his life is in danger due to ♘f4 and e4-e5.

b) 14 ♖c1!? ♗xa2 15 ♕a4 ♗e6 16 d5 ♗d7 17 ♕b4 is equal, e.g. 17...b6 18 ♗a6 ♗c8 or 17...e6 18

♘c3 exd5 19 ♘xd5 with sufficient activity for the pawn. On the more direct 15 d5 (instead of 15 ♕a4), 15...♗b3 16 ♕e1 e6 is equal (16...a6? 17 ♕f2!).

c) 14 ♕a4 a6!? 15 d5 (15 ♖ad1?! b5! 16 ♕a3 ♘c4 ∓) 15...b5 16 ♕b4 ♗xa1 17 ♖xa1 ♗d7 18 ♕d4 f6 19 e5 fxe5 20 ♕xe5 ♕b8 21 ♕xe7 ♖e8 22 ♕c5 ♘b7 is also about equal.

C. 1 d4 ♘f6 2 c4 g6 3 ♘c3 d5 4 cxd5 ♘xd5 5 e4 ♘xc3 6 bxc3 ♗g7 7 ♗b5+

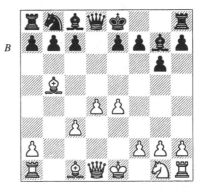

The point of this interesting check is that no matter how Black reacts, he does not achieve his usual counter-attacking plan (...c7-c5, ...♘c6 and ...♗g4).

7...c6
After 7...♘c6 or 7...♘d7 Black will struggle to generate any activity. 7...♗d7 8 ♗e2 c5 9 ♘f3 cxd4 10 cxd4 ♗c6 11 ♕d3 f5!? 12 exf5 ♕a5+ 13 ♗d2 ♕xf5 is equal but after 8 ♗xd7+ ♕xd7 9 ♘f3 White stands more freely.

8 ♗a4 b5!? 9 ♗b3 b4 10 ♕f3

10 ♗e3 bxc3 11 ♖c1 ♘d7 12 ♘e2 ♗a6 is uncomfortable for White because Black has the obvious moves: ...c7-c5, ...♕a5, ...0-0, etc.

10...0-0 11 ♘e2 bxc3 12 h4!?

12 ♕xc3 is met by 12...♗b7 followed by ...♘a6 and ...c7-c5. On 12 0-0 ♗a6 13 ♖d1, 13...c5! is strong.

Plans and Counterplans:

White threatens to play h4-h5, h5xg6, ♕g3 and then either to take on g6 or mate with ♕h4-h7. For example, **12...c5?** 13 h5 cxd4 14 hxg6 hxg6 15 ♕g3 e6 (15...d3 16 ♕xg6 d2+ 17 ♗xd2! is curtains) 16 ♕h2 ♖e8 17 ♕h7+ ♔f8 18 ♗a3+ ♖e7 19 ♕h8+ wins the house.

Black's only move is **12...h5!**, when after 13 ♕xc3 ♗b7 14 ♗g5 ♘a6! he has excellent prospects with ...c6-c5. Instead of 14 ♗g5 White can also play 14 ♕b4 ♕b6 or 14 ♖b1 c5! with an unclear position.

VI. Grünfeld against fianchetto set-ups

There are two situations when Black can play d5: either immediately after 1 d4 ♘f6 2 c4 g6 3 g3 (section A) when following 3...d5 4 cxd5 '**Black captures on d5 with the knight**', or on 1 d4 ♘f6 2 c4 g6 3 g3 Black can play 3...c6 first and then 4 ♗g2 d5 5 cxd5 cxd5 6 ♘f3 ♗g7 7 0-0 0-0 leads to the '**Symmetrical Grünfeld**'. The latter may interest those who play the King's Indian but want to avoid the g2-g3 lines. Note that with the move order 1 d4 ♘f6 2 c4 g6 3 ♘c3 d5 4 cxd5 ♘xd5 5 g3 Black is forced into section A, but now the white knight is already on c3 so Black has the opportunity to trade knights.

A. Black captures on d5 with the knight

1 d4 ♘f6 2 c4 g6 3 g3 d5 4 cxd5 ♘xd5 5 ♗g2 ♗g7

6 ♘f3

White would first like to develop and only then occupy the centre. He may instead accelerate actions with:

a) 6 ♘c3 (this position can also be reached via 1 d4 ♘f6 2 c4 g6 3 ♘c3 d5 4 cxd5 ♘xd5 5 g3 ♗g7 6 ♗g2) 6...♘xc3 7 bxc3 c5 8 e3 ♘c6 (also playable is 8...0-0 9 ♘e2 ♘c6 10 0-0 cxd4 11 cxd4 ♗f5 with ...♕d7, ...♖ac8 and ... ♖fd8 to

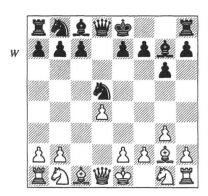

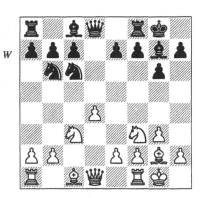

follow =) 9 ♘e2 ♗d7 10 0-0 ♖c8 and Black has cleared his pieces from the dangerous long diagonal. His plan is ...0-0 and ...♘a5 with the target square being c4 (=).

b) 6 e4 ♘b6 **7** ♘e2 **0-0 8 0-0** ♗g4 (also interesting is 8...c6 and 9...e5!?) **9 f3** ♗d7 **10** ♘bc3 **e5 11 dxe5** ♗xe5 **12** ♗h6 ♗g7 **13** ♕c1 ♘c6 **14** ♗xg7 ♔xg7 **15 f4 f6!** followed by ...♕e7, ...♖ad8 and ...♖fe8 with equality.

6...0-0 7 0-0 ♘b6
This is more precise than 7...c5 8 dxc5 ♘a6 9 c6!? ± or 7...♘c6 8 e4 and 9 d5 ±.

8 ♘c3
Not 8 e4?! ♗g4! 9 d5 c6!

8...♘c6

Plans and Counterplans:
White can either push with d4-d5 or protect the pawn with e2-e3, viz.

a) 9 d5 ♘a5! (when the bishop is on g2, the c4-square is weakened) **10 e4 c6 11** ♗g5 **h6 12** ♗f4 **cxd5 13 exd5** ♘ac4 when play can follow tactical paths, e.g. **14** ♕e2 ♘xb2!? **15** ♕xb2 ♘a4 **16** ♘xa4!? ♗xb2 **17** ♘xb2 ∞ or **14 b3!?** ♗xc3 (14...♘d6 15 ♗e5) **15** ♖c1 ♘b2 **16** ♕e2 ♗g7 **17** ♗e5 ♗xe5 **18** ♘xe5 ∞.

b) 9 e3 e5!? 10 d5 ♘a5 (the idea 10...♘e7 11 e4 ♗g4 and ...c7-c6 is also perfectly playable) **11 e4 c6 12** ♗g5 (on 12 d6 Black plays ...♗g4 and ...♘c8) **12...f6 13** ♗e3 **cxd5 14** ♗xb6 ♕xb6 **15** ♘xd5 ♕d8 **16** ♖c1 ♘c6 **17** ♕b3 ♖f7 **18** ♖fd1 ♗e6 with complicated play. A typical motif of this line is that after d4-d5 (which is often provoked by Black) the black knight goes to a5. The reason for this is the weakness of square c4 and that White is unable to play b2-b4 due to the strength of the bishop on g7.

B. Symmetrical Grünfeld

1 d4 ♘f6 **2 c4 g6 3 g3 c6**
A similar principle applies in the Réti Opening: Black wants to seal the diagonal of bishop g2 with ...c7-c6 and ...d7-d5.

4 ♗g2

White cannot prevent Black from playing d5 as after 4 d5?! cxd5 5 cxd5 d6 6 ♘c3 ♗g7 7 ♗g2 ♕a5 8 ♗d2 0-0 9 e3 ♘bd7 10 ♘ge2 ♘e5, followed by ...♘c4 or ...♗g4, Black is very active. A golden rule is that White should never play d4-d5 'for nothing'. This thrust is only effective if it attacks a piece (for example a knight on c6), and thus forces the opponent to lose a tempo, or if it locks in the bishop on b7 (see the Queen's Indian Defence). Otherwise Black can 'pick on' the pawn on d5 with ...c7-c6 and ...e7-e6 or, as in the above example, he can simply evade it with ...♕a5, ...♘d7-e5, ...♗g4, etc.

4...d5 5 cxd5

If Black lines up with ...c7-c6 and ...d7-d5 then White should be aware of ...d5xc4 since the stolen pawn can be protected with ...b7-b5. Thus 5 ♘f3?! dxc4!? 6 ♘a3 b5 7 ♘e5 ♕b6 or 6 ♘e5 (instead of 6 ♘a3) 6...♗e6 7 ♘a3 ♗d5! is better for Black. On 5 ♕b3 ♗g7 6 ♘f3 interesting is 6...a5!? 7 ♗f4 a4 8 ♕b4 ♘bd7 9 0-0 ♕b6 10 ♕xb6 ♘xb6 11 c5 ♘c4! and Black is on top in view of White's gaping holes on the queenside (c4, b3). But 5 ♘d2 ♗g7 6 ♘gf3 0-0 7 0-0 ♗f5 8 b3 a5!? with the plan ...a5-a4 is equal.

5...cxd5 6 ♘f3 ♗g7 7 0-0 0-0

Plans and Counterplans:
We do not need a crystal ball to see that after 8 ♘c3 ♘c6 White

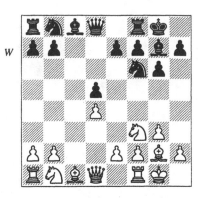

intends to break the symmetry with 9 ♘e5. Black can prevent this with 8 ♘c3 ♘e4, but White may pre-empt this with 8 ♘e5. For example:

a) 8 ♘e5 e6 (8...♘g4 9 ♘xg4 ♗xg4 10 ♘c3 ♘c6 11 h3 ♗d7 12 e3 e6) 9 ♘c3 ♘fd7 10 f4 f6 11 ♘f3 ♘c6 with a complicated game.

b) 8 ♘c3 and now:

b1) 8...♘e4 9 ♘xe4 dxe4 10 ♘e5 ♕d5 (this seems better than 10...f6 11 ♕b3+ e6 12 ♘c4 ♘c6 13 e3, when White's plan is ♗d2, ♖ac1 and f2-f3!?) 11 b3 and lately Black has been successful with two plans:

b11) 11...♘c6 12 ♗b2 ♖d8!? 13 ♘xc6 bxc6 14 ♕c2 ♗f5 15 e3 ♖ac8 16 ♖ac1 c5 =.

b12) 11...♘d7!? 12 ♗b2 ♘f6 13 ♖c1 ♗f5 14 ♖c5 (14 ♖c7 ♖ac8! 15 ♖xe7 ♕b5 and ...♘d5 or ...♕b4) 14...♕e6 and Black has a nice game: ...♗h3 or ...♖ad8, ...h7-h5. Finally we have

b2) 8 ♘c3 ♘c6 9 ♘e5, when Black does not obtain complete equality after either:

b21) 9...♘xe5 10 dxe5 ♘g4 11 ♘xd5 ♘xe5 12 ♕b3 followed by ♖d1 ±.

b22) 9...e6 10 ♘xc6 bxc6 11 ♘a4 ♘d7 12 b3! c5 13 ♗b2 ♗b7 14 ♖c1 ♖c8 15 ♕d2 and White awaits the exchanges on d4, after which his upper hand on the queenside becomes dominant (±). General chess theory would suggest that Black should not copy White for too long. So on 8 ♘c3, as we have seen, he should grab the opportunity to play 8...♘e4! In this symmetrical line Black can obtain equality but only if he does not underestimate White's initiative and opts for active counterplay.

King's Indian Defence

In the **King's Indian Defence** Black chooses the following structure:

This set-up is suitable against nearly every opening sequence for White but is best in the closed games (that is when the first move is not 1 e4). Often it leads to an exciting battle in which Black will later strike at the centre with ...c5 or ...e5. White can choose between the following lines:

I. Set-ups with g2-g3
II. Set-ups with e2-e4
III. With minimal risk viz. 1 d4 ♘f6 2 ♘f3 g6 3 ♗g5 or 3 ♗f4.

I. Set-ups with g3

1 d4 ♘f6 2 c4 g6 3 ♘c3 ♗g7 4 ♘f3 d6 5 g3 0-0 6 ♗g2
Black has three common King's Indian plans at his disposal:

A. 6...♘bd7 followed by ...e7-e5,
B. 6...c5, and a line that is frequently seen in the fianchetto variation:
C. 6...♘c6 with the idea of ...a7-a6, ...♖b8 and ...b7-b5.

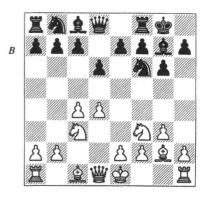

Another line that warrants attention is 6...c6 7 0-0 ♕a5, when Black prepares either ...♕h5 and ...♗h3 or an attack on the c-pawn with ...♗e6. However, White may play 8 e4!? e5 (8...♕h5 9 h4 ♗g4 10 ♕d3 and the threat is 11 ♘h2!) 9 h3 (9 d5 cxd5 10 cxd5 b5! is unclear) 9...exd4 10 ♘xd4 ♕c5 11 ♘b3 ♕xc4 12 ♕xd6 with an advantage. White now has the option of ♗f4, ♖fd1, ♖ac1, ♗f1 and e4-e5.

A. 1 d4 ♘f6 2 c4 g6 3 ♘c3 ♗g7 4 ♘f3 d6 5 g3 0-0 6 ♗g2 ♘bd7

7 0-0 e5

After 6...♘bd7, it is bad to follow up with 7...c5? 8 d5 a6 9 a4, as Black is completely tied up and White can start preparing for e4-e5 with e2-e4 and ♖e1.

8 e4

On 8 d5 a5 followed by 9...♘c5, or on 8 dxe5 dxe5 and ...c7-c6, ...♕e7 =, while on 8 e3?! ♖e8 and after 9...c6 Black is threatening ...e5-e4 and ...d6-d5.

8...c6

Also interesting is 8...exd4, liberating the squares e5 and c5 for the black knights and opening up the e-file and the long diagonal for the bishop on g7. On the other hand, this makes the pawn on d6 vulnerable. 9 ♘xd4 ♘c5 10 h3 (it is vital to secure the g4-square, especially against ...♘g4) 10...♖e8 11 ♖e1 ♗d7 12 ♖b1 ♕c8 13 ♔h2 h6 (13...♖e5?! is too optimistic: 14 f4! ♖h5 15 f5! gxf5 16 ♘d5! ±) 14 b3 and now Black has the plan ...♖b8, ...a7-a6 and ...b7-b5 or ...♘h7 and ...f7-f5 whereas White can operate with ♗f4 and ♘bd5 or ♗b2 and ♕c2. With 8...c6 Black does not commit himself while the queen's route to b6 or a5 is cleared.

9 h3

Again to prevent ...♘g4. If for example 9 ♖e1 exd4 10 ♘xd4 ♘g4! 11 ♕xg4 ♗xd4 12 ♕d1 ♕f6 ∞.

Plans and Counterplans:
On **9...♖e8** 10 ♗e3 exd4 11 ♘xd4 ♘c5 12 ♕c2 ♕e7 13 ♖fe1 ♗d7

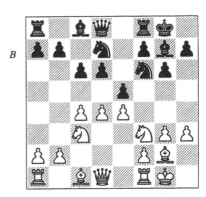

(13...♘fxe4 14 ♘xe4 ♘xe4 15 ♗xe4 ♕xe4 16 ♗d2!) 14 ♘b3! ♘xb3 15 axb3 Black's queenside is in difficulties. A sharper continuation is **9...♕b6!?** Now 10 d5 is harmless in view of 10...♘c5 11 ♖e1 cxd5 12 cxd5 ♗d7 13 ♖b1 a5 with equal chances. White opts for ♗e3, ♘d2-c4 while Black's plan is ...♖ac8, ...♕d8, ...♘e8 and ...f7-f5 or ...♖fc8, ...♕d8 and ...b7-b5. Also unclear is 10 ♖e1 exd4 11 ♘xd4 ♖e8 due to Black's threats of ...♘xe4, ...♘g4 and ...♕b4. The real thrills start after 10 c5!?: 10...dxc5 11 dxe5 ♘e8 12 e6!? (not 12 ♘a4 ♕a6 followed by ...b7-b5 and ...♘c7-e6, when Black has an active position) 12...fxe6 13 ♘g5 ♘e5 14 f4 ♘f7 15 ♘xf7 ♗d4+ 16 ♔h2 ♖xf7 17 e5 ♘c7 18 ♘e4 ♘d5 19 h4!? with a complicated fight in which White's attacking prospects offer him compensation for the pawn.

B. 1 d4 ♘f6 2 c4 g6 3 ♘c3 ♗g7 4 ♘f3 d6 5 g3 0-0 6 ♗g2 c5

7 0-0

7 d5 e6 8 0-0 exd5 9 cxd5 transposes to the Fianchetto variation of the Benoni, while 7...♘a6 instead of 7...e6 leads to a slightly inferior position: 8 0-0 ♘c7 9 a4 ♖b8 10 e4 a6 11 a5 b5 12 axb6 ♖xb6 ±. An interesting alternative is 7...e5!? 8 dxe6 (or 8 0-0 ♘a6 9 e4 ♘c7 10 a4 b6 and Black can aim for ...♘h5 and ...f7-f5) 8...♗xe6 9 ♘g5 ♗xc4 10 ♗xb7 ♘bd7 11 ♗xa8 ♕xa8 12 0-0 d5 with pleasant play for Black.

7...♘c6

For 7...cxd4 8 ♘xd4 ♘c6 see the 'Typical English'. After 9 ♘xc6 bxc6 10 ♗xc6 Black should not play 10...♗h3, but instead 10...♖b8, 11...♕a5 with pressure on the queenside.

8 d5

Or 8 dxc5 dxc5 and in the symmetrical position Black's lack of one tempo is not significant: 9 ♗e3 ♗e6 10 ♗xc5 ♕a5! 11 ♗a3 ♗xc4 =; or 9 ♗f4 ♗d7 10 ♘e5 ♘xe5 11 ♗xe5 ♕c8, when with ...♖d8, ...♗c6 Black maintains equality.

8...♘a5!

This is a rare occasion on which the knight stands well on the sidelines, as it threatens the pawn on c4, and White cannot easily chase the knight away with a2-a3 and b2-b4 owing to the scope of the bishop on g7.

9 ♘d2

This is better than 9 ♕d3 as it allows White to play e2-e4 and f2-f4 and also counterbalances the

knight on a5 by defending the b3 and c4 squares.

9...a6

Also not bad is 9...e6. If White takes then after ...♗xe6 the c4-pawn becomes weak, while if he does not capture, Black can play 10...exd5 11 cxd5, when after ...♖b8 he is ready for ...b7-b5. Also playable is the routine King's Indian plan of 9...e5 10 e4 ♘e8 and ...f7-f5. Instead of 10 e4, White can also try 10 a3 b6 11 b4 ♘b7, when again Black plays ...♘e8 and ...f7-f5.

10 ♕c2 ♖b8 11 b3 b5 12 ♗b2

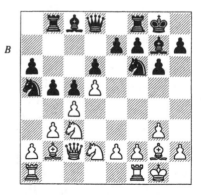

B

Plans and Counterplans:

Black will try to compensate the offside position of his a5-knight with active play on the queenside. The most aggressive follow-up is 12...♗h6!?, indirectly attacking the pawn on c4. One possible continuation is 13 f4 bxc4 14 bxc4 e5 (14...♘g4 15 ♘d1) 15 dxe6 (15 fxe5? ♘g4 16 ♘d1 ♘e3 17 ♘xe3 ♗xe3+ followed by ...♗xd2 and ...♘xc4, and Black wins) 15...♗xe6

16 ♘d5 ♖xb2!? 17 ♕xb2 ♗g7 and, with threats of ...♘xd5, ...♘g4 and ...♘xc4 Black stands well.

C. 1 d4 ♘f6 2 c4 g6 3 ♘c3 ♗g7 4 ♘f3 d6 5 g3 0-0 6 ♗g2 ♘c6

7 0-0

7 d5 ♘a5 8 ♘d2 c5 transposes to the previous section.

7...a6

7...♗g4 comes into consideration, with the idea of 8 h3 ♗xf3 9 ♗xf3 ♘d7 10 e3 e5 11 d5 ♘e7 12 e4 f5. The continuation 7...e5 8 d5 ♘e7 strongly resembles the Classical Main Line with the exception that here White has played g2-g3 and ♗g2 instead of e2-e4 and ♗e2. This is a significant difference because in these positions White attacks on the queenside while Black's play is on the kingside. And a g2-g3 and ♗g2 set-up is almost impossible to crack with a pawn-storm. White can play 9 b4!? ♘d7 10 ♖b1 a5 11 a3 h6 (11...f5 12 ♘g5!) 12 e4 f5 13 exf5 gxf5 14 ♘h4 e4 15 ♕b3!, preparing c4-c5 and threatening to eliminate Black's advanced pawn with f2-f3. Why doesn't Black play 9...a5 instead of 9...♘d7? Because after 10 bxa5! ♖xa5 11 ♘d2 White is threatening ♘b3 and c4-c5, when he will quickly seize control with the moves c5xd6, a2-a4, ♘b5, ♗a3 and ♖c1. For example, 11...b6 12 ♘b3 ♖a8 13 a4! followed by a4-a5 and later c4-c5, when White is on top.

8 h3

A very sharp alternative is 8 b3 ♖b8 9 ♗b2 b5 10 cxb5 axb5 11 d5 ♘a5 12 ♘d4 b4 13 ♘a4 e5 14 dxe6 fxe6 ∞, while again 8 d5 ♘a5 9 ♘d2 c5 leads to section B.

8...♖b8

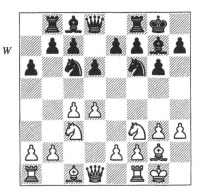

W

Plans and Counterplans:

White has two typical plans here: an immediate advance in the centre and a simple developing move:

a) 9 e4 b5 10 e5 dxe5 11 dxe5 ♕xd1 12 ♖xd1 ♘d7 13 e6 fxe6 14 cxb5 axb5 15 ♗f4 ♘de5 ∞.

b) 9 ♗e3!? (perhaps a more logical follow-up to h2-h3) 9...b5 10 ♘d2 ♗d7 11 ♖c1!? e5!? 12 dxe5 ♘xe5 13 cxb5 axb5 14 b3 ♖e8 15 ♘de4 , when the outcome will depend on whether Black can ever mobilize his b-, c- and d-pawns.

II. Set-ups with e2-e4

---

1 d4 ♘f6 2 c4 g6 3 ♘c3 ♗g7 4 e4 d6

After 4...0-0, 5 e5?! is premature: 5...♘e8 6 f4 d6 7 ♗e3 c5!? 8

dxc5 ♘c6 and Black's development plus may easily evolve into a dangerous initiative. White cannot occupy the whole centre as Black would be able to blow it up. But after 4...0-0 White can simply play the same as on 4...d6, when Black has nothing better than to transpose to theoretical lines with 5...d6.

After 4...d6, White's choices are:

A. Four Pawns Attack, viz. 5 f4.
B. Sämisch Variation, viz. 5 f3.
C. h2-h3 set-ups and other delicacies
D. Averbakh Variation, viz. 5 ♗e2 0-0 6 ♗g5.
E. Classical Main Line, viz. 5 ♘f3 followed by ♗e2, 0-0.

A. Four Pawns Attack

1 d4 ♘f6 2 c4 g6 3 ♘c3 ♗g7 4 e4 d6 5 f4

This line certainly has its pros and cons: White follows the general rule of development, first the pawns, then the knights, but the counter-argument is that it is bad to make too many pawn moves in the opening as it creates a wide front without developing pieces and castling. As we shall see, these arguments as roughly of equal merit, and this coincides with the theoretical evaluation of this line.

5...0-0 6 ♘f3

Black has to undermine the white centre quickly, otherwise

his opponent will complete his development with ♗e2, 0-0 and start to advance his four central pawns (e4-e5). Black's possibilities are the usual:

A1. 6...♘a6!?, playing for ...e7-e5 or
A2. 6...c5.

6...♗g4?! is of little merit, due to 7 ♗e3 ♘fd7 (preparing ...♘c6 and ...e7-e5) 8 h3 ♗xf3 9 ♕f3 followed by 0-0-0 and g4 ±.

A1. 1 d4 ♘f6 2 c4 g6 3 ♘c3 ♗g7 4 e4 d6 5 f4 0-0 6 ♘f3 ♘a6!?

Black aims for ...e7-e5, after which the knight will gain access to the c5-square. It is better to await this on a6 than on d7 in order to keep the diagonal of the bishop on c8 open. On the immediate 6...e5 7 dxe5 dxe5 8 ♕xd8 ♖xd8 9 ♘xe5 Black cannot achieve sufficient compensation for the pawn.

7 ♗e2

7 e5 is met by 7...♘d7 followed by 8...c5.

7...e5 8 dxe5

Alternatively 8 fxe5 dxe5 9 d5 (9 dxe5? ♘g4; or 9 ♘xe5 c5 10 d5 ♘xe4 11 ♘xe4 ♗xe5 threatening 12...♕h4+) 9...c6 (9...♘c5 10 ♗g5 h6 11 ♗xf6! ♕xf6 12 b4 ±) 10 0-0 cxd5 11 cxd5 ♘e8 followed by ...♘d6, whereupon the manoeuvre ...♘c7-e8 will secure the knight as a blockader on d6. Later Black can play ...h7-h6 and ...f7-f5 while White may go ♗e3-c5 and/or ♘d2-c4.

8...dxe5 9 ♕xd8 ♖xd8 10 ♘xe5 ♘c5 11 ♗f3 ♗e6

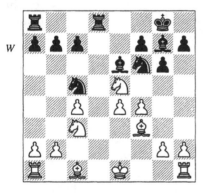

Plans and Counterplans:

Black prepares for ...♘fd7, when after the exchange of knights, the pawn on c4 is hanging and the d3-square is wide open. This cannot be prevented by **12 ♘d5 ♘fd7 13 ♘xd7** (not 13 ♘xc7? ♘xe5 14 fxe5 ♘d3+ 15 ♔e2 ♗xc4 ∓) **13...♖xd7 14 ♔e2 ♖e8 15 e5 c6 16 ♘e3 f6!**, because the white king faces a terrible onslaught. White should

maintain an equal position with **12 0-0 ♘fd7 13 ♘xd7 ♗d4+ 14 ♔h1 ♖xd7 15 ♘d5 c6 and now16 ♗e3 (16 ♘e3? ♘d3) 16...cxd5 17 ♗xd4 dxe4 18 ♗xc5 exf3 19 ♖xf3 ♗xc4.**

A2. 1 d4 ♘f6 2 c4 g6 3 ♘c3 ♗g7 4 e4 d6 5 f4 0-0 6 ♘f3 c5

7 d5

On 7 dxc5 ♕a5 8 ♗d3 ♕xc5 9 ♕e2 ♘c6 10 ♗e3 ♕a5 11 0-0 ♗g4 12 ♖ac1 ♘d7!? ∞, while 7 ♗e2 transposes to the Maroczy Bind (Sicilian Defence): 7...cxd4 8 ♘xd4 ♘c6 9 ♗e3 but since White has played f2-f4 instead of castling Black can easily equalize: 9...e5!? 10 ♘xc6 (10 ♘db5 ♘e8 and then 11...a6) 10...bxc6 11 fxe5 (otherwise Black would capture on f4 and take aim at the pawn on e4 with ...♖e8) 11...dxe5 12 ♗c5 ♖e8 =. Black can play for either ...♗e6 and ...♘d7 or for the g4-square.

7...e6

Similar to the Benko Gambit is 7...b5!? 8 cxb5 a6 9 a4 (9 bxa6 ♕a5 10 ♗d2 ♗xa6 11 ♗xa6 ♕xa6 with ...♘bd7 and ...♖b8 to follow) 9...e6!? 10 dxe6 ♗xe6 11 ♗e2 axb5 12 ♗xb5 d5! 13 exd5 ♘xd5 14 ♘xd5 ♗xd5 15 0-0 ♘c6 with good play for Black, owing to the strong bishop on g7 and the fact that the pawn on f4 weakens White's position.

8 dxe6

8 ♗e2 exd5 9 cxd5 is the basic position of the Benoni with f2-f4.

On 9 exd5 (instead of 9 cxd5) 9...a6 10 a4 a5! the black knight infiltrates via a6 to the b4-square.

8...fxe6

Less effective is 8...♗xe6 9 ♗d3 ♘c6 10 f5! ♗d7 11 0-0 ♖e8 12 ♗g5 ±.

9 ♗e2

On 9 ♗d3 ♘c6 10 0-0 a6!? and if 11 a4 then 11...b6 and Black has obtained the chance to regroup with ...♖a7-e7, ...♘c6 and ...♗b7.

9...♘c6 10 0-0 ♕e7

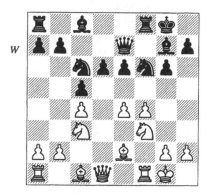

Plans and Counterplans:
It is difficult for White to continue quietly because on **11 ♗e3** ♘g4 while on **11 h3** the reply is 11...♘h5. The real test is **11 e5** dxe5 12 fxe5 ♘g4 13 ♗g5 and now 13...♕e8 14 ♕d2, when the move ♘c3-e4 will compensate White for the pawn on e5. Instead of 13...♕e8, also interesting for Black is 13...♕d7!? 14 ♕e1 ♘gxe5 15 ♖d1 ♘xf3+ 16 ♖xf3 ♗d4+ 17 ♔h1 ♖xf3 18 ♗xf3 ♕g7!?, with ...♗d7 to follow (∞).

B. Sämisch Variation

1 d4 ♘f6 2 c4 g6 3 ♘c3 ♗g7 4 e4 d6 5 f3

With this move, White first builds a massive pawn structure to secure his spatial plus and then plans to fill up the space with his pieces: ♗e3, ♕d2, ♗d3 and ♘ge2.

5...0-0

5...e5 immediately is also playable. For example 6 dxe5 dxe5 7 ♕xd8+ ♔xd8 8 ♗e3 ♗e6 9 0-0-0+ ♘fd7 10 g3 ♘c6 11 ♗h3 ♘d4 12 ♗xe6 fxe6 13 f4 c5 =. White should instead play 6 d5, when if Black does not transpose to the main lines with 6...0-0 but plays for instance 6...♘fd7 7 h4!? f5, then after 8 g3!? (against 8 f4!?) and 9 h5 White has the upper hand.

6 ♗e3

On 6 ♗g5 c5 7 d5 (or 7 dxc5 ♕a5 8 ♕d2 dxc5 followed by ...♖d8) 7...e6 8 ♕d2 exd5 9 cxd5 (or 9 ♘xd5 ♗e6 10 ♘e2 ♗xd5 11 cxd5 ♘bd7 12 ♘c3 a6 = since Black has got rid of his problem bishop on c8) and we find ourselves in a 'Sämisch-like' Benoni. The difference is that Black, due to the different move-order, has up to now been unable to play ...h7-h6, and now it is too late: 9...h6? 10 ♗xh6! ♘xe4 11 ♘xe4 ♕h4+ 12 g3 ♕xh6 13 ♕xh6 ♗xh6 14 ♘xd6 with f2-f4 and 0-0-0 to come (±). That leaves us with 9...a6 10 a4 ♕a5 11 ♖a3! and White is better. 11 ♖a3! is worth remembering because it is a unique way to protect the rook against the threat of ...b7-b5.

On 6 ♗g5 Black can also play 6...♘c6 7 ♘ge2 and now either ...a7-a6, ...♖b8, ...b7-b5 and ...♗d7 or 7...e5 8 d5 ♘e7 9 ♕d2 h5! followed by ...♘h7 and ...f7-f5 ∞. This line can also appear through the move-order 6 ♘ge2 e5 7 ♗g5 ♘c6 8 d5 ♘e7.

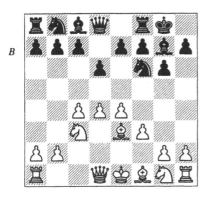

Black now has a choice of various set-ups, and the following are worth examining closely:

B1. 6...c5 and
B2. 6...e5.

Other lines are also instructive:

a) 6...c6 7 ♗d3 (more direct than 7 ♕d2) 7...a6 8 ♘ge2 b5 9 0-0 bxc4 (9...♘bd7 10 b3 e5 11 d5 cxd5 12 cxd5 ♘h5 13 ♖c1 f5 14 exf5 gxf5 15 ♕d2 with a tough game) 10 ♗xc4 d5 11 ♗b3 dxe4 12 ♘xe4 ♘d5 13 ♗f2 a5 ∞.

b) 6...♘bd7 7 ♕d2 c5 (7...a6!? 8 0-0-0 b5! 9 cxb5 axb5 10 ♗xb5 ♘b6 and 11...♗a6 with a pleasant attack on the queenside) 8 d5!? (or 8 ♘ge2 a6 9 0-0-0 ♕a5 followed by 10...b5) 8...♘e5 9 ♗g5!? a6 10 f4 ♘ed7 11 ♘f3 b5 12 cxb5 ♕a5!? 13 e5 dxe5 14 fxe5 ♘g4 15 e6! (15 ♗xe7? ♖e8 16 d6 ♗h6! ∞) 15...fxe6 16 ♗xe7 and d5-d6, when the position is Byzantine.

c) 6...♘c6 7 ♘ge2 a6 8 ♕d2 ♖b8 9 h4 (9 ♘c1 e5! 10 d5 ♘d4 ∞) 9...h5 10 ♘c1 e5!? 11 d5 ♘d4 and now on both 12 ♘b3 and 12 ♘1e2 a fresh idea is 12...c5! 13 dxc6 bxc6 14 ♘xd4 exd4 15 ♗xd4 ♖e8 16 ♗e2 d5 17 cxd5 ♖b4! and for example, 18 ♗c5 ♘xe4! 19 fxe4 (19 ♘xe4 ♖xb2 and 20...cxd5) 19...♗xc3 20 ♕xc3 ♖bxe4 21 0-0 ♖xe2 and Black is very active: 22 d6? is met by 22...♗e6! followed by 23...♗d5, therefore of course White should prefer 22 dxc6 ♕xh4 with a double-edged position.

B1. 1 d4 ♘f6 2 c4 g6 3 ♘c3 ♗g7 4 e4 d6 5 f3 0-0 6 ♗e3 c5

7 dxc5

7 d5 e6 8 ♕d2 exd5 9 cxd5 leads to the Benoni. Also possible is 7 ♘ge2 ♘c6 8 ♕d2 cxd4 9 ♘xd4 ♘xd4 10 ♗xd4 ♗e6 11 ♗e2 ♕a5 12 ♖b1 ♖fc8 13 b3 a6!? and if White stops ...b7-b5 with 14 a4 then 14...♕b4! 15 ♘d5 ♕xd2+ 16 ♔xd2 ♘xd5 17 ♗xg7 ♘f4!? 18 ♗h6 ♘xe2 19 ♔xe2 b5!? with a

promising endgame for Black.
(Just like the Sicilian Maroczy!)

7...dxc5 8 ♕xd8

8 e5 is met by 8...♘fd7 9 f4 f6!
(the very first opportunity should
be taken to blow up the enemy
centre) 10 exf6 (10 e6 ♘b6 and
the pawn on e6 falls) 10...♘xf6!
11 ♕xd8 ♖xd8 12 ♗xc5 ♗f5! 13
♘f3 ♘e4! with a good deal of compensation for the pawn.

8...♖xd8 9 ♗xc5 ♘c6 10 ♗a3

The threat was 10...♘d7 and
11...♗xc3+ disconnecting White's
queenside pawns. Or 10 ♘d5 ♘d7
11 ♗a3 e6 12 ♘c7 ♖b8 13 0-0-0
b6!? followed by ...♗b7, ...♖bc8
and Black's play with the strong
dark-squared bishop, initiative on
the c-file and White's jammed
queenside leads to an equal game.

10...a5!?

Preparing ...♘c6-b4.

11 ♖d1 ♗e6

Also interesting is 11...♖xd1+
12 ♔xd1 ♘b4 13 ♘ge2 ♗e6 14
♘d5 ♗xd5 15 cxd5 e6!?

12 ♘d5

Plans and Counterplans:

White plans to secure his position
and extra pawn with ♘e2-c3.
However, he is still so undeveloped that Black can convert his
development advantage into an
equal material balance. On the
older line **12...♗xd5** 13 cxd5 ♘b4
14 ♔f2! (14 ♗b5 ♘c2+ 15 ♔f2
♘xa3 16 bxa3 e6 ∞) Black does
not get the bishop on a3! However **12...♘b4!** is an important

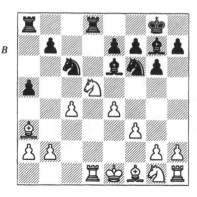

new move: 13 ♗xb4 axb4 14 ♘xb4
♘d7 15 ♖d2 ♘c5 and the white
queenside gets into trouble or 13
♘xe7+ ♔h8 14 ♘d5 ♘c2+ 15 ♔f2
♘xa3 16 bxa3 b5! 17 ♘h3 ♖ac8!
and Black is on top. Maybe White
can seek reinforcement with 13
♔f2.

**B2. 1 d4 ♘f6 2 c4 g6 3 ♘c3 ♗g7 4
e4 d6 5 f3 0-0 6 ♗e3 e5**

Now White gains nothing from 7
dxe5 dxe5 8 ♕xd8 ♖xd8 9 ♘d5 in
view of 9...♘xd5 10 cxd5 c6 11
♗c4 b5 12 ♗b3 ♗b7 =.

So White can either keep up
the tension in the centre – at least
for a while – with **7 ♘ge2** (section
B2a), or immediately close the
centre with **7 d5** (section B2b).

**B2a. 1 d4 ♘f6 2 c4 g6 3 ♘c3
♗g7 4 e4 d6 5 f3 0-0 6 ♗e3 e5 7
♘ge2**

7...c6

This is better than 7...♘c6?! 8
♕d2 exd4 9 ♘xd4, when White

guards his spatial plus with ♗e2 and 0-0. An important difference compared to the Maroczy set-up is that there the c-pawn is missing instead of the e-pawn and therefore in the Maroczy Black has some counterplay on the c-file, attacking the pawn on c4 after ...♘xd4, ...♗e6, ...♕a5 and ...♖fc8. The open e-file instead of the c-file does not offer such active possibilities.

8 ♕d2 ♘bd7

Or 8...exd4 9 ♘xd4 d5 10 cxd5 cxd5 11 e5 ♘e8 12 f4 f6 13 ♘f3!? fxe5 14 ♗c4! and in the course of blasting open the centre Black has become passive.

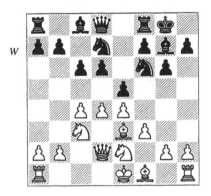

Plans and Counterplans:
White can either close the centre with d4-d5 or keep the option fluid by playing ♖d1 or 0-0-0:

a) 9 d5 cxd5 10 ♘xd5 (10 cxd5 a6 11 g4!? h5! 12 g5 ♘h7 13 ♖g1 f6 14 gxf6 ♖xf6 ∞) 10...♘xd5 11 ♕xd5 (11 cxd5 f5 12 ♘c3 ♘f6 13 ♗d3!?) 11...♘f6!? (a rare line is 11...♘b6 12 ♕b5 ♗h6!? and the

bishop is protected by ...♕h4+. It is a pity that after 13 ♗f2! followed by ♘c3, ♗e2 and 0-0 White is slightly better) 12 ♕d2 b5! and 13 cxb5 d5 14 exd5 ♘xd5 15 ♖d1 ♗e6 or 13 ♘c3 bxc4 14 ♗xc4 ♗e6!? with good play for Black. The breakthrough ...b7-b5 and ...d6-d5 is very attractive!

b) 9 ♖d1 a6!? 10 dxe5 ♘xe5 11 b3 b5! 12 cxb5 axb5 13 ♕xd6 ♘fd7 and on, for example 14 ♕d2 b4 15 ♘a4 ♖xa4 16 bxa4 ♘c4 17 ♕c1 ♘xe3 18 ♕xe3 ♕a5 with a tremendous attack for Black. For that matter, after 13...♘fd7 Black was already threatening 14...b4! 15 ♕xb4 c5 16 ♗xc5 ♘xc5 17 ♖xd8 ♘ed3+. 10 d5!? instead of 10 dxe5 comes into consideration, and on 10...cxd5? 11 ♘xd5! ♘xd5 12 ♕xd5 ±. Black must therefore close the d-file before the white forces invade: 10 d5!? c5!? and Black may consider a future ...b7-b5 sacrifice or the manoeuvre ...♘e8 and ...f7-f5.

c) 9 0-0-0 a6!? 10 ♗h6!? (10 d5 c5 and 11...b5 ∞ or 10 ♔b1 b5 11 ♘c1 exd4 12 ♗xd4 b4!? 13 ♘a4 c5 14 ♗xf6 ♗xf6 15 ♕xd6 ♗e7 and Black's control over the dark squares yields him good play. He can even dream about ...♕a5, ...♗f6, ...♘e5-c6-d4 and ...♗d7). 10...b5!? 11 h4 ♕a5 12 h5 b4 13 ♘b1 ♕xa2 14 ♘g3 (if Black had interpolated ...♗xh6, ♕xh6, another interesting defensive move would be ♖d1-d2) 14...♗xh6 15 ♕xh6 and Black's bilateral attack can be continued with ...♘b6-c4 or ...e5xd4 and ...♘c5, whereas White can operate with a combination of the moves ♕g5, ♘f5 and h5xg6.

B2b. 1 d4 ♘f6 2 c4 g6 3 ♘c3 ♗g7 4 e4 d6 5 f3 0-0 6 ♗e3 e5 7 d5

7...♘h5

With the centre closed, Black can try for ...f7-f5, as he no longer needs to fear d4xe5. 7...c6 8 ♘ge2 cxd5 9 cxd5 ♘bd7 10 ♕d2 transposes into section B2a, while on 8 ♗d3!? (instead of 8 ♘ge2) 8...cxd5 9 cxd5 ♘h5 10 ♘ge2 f5 11 exf5!? gxf5 12 0-0 ♘d7 13 ♖c1 a6 14 ♔h1!? White has a fantastic positional trap: 14...♔h8?! 15 ♕d2 b5? 16 ♗xf5!! ♖xf5 17 g4 and on any rook move White has a tremendous attack with g4xh5, ♘e4, ♗h6, ♖g1 and ♘g5. Better is 14...♘df6 15 ♗g5!? and White has a somewhat more harmonious position as Black's knights are tied up.

8 ♕d2

White prepares to castle queenside.

8...f5

The queen sacrifice 8...♕h4+ 9 g3 (9 ♗f2 ♕e7 followed by f7-f5 or 9...♕f4) 9...♘xg3 10 ♕f2 ♘xf1 11 ♕xh4 ♘xe3 is the subject of a long-standing debate. Besides the two pieces Black also has a pawn for the queen, but after 12 ♔e2! ♘xc4 13 ♖c1 ♘a6 14 ♘d1 (14 b3? ♘a3 and ...♗d7) 14...♘b6 15 ♘e3

♗d7 16 ♘h3 f6 17 ♘f2 ♘c8! 18 ♘d3 c5 19 ♕g3, followed by h2-h4, White is ahead in 'weight', although Black can play ♗h6xe3 and if h4-h5 then ...g6-g5 stopping White's kingside attack.

9 0-0-0 ♘d7

The premature ...f5-f4 would simply release the pressure on White's position.

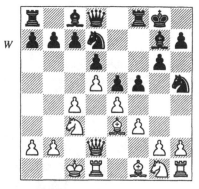

Plans and Counterplans:

After completing his development, White will advance his kingside plans with ♗d3, ♘ge2, g2-g3, ♗h6 and naturally e4xf5. For his part, Black can generate play on the queenside with ...a7-a6 and ...b7-b5, play ...♘c5 and ...a7-a5, or play ...♘df6 followed by a capture on e4. One interesting possibility is 10 exf5 gxf5 11 ♗d3 ♘c5 12 ♗c2 ♕h4! forcing a weakness: 13 b3 (now the threat is 14 ♗g5) 13...♕e7! and Black has play on the weakened long diagonal. He still needs to be careful, however, because White still has the d4-square.

C. h2-h3 set-ups and other delicacies

1 d4 ♘f6 2 c4 g6 3 ♘c3 ♗g7 4 e4 d6 5 h3

White is planning to play ♗g5 and ♕d2 but the immediate 5 ♗g5 h6 6 ♗e3 allows 6...♘g4, therefore White first protects the g4-square.

Another, quite rare continuation, also deserves attention: 5 ♗d3!? 0-0 6 ♘ge2. Now Black can make use of White's lack of control over d4 and e5 with 6...♘c6 7 0-0 ♘d7!? 8 ♗e3 e5 9 d5 ♘d4 and he need not fear 10 ♗xd4 exd4 11 ♘b5 in view of 11...♘e5 12 ♘bxd4 c5! 13 dxc6 (if the knight moves, there follows ...♘xd3 and ...♗xb2) 13...bxc6 and the black bishops are very strong (Black's plan is ...♗a6 and ...d6-d5).

Also interesting is the set-up 5 ♘ge2 with ♘g3 and ♗e2 to follow. The logical reply is 5...0-0 6 ♘g3 e5 7 d5 a5 8 ♗e2 ♘a6 9 0-0 ♘c5 10 b3 ♗d7 11 ♖b1 h5 12 ♗g5 ♕e8! 13 ♕d2 ♘h7 and on 14 ♗h6 h4! completely upsetting the position.

5...0-0 6 ♗g5

White can still switch to a well-trodden path with 6 ♘f3 c5 7 d5 e6 8 ♗d3 exd5 9 exd5 (9 cxd5 is a fashionable line of the Benoni) 9...♖e8+ 10 ♗e3 ♗h6 11 0-0 ♗xe3 12 fxe3 and 12...♖xe3? is fatal because 13 ♕d2 followed by ♕h6 and ♘g5 gives White a decisive

attack. Better is 12...♘bd7 and then ...♔g7, ...♘g8 and ...f7-f6 with a blockade on the dark squares.

6...c5!?

This is more accurate than 6...h6?! 7 ♗e3 e5 8 d5 followed by ♗d3, ♕d2 and ♘ge2 ±.

7 d5 e6 8 ♗d3 exd5 9 exd5 ♘bd7

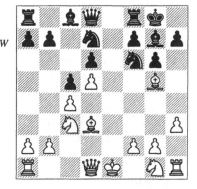

Plans and Counterplans:
White faces a difficult decision. After **10 ♘f3 ♖e8+** the king must depart: 11 ♔f1 (11 ♗e3 ♗h6), although this is ugly only to the eye since after 11...h6 12 ♗f4 ♘e5 13 ♘xe5 dxe5 14 ♗e3 b6 15 ♕d2 h5 the game is double-edged. White can attack with a2-a4-a5 while Black can proceed with ...f7-f5 after the f6 knight has moved. An interesting alternative is **10 f4!? ♕a5 11 ♔f2!?** (the threat was 11...b5 12 cxb5 ♘xd5) 11...h6 12 ♗h4 a6 13 a4 ♘h5 14 ♘ge2 f5 with a difficult fight.

The variation 5 h3 or perhaps 5 ♗d3 with the idea ♘ge2 is best suited to those who seek novel ideas brought about by tiny differences or variances in move-orders right at the start.

D. Averbakh Variation

1 d4 ♘f6 2 c4 g6 3 ♘c3 ♗g7 4 e4 d6 5 ♗e2 0-0 6 ♗g5

White immediately exerts pressure on the knight f6, thereby preventing Black from playing ...e7-e5 right away: 6...e5? 7 dxe5 dxe5 8 ♕xd8 ♖xd8 9 ♗xf6 ♗xf6 10 ♘d5 and major material losses can only be avoided with 10...♘d7 ±. Of course Black can play 6...h6, but then the bishop retreats to e3 and later the pawn on h6 will need defence. Black's usual plans are:

D1. 6...c5
D2. 6...h6 7 ♗e3 e5 and
D3. 6...♘a6!?

D1. 1 d4 ♘f6 2 c4 g6 3 ♘c3 ♗g7 4 e4 d6 5 ♗e2 0-0 6 ♗g5 c5

Those who plan to play ...c7-c5 can first interpolate 6...h6 7 ♗e3 and now 7...c5 8 e5!? (on 8 dxc5 ♕a5 while 8 d5 is only a different move-order leading to 6...c5) 8...dxe5 9 dxe5 ♕xd1+ 10 ♖xd1 ♘g4 11 ♗xc5 ♘xe5 12 ♗xe7 ♖e8 13 ♘d5 ♘a6 14 b3 ♗f5 15 ♔f1 ♘c6 16 ♗f6 ♘cb4 and Black's development plus is ample reward for the pawn.
7 d5
When one has not yet castled one should keep the position

closed. On 7 dxc5?! ♕a5 8 ♗d2 (8 ♕d2 dxc5 and ...♖d8) 8...♕xc5 9 ♘f3 ♗g4 10 ♗e3 ♕a5 followed by ...♘c6 Black has comfortable play.
7...h6
Slightly worse for Black is 7...e6 8 ♕d2 exd5 9 exd5 (9 cxd5 leads to the Benoni but 9 exd5 is free from risk and is to White's advantage) 9...♖e8 10 ♘f3 ♗g4 11 0-0 ♘bd7 12 h3 ♗xf3 13 ♗xf3 a6 14 a4 and Black has no counterplay while White can either consider a slow kingside expansion with ♗e2, f2-f4, ♗d3 and g2-g4 or he can opt for an endgame with exchanges on the e-file where his bishop pair and Black's vulnerable pawn on d6 secure White's advantage (±).

After 7...♕a5, 8 ♕d2?! is wrong on account of 8...a6 9 a4 ♘bd7, threatening 10...♘b6 and ...♗d7, ...♕b4 with an attack on the white pawns. Another interesting concept is 10 ♘f3 b5!? 11 cxb5 axb5 12 ♗xb5 (the pawn on a4 is pinned!) 12...♘xe4!? 13 ♘xe4 ♕xb5 14 axb5 ♖xa1+ followed by ...♖xh1. So on 7...♕a5 White should play 8 ♗d2! and then simply ♘f3 and 0-0, when the black queen is misplaced on a5 whereas White can even prepare ♗h6 with ♕c1.

Again playable is the Benko Gambit-like 7...b5!? 8 cxb5 a6: 9 a4!? ♕a5 10 ♗d2 axb5 11 ♗xb5 ♘a6 and then ...♘b4 and ...♗a6.
8 ♗f4
Also possible is 8 ♗e3 ♘bd7 9 ♕d2 ♔h7 10 ♘f3 a6! 11 a4 ♕a5 12

0-0 ♘g4 13 ♗f4 ♘ge5 14 ♕c2!? ♘xf3+ 15 ♗xf3 ♘e5 16 ♗e2 f5! with mutual chances.

8...e6!?

Or 8...♕b6 9 ♕d2 ♔h7 10 h3 and ♘f3, 0-0 ±.

9 dxe6

The bishop has been chased from g5 so after 9 ♕d2 exd5 10 exd5 ♔h7 11 ♘f3 Black can play 11...♘h5! 12 ♗e3 f5!

9...♗xe6

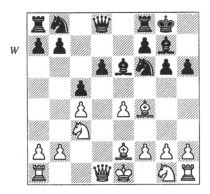

Plans and Counterplans:
Black threatens to take over with ...♕b6 and ...♘c6 so White has to bite at the pawn on d6 in one of two ways:

a) 10 ♗xd6 ♖e8 11 ♘f3 ♘c6 12 0-0 (12 ♗xc5 ♕a5 ∓) 12...♘d4 13 e5 (13 ♗xc5 ♘xe2+ 14 ♕xe2 ♕c7 and ...♗xc4 −+) 13...♘d7 14 ♘xd4 cxd4 15 ♕xd4 ♘xe5! 16 ♗xe5 ♕xd4 17 ♗xd4 ♗xd4 and Black maintains equality with ...♖ad8, ...♗xc3 and ...♖d2.

b) 10 ♕d2!? sets a trap, since on 10...♔h7? White can play 11 ♗xd6 ♖e8 12 e5! ♘fd7 13 f4 f6 14

h4! fxe5 15 h5! and Black's monarch has become the target. So Black should play 10...♕b6!? 11 ♗xh6 ♗xh6 12 ♕h6 ♕xb2 13 ♖c1 ♘c6 14 h4 ♘e5 15 ♘h3!? (15 h5? ♘fg4! 16 ♕f4 ♘xf2! and White cannot recapture) and now Black can choose between 15...♗xh3 16 ♖xh3 ♘fg4 and ...f7-f5; 15...♖fe8 16 h5 ♗xh3 17 hxg6 ♘xg6 18 ♖xh3 ♘xe4; or 15...b5!? In each case his counterattack balances White's offensive.

D2. 1 d4 ♘f6 2 c4 g6 3 ♘c3 ♗g7 4 e4 d6 5 ♗e2 0-0 6 ♗g5 h6 7 ♗e3

Not 7 ♗f4 ♘c6! 8 d5 (8 ♘f3 e5! 9 dxe5 ♘h5 and 10...dxe5) 8...e5! 9 ♗e3 ♘d4!? 10 ♗xd4 exd4 11 ♕xd4 ♖e8 12 ♕d3 ♘d7 with excellent play on the dark squares, while on 7 ♗h4 ♘a6!? followed by ...e7-e5 White's pressure on diagonal c1-h6 has evaporated. On 8 ♘f3 Black can even consider 8...g5 9 ♗g3 ♘h5.

7...e5 8 d5

The only move as after 8 ♘f3 ♘g4 or 8 dxe5 dxe5 9 ♕xd8 ♖xd8 10 ♘d5 ♘a6 White has achieved nothing.

8...c6

8...♘bd7 is also important: 9 ♕d2 ♘c5 10 f3 a5 and now the mistake 11 ♗xh6? allows 11...♘fxe4 followed by ...♕h4+ and ....♕xh6 and Black has won the pawn back with a superior position. On 11 g4 h5! White's attack is halted, but with 11 ♗d1 and ♗c2, ♘ge2 to follow, White can develop and castle kingside with the plan of b2-b3, a2-a3 and b3-b4 or he can castle queenside and start things rolling on the other flank.

9 ♕d2 cxd5 10 cxd5 h5

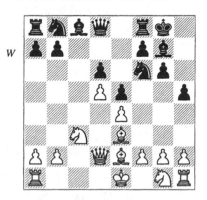

Plans and Counterplans:
It is hardly desirable for White to allow an exchange dark-squared bishops here, as the bishop on g7 will be rather passive in the middlegame, but of course he still needs to complete his development. So 11 h3!? ♘a6 12 ♘f3 ♘c5 13 ♕c2 and on account of his material advantage on the queenside White's chances are better both after 13...a5 14 0-0 followed by ♘d2 and after 13...♕c7 14 ♖c1 ♗d7 15 b4!? ♘a4 16 ♕b3.

D3. 1 d4 ♘f6 2 c4 g6 3 ♘c3 ♗g7 4 e4 d6 5 ♗e2 0-0 6 ♗g5 ♘a6!?

This makes 7...e5 possible, after which the knight will find its place on c5. Note that 7...e5 8 dxe5 dxe5 9 ♕xd8 ♖xd8 10 ♗xf6

♗xf6 11 ♘d5 is no longer a double attack since c7 is protected! The similar 6...♘bd7 is weaker: 7 ♕d2 e5 8 ♘f3 c6 9 ♖d1 (9 0-0?! exd4 10 ♘xd4 ♘c5 11 f3? ♘fxe4! 12 fxe4 ♗xd4+ −+) and on 9...♖e8 10 d5! ± owing to White's spatial plus. To make matters worse, the rook would now be better placed on f8, supporting the plan of ...f7-f5.

7 ♕d2
After 7 f4 c6!? 8 ♘f3 ♘c7!, the central blow ...d6-d5 is an adequate plan, while on 7 ♘f3 h6 8 ♗e3 e5 9 dxe5 ♘g4!? (9...dxe5 10 ♘xe5 ♘xe4 is also not bad) 10 ♕d2 ♘xe3 11 ♕xe3 dxe5 and after ...c7-c6 and ...♕e7 Black is somewhat better.

7...e5 8 d5
After 8 ♘f3 ♕e8 the merits of 6...♘a6 compared to 6...♘bd7 become clear because now besides 9...exd4, Black is also threatening 9...♗g4.

8...c6!?
After 8...♕e8 9 f3 White can play ♗d1, ♘ge2 and ♗c2 while Black can opt for ...♘c5, ...a7-a5, ...♘h5 and ...f7-f5. However, White's spatial plus is the dominant factor.

9 ♗d3
In order to thwart ...♗g4, White once again hands over the e2-square to the knight.

9...♘c5 10 ♗c2 a5 11 ♘ge2 cxd5 12 cxd5

Plans and Counterplans:
White is planning 0-0, f2-f3, ♗e3, b2-b3, a2-a3 and b3-b4. With

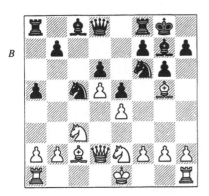

12...b5!? 13 ♘xb5 h6 14 ♗xf6 ♗xf6 Black can obtain the bishop pair, but it has cost him a pawn. Therefore it is better to prepare this with **12...♗d7!?** and now on 13 0-0 b5 while on 13 a4 ♕b6 and ...♖fc8, when the black queen can even tease White from the b4-square.

E. Classical Main Line

---

1 d4 ♘f6 2 c4 g6 3 ♘c3 ♗g7 4 e4 d6 5 ♘f3 0-0 6 ♗e2

Not 6 ♗g5 h6! 7 ♗h4 g5 8 ♗g3 ♘h5 =.

6...e5

6...c5 has no independent value as after 7 d5 e6 8 0-0 exd5 9 cxd5 it transposes to the Benoni, while after 7 0-0!? cxd4 (not 7...♘c6?! 8 d5 ♘a5 9 ♗d2 ♗g4 10 b3 a6 11 ♖c1 ± followed by ♕e1, when White is threatening the knight on a5 as well as the breakthrough e4-e5) 8 ♘xd4 and we have reached a Sicilian Maroczy.

On 6...♗g4 7 ♗e3 ♘fd7 White should play 8 ♘g1! ♗xe2 9 ♘gxe2,

when after 0-0, ♕d2 and f2-f3 he has a spatial advantage (±).

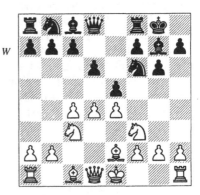

This is the starting position for three main variations:

E1. 7 d5
E2. 7 0-0 ♘bd7 and
E3. 7 0-0 ♘c6.

Besides 7 d5 and 7 0-0 White also has:

a) 7 dxe5 dxe5 8 ♕xd8 ♖xd8 9 ♗g5 (9 ♘xe5 ♘xe4 ∓ or 9 ♘d5 ♘xd5 10 cxd5 c6 11 ♗c4 cxd5 12 ♗xd5 ♘d7 =) 9...c6!? 10 ♘xe5 ♖e8 11 f4 (11 0-0-0 ♘a6! 12 ♖d6 ♗e6 13 f4 h6 14 ♗xf6 – 14 ♗h4 g5! – 14...♗xf6 ∞) 11...♘h5!? 12 ♗xh5 gxh5 13 ♗h4 ♘d7 14 ♗g3 ♘xe5 =.

b) 7 ♗e3 Now this is a dangerous move! For example 7...♘c6 8 d5 ♘e7 9 ♘d2! and White has achieved the ideal set-up of ♗e3 and ♘d2. Why is it ideal? Because on the kingside it obstructs the moves ...♘h5, ...♘g4 and ...♗g4 and when ...f7-f5 arrives White can answer f2-f3. Meanwhile the knight on d2 is ready to occupy the c4-square after b2-b4 and c4-c5 and exert strong pressure on b6 and d6. So instead of 7...♘c6?, Black should play 7...♘g4 8 ♗g5 f6 9 ♗h4 ♘c6 10 d5 ♘e7 11 ♘d2 ♘h6, followed by ...f7-f5, or prepare this by 7...h6!? 8 0-0 ♘g4 9 ♗c1 ♘c6 10 d5 ♘e7 11 ♘e1 f5!? and after 12 ♗xg4 fxg4 Black can even think about the exchange sacrifice ...g6-g5 and ...♖f4.

E1. 1 d4 ♘f6 2 c4 g6 3 ♘c3 ♗g7 4 e4 d6 5 ♘f3 0-0 6 ♗e2 e5 7 d5

White does not allow the knight on b8 to go to e7 after 7 0-0 ♘c6 8 d5, but shuts off this route well in advance.

7...a5

On 7...♘h5 White can play 8 g3! which impedes 8...♘f4 while 8...♗h3? is harmless as well due to 9 ♘g5! On 8...f5 9 exf5 ♕f6 10 ♘g5! ♕xf5 11 0-0 ♘f6 12 f3 and, with sufficient control over the e4-square to be able to locate a piece there, White is on top. This line demonstrates that when the knight is on h5 Black has difficulties recapturing on f5, e.g. 9 exf5 gxf5 10 ♘xe5 and the knight on h5 is hanging. On 9...♖xf5, 10 g4 is a fork while on 9...♗xf5 10 ♘g5! ♘f6 11 g4! White again has the e4-square in his control while e6 is also weak.

After 7...♘bd7 8 ♗g5! h6 9 ♗h4 g5 10 ♗g3 ♘h5 White can make

use of the fact that he has not yet castled and with 11 h4! start picking on the loose black kingside,. e.g. 11...♘xg3 12 fxg3 gxh4 13 ♘xh4 ♕g5 14 ♗g4! ♘c5 15 ♗xc8 and 16 ♘f5! ± or 11...g4 12 ♘h2 ♘xg3 13 fxg3 h5 14 0-0! ♗h6 15 ♗d3 ♘c5 16 ♗c2 followed by ♕e2, ♖f2, ♘h2-f1-e3 and White examines the loose enemy kingside. Finally on 7...♘bd7 8 ♗g5 a5, again 9 ♘d2! h6 10 ♗e3 and White has 'switched' the bishop on c1 and knight on f3, thus obtaining the maximum efficiency of his pieces. Later, on ...f7-f5 he answers f2-f3 and with a2-a3, b2-b4 (or if Black threatens to block with ...a5-a4 then with b2-b3, a2-a3 and b3-b4) he can start a queenside expansion.

8 ♗g5! h6!

On 8...♘a6?! 9 ♘d2 h6 10 ♗e3 ±.

9 ♗h4

9 ♗e3 is met by 9...♘g4 and 9 ♗d2 takes away the knight's natural square.

9...♘a6 10 0-0 ♕e8!

The knight on f6 must be set free in order to enable Black's standard plan of ...f7-f5. 10...g5? is a major blunder, as later this pawn will have to recapture on f5.

11 ♘d2

Also possible is 11 ♘e1 ♘c5 12 f3 and 13 ♘d3 with an exchange of knights on c5.

11...♘h7

11...♘c5?! 12 ♘b5! is unpleasant.

12 a3 ♗d7!
This move both develops and irritates White: the threat is to block the white queenside with ...a5-a4 and thus shelter the position of the knight after ...♘a6-c5.

13 b3!?
Another interesting move is 13 ♘b5!? The knight on a6 is now doomed to stay where it is and White is threatening 14 b4! axb4 15 axb4 ♗xb5 16 cxb5 ♘xb4 17 ♕b3 +–. The best choice for Black is 13...h5! 14 f3 ♗h6!? ∞ with the possible follow-up ...♗e3+. White can also try to avoid this line with 13 ♔h1!?, when 13...a4 14 ♘b5! ♗xb5 15 axb5 ♘c5 16 f3 and ♗f2 leads to great complications. But back to 13 b3!

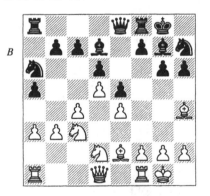

Plans and Counterplans:
If Black is feeling brave, he can try **13...f5!?** 14 exf5 gxf5 15 ♗h5 ♕c8 16 ♗e7 ♖e8 17 ♗xe8 ♕xe8 18 ♗h4 e4 19 ♖c1 ♘c5, when he has sufficient play for the exchange. His next task will be to improve the placement of the knight on h7

via either f8-g6 or f6-h5-f4. Black's other possibility is to activate his g7-bishop: **13...h5** (threatening 14...g5) 14 f3 ♗h6 and now on 15 ♗f2 ♕e7 followed by ...h5-h4, on 15 ♔h1 ♗e3 and ...f7-f5, while on 15 ♖b1 ♗e3+ 16 ♗f2 ♗xf2+ 17 ♖xf2 ♕e7 18 b4 axb4 19 axb4 c5!? with mutual chances.

E2. 1 d4 ♘f6 2 c4 g6 3 ♘c3 ♗g7 4 e4 d6 5 ♘f3 0-0 6 ♗e2 e5 7 0-0

White need not fear the premature 7...exd4 8 ♘xd4 as he obtains a slight central plus: 8...♖e8 9 f3 ♘c6 10 ♗e3 ♘h5 11 f4! ♘f6 12 ♗f3.

7...♘bd7
Again Black has the option of the popular King's Indian move 7...♘a6: 8 ♗e3 ♘g4 9 ♗g5 ♕e8 10 dxe5 h6 11 ♗d2 ♘xe5!? (11...dxe5 12 ♘e1! ♘f6 13 ♘d3 c6 14 ♗e3 ♕e7 15 b4 ♘d7 16 b5 ♘c7 17 bxc6 bxc6 18 ♕a4 ±) 12 ♘d4!? c6 13 ♗e3 h5! 14 h3 ∞ or 8 ♖e1 c6 9 ♗f1 ♗g4 10 d5 ♘b4 11 ♗e2 a5 12 ♗e3 c5 13 a3 ♘a6 14 ♖f1! and 15 ♘e1. Now White's idea is ♘d3 and carrying through b2-b4, while Black opts for ...f7-f5.

8 ♖e1
Also possible is 8 d5 ♘c5 9 ♕c2 a5 10 ♗g5 h6! 11 ♗e3 (11 ♗h4 g5 with ...♘h5-f4 and ...h7-h5 to follow is strong) 11...♘g4 12 ♗xc5 dxc5 ∞. Alternatively, 8 ♗e3!? ♘g4 9 ♗g5 f6 (9...♕e8?? 10 ♘d5 +–) 10 ♗d2 ♘h6 (10...f5? 11 dxe5 dxe5 12 ♘g5! ±) 11 ♕c2 and White is

slightly better. Another modern concept is 8 ♕c2 c6 9 ♖d1: 9...♕e7 10 d5 (crossing Black's plan of 10...exd4 11 ♘xd4 ♘c5 12 f3 ♘h5 followed by ...f7-f5) 10...c5 11 g3 ♘g4!? 12 ♘h4 ♘b6 13 a3 f5 ∞.

8...c6

If White does not push d4-d5 then the plan of ...f7-f5 does not work since White can open up the centre and exploit his lead in development; not to mention the weakness of Black's king. So on occasions such as this, Black should opt for play on the dark squares with his bishop. For this he will need his queen to join the game, preferably from b6.

9 ♗f1

Or 9 d5 c5 followed by ...♘e8 and ...f7-f5 ∞.

9...exd4

On 9...♖e8?, correct is 10 d5! as the rook is badly placed for the break ...f7-f5: it even occupies a square that the knight on f6 would like.

10 ♘xd4

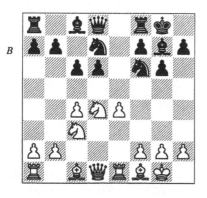

Plans and Counterplans:

Black has two original continuations:

a) 10...♘g4 11 ♕xg4 (11 h3 ♕b6 12 hxg4 ♕xd4 13 ♗e3 ♕e5 14 ♕d2 ♕e7 15 ♖ad1 ♘e5 is unclear) 11...♗xd4 12 ♕g3! ♘f6 13 ♕d3 ♕b6 14 ♗e3 ♗xe3 15 ♖xe3 and White stands somewhat better due to the weakness of the pawn on d6. And of course pawn b2 is taboo: 15...♕xb2? 16 ♖b1 ♕a3 17 ♕d4! ♘e8 18 ♘d5 ♕c5 19 ♘e7 mate! The other line is even more exciting:

b) 10...♖e8 11 ♗f4 (11 ♘b3 a5!) 11...♘c5 12 ♕c2 ♘g4 13 ♖ad1 ♗xd4! 14 ♖xd4 ♕f6 15 ♘e2 ♘xf2! 16 ♔xf2 g5 17 ♖xd6 ♕e7 18 e5 gxf4 19 ♘xf4 ♕g5 20 g3 ♗f5 21 ♗d3 ♘xd3+ 22 ♘xd3 ♗xd3 23 ♕xd3 ♖xe5, when things have resolved into a drawish endgame. Instead of 12 ♕c2 White can play 12 f3!? and now not 12...d5 13 cxd5 ♘xd5 14 exd5 ♖xe1 15 ♕xe1 ♗xd4+ 16 ♗e3 ±, but 12...♘h5!? 13 ♗e3 a5!? with an interesting game and chances for both sides (...a5-a4, ...♕a5 or ...♕h4, ...f7-f5).

E3. 1 d4 ♘f6 2 c4 g6 3 ♘c3 ♗g7 4 e4 d6 5 ♘f3 0-0 6 ♗e2 e5 7 0-0 ♘c6

Black virtually forces d4-d5 with the threat of 8...♗g4, after which Black would overpower the pawn on d4. The knight will go to e7 where it will be of use for Black's kingside actions. Of course this plan has its price as well: Black will have fewer defensive forces with which to meet White's attack on the queenside.

8 d5

8 dxe5 dxe5 9 ♕xd8 ♘xd8! followed by ...♘e6-f4(d4) is promising for Black and on ♘xe5 the reply is always ...♘xe4. However things are more complicated after 8 ♗e3!?, again threatening the ideal set-up 9 d5 ♘e7 10 ♘d2 and provoking 8...♗g4?! 9 d5 ♘e7 10 ♘d2 or 10 c5!?, when the bishop is misplaced on g4. White's plans can be hindered by the tricky 8...♖e8 and now on 9 d5?! ♘d4! 10 ♘xd4 exd4 11 ♗xd4 ♘xe4 =, while 9 dxe5 dxe5 10 h3 ♗e6 11 c5!? ♘h5!? is unclear. Besides this tricky solution there is the typical 8...♘g4 9 ♗g5 f6 10 ♗c1 (10 ♗h4 g5 11 ♗g3 ♘h6 12 dxe5 fxe5 ∞) 10...f5!? 11 ♗g5 ♗f6 12 ♗xf6 ♘xf6 (12...♕xf6 13 d5 ♘e7? 14 ♘b5 +−) 13 exf5 gxf5 14 dxe5 dxe5 15 ♕xd8 ♖xd8 16 ♘d5 ♘e8 17 ♖ad1 ♔g7 18 ♖fe1 ♗e6 with double-edged play.

8...♘e7

This position is the very essence of the King's Indian. Black plays for a kingside storm by means of ...♘e8, ...f7-f5-f4, ...g6-g5 (of course only if it is not hanging), ...h7-h5, ...g5-g4 and ...♘f6, while White prepares b2-b4 and c4-c5 with ♘e1, f2-f3 and ♗e3, or he plays ♘d2 to undertake action from c4. Of course neither side will rush headlong: they will also

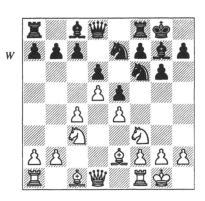

attempt to obstruct the opponent's plan as much as possible. White's queenside action is faster but Black's kingside threats are more dangerous!

There are three ways for White to start his queenside actions:

E3a. 9 b4
E3b. 9 ♘d2 and
E3c. 9 ♘e1.

E3a. 1 d4 ♘f6 2 c4 g6 3 ♘c3 ♗g7 4 e4 d6 5 ♘f3 0-0 6 ♗e2 e5 7 0-0 ♘c6 8 d5 ♘e7 9 b4

9...a5

This considerably slows down White's queenside play, but Black can also play his own game with 9...♘h5!? 10 c5 (10 g3 f5 11 ♘g5 ♘f6 12 f3 f4 ∞) 10...♘f4 11 ♗xf4 exf4 12 ♖c1 h6 13 ♘d4 g5 ∞.

10 ♗a3

Also interesting is 10 bxa5 ♖xa5 (10...c5!?) 11 ♘d2 followed by ♘b3. If Black plays ...b7-b6 to defend against c4-c5, White's plan is a2-a4-a5.

10...♘d7 11 bxa5 ♖xa5 12 ♗b4 ♖a8 13 a4 ♘c5

Also playable is 13...♗h6!?

14 ♘d2 ♘a6 15 ♗a3 f5 =

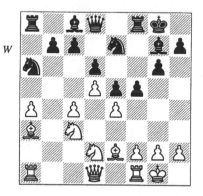

Plans and Counterplans:

White can aim for ♘b3 and c4-c5 whereas Black will play for ...f5xe4 and ...♘f5-d4 or on White's f2-f3 he can go ...♗h6-e3.

E3b. 1 d4 ♘f6 2 c4 g6 3 ♘c3 ♗g7 4 e4 d6 5 ♘f3 0-0 6 ♗e2 e5 7 0-0 ♘c6 8 d5 ♘e7 9 ♘d2

This move prepares 10 b4 a5 11 bxa5 ♖xa5 12 ♘b3 ♖a8 13 c5!

9...a5

Black's other attempt to slow up White's attack is 9...c5 10 ♖b1 ♘e8 11 b4 b6 (11...cxb4 12 ♖xb4 and then a2-a4, ♗a3, ♖b1, ♘b3, a4-a5 and c4-c5, when the black cavalry is far from the important c5-square) 12 bxc5 bxc5 and after ♘b3, ♗d2, ♘b5 White will try to invade via the a5-square. The other alternative is better: 9...c6!? 10 b4 a5! 11 bxa5 ♕xa5 12 ♕c2 c5 =. Instead of 10 b4, it is first necessary to play 10 a3 and then b2-b4, ♗b2, ♘b3, d4xc6 and c4-c5. But this plan is slightly too elaborate; in the meantime, of course, Black plays ...♘e8 and ...f7-f5.

10 a3 ♘d7

On 10...♗d7, correct is 11 b3 followed by ♖b1 and b3-b4, due to the threat of ...a5-a4, while 10...c5 11 ♖b1 ♘e8 12 b4 axb4 13 axb4 b6 14 bxc5 bxc5 leads to the exchange of the a- and b-pawns. This favours White as he can easily invade on the queenside with and threaten the pawn on d6 right through to the endgame: 15 ♘b3 ♔h8 16 ♗d2 f5 17 ♖a1 ♖xa1 18 ♕xa1 ♘g8 19 ♕a5!? ±.

11 ♖b1 f5 12 b4 ♔h8!? 13 f3 ♘g8 14 ♕c2

Plans and Counterplans:

If Black is to contemplate an attack, he should first place his pieces on healthy squares. For example, he can continue the manoeuvre ...♔h8 and ...♘g8 with ...♘gf6, ...f5-f4, ...♖g8, ...♗f8 and

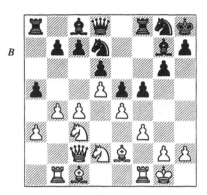

...g5-g4, or instead play ...♗h6 and ...♘df6 maybe later combined with f5xe4. White plays for c4-c5, often sacrificing a pawn. For example, 14...♘gf6 15 ♗d3 f4 16 ♗e2 (White has fixed the centre to play c4-c5) 16...h5 17 c5! dxc5 18 bxc5 ♘xc5 19 ♘b5 b6 20 a4 and 21 ♗a3 and White has achieved his plan. Instead of 16...h5 it is better to play 16...♖g8!?, as this fits into Black's plan and in the former line, after ♗a3, the knight on c5 is no longer pinned if the rook has moved from f8. In that case White can prepare c4-c5 with 17 ♘a4.

E3c. 1 d4 ♘f6 2 c4 g6 3 ♘c3 ♗g7 4 e4 d6 5 ♘f3 0-0 6 ♗e2 e5 7 0-0 ♘c6 8 d5 ♘e7 9 ♘e1

White pictures his knight on d3, where it would control all-important battle squares (b4, c5, e5 and f4).
   9...♘d7
   Also playable is the alternative 9...♘e8, which leaves the route open for the bishop on c8 but does

not impede White's c4-c5 advance.
   10 f3 f5

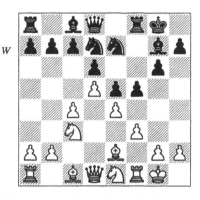

Plans and Counterplans:
White can develop his bishop via **11 ♗e3 f4 12 ♗f2 g5**, when he has all sorts of plans to continue on the queenside, for example b2-b4 and c4-c5 or first a2-a4-a5 and then b2-b4 and c4-c5, or he can even provoke Black with **13 ♘b5:** 13...a6?! 14 ♘a7! ♖xa7 15 ♗xa7 b6 16 b4 and 17 c5 is better for White. Instead of 13...a6?!, correct is 13...b6!? 14 b4 a6 15 ♘c3 ♖f6!? and then ...♖g6, ...♘f6, ...h7-h5 and ...g5-g4. Instead of 11 ♗e3, White can also play **11 ♘d3 f4 12 ♗d2 ♘f6 13 c5 g5 14 cxd6 cxd6 15 ♖c1 ♘g6 16 ♘b5**, when Black can thwart the invasion along the c-file with 16...♖f7 and ...♘e8. In this line, instead of 13 c5 White can play **13 g4!?**, which is perhaps his most efficient weapon against Black's attack. Then he can defend with h2-h3, ♗e1, ♔g2, ♗f2 and ♖h1. In fact, this idea can be

realized at once with **11 g4**, although Black has the interesting reply 11...♔h8 12 ♗e3 ♘g8 with the intention of 13...♗h6, and if White stops this with 13 ♕d2, then 13...f4 14 ♗f2 h5 15 h3 ♖f7 16 ♔g2 ♗f6 17 ♘d3 ♖h7 18 ♖h1 with a difficult position for both sides.

III. With minimal risk

1 d4 ♘f6 2 ♘f3

Those who prefer safe variations might prefer this line to the complexities of the King's Indian 'proper'. Of course it is necessary that they make sure that it fits into their repertoires. For example after 2...e6 3 c4 we have a Queen's Indian, while after 2...d5 3 c4 c6 the Meran can only be reached via the move-order 4 ♘c3 e6 5 e3 since on the immediate 4 e3, 4...♗f5 equalizes at once. But on 4 ♘c3 White also has to know 4...dxc4, which transposes to the Slav Queen's Gambit Accepted. Many things have to be adjusted if you want to play 2 ♘f3 but it is also true that quite a few gambits are sidestepped (Benko Gambit, Budapest Gambit).

2...g6 3 ♗g5

Well, this is a reversed Réti! The same could be said about 3 ♗f4 ♗g7 4 ♘bd2 0-0 5 e3 d6 6 h3 ♘bd7, when Black can prepare the counter-thrust ...e7-e5 with ...♕e8. The seemingly colourless 3 g3 ♗g7 4 ♗g2 0-0 5 0-0 d6 6 b3

♘bd7 7 ♗b2 can be 'brought to life' by Black's 7...e5!? 8 dxe5 ♘g4, although 9 c4 ♘gxe5 10 ♘c3 is a little better for White. So this motif is better a move earlier: 6...e5! (instead of 6...♘bd7) 7 dxe5 ♘g4 8 ♗b2 ♘c6! 9 c4 dxe5 10 h3 ♘h6 =. Black can flirt with ...♘f5-d4 or ...e5-e4.

3...♗g7 4 ♘bd2 d5!?

A slightly inferior alternative is 4...c5?! 5 ♗xf6! ♗xf6 6 ♘e4 ♗xd4 7 ♘xd4 cxd4 8 ♕xd4 ± with a spatial advantage for White. Of course 4...d6 is also playable, with the plan ...♘bd7, ...0-0 and ...e7-e5.

5 e3 0-0 6 ♗d3 c5! 7 c3 ♕b6 8 ♖b1 ♘c6 9 0-0

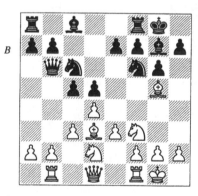

Plans and Counterplans:
Black's obvious plan is ...e7-e5. This can be prepared by 9...♖e8 but the instant 9...e5!? is also good: 10 ♘xe5 ♘xe5 11 dxe5 ♘g4 12 ♘f3 ♘xe5 =. The tempo difference does not change the evaluation compared to the Réti: the position is still equal.

Modern Defence

1 d4 g6

Black offers White a transposition to the Pirc Defence (2 e4) but here we look at the alternative King's Indian set-up.

2 c4 &g7 3 e4 d6 4 ©c3 ©c6

After 4...e5 5 dxe5 dxe5 6 ♕xd8+ ♔xd8 7 f4! ± Black does not reach the ideal arrangement ...&e6, ...c7-c6, ...©d7 and ...♔c7.

5 d5!

On any other move Black would play 5...e5 6 d5 ©ce7 and launch a quick assault on the white centre with ...f7-f5. And on 5 ©f3? first 5...&g4! followed by 6...e5 is already ∓!

5...©d4!? 6 ©ge2

White can instead draw at once with 6 &e3 c5 7 ©ge2 (7 dxc6? ©xc6 is good for Black, his plan being ...♕a5, ...©f6, ...0-0, ...&e6, ...Ic8 and ...©e5, etc.) 7...♕b6 8 ©xd4 cxd4 9 ©a4 ♕a5+ 10 b4 ♕xb4 11 &d2 ♕a3 12 &c1 ♕b4+ 13 &d2 and a draw by repetition.

6...c5

Alternatively, 6...e5 7 dxe6 ©xe6 8 g3 ± or 6...©xe2 7 &xe2 followed by &e3, f2-f3, ♕d2, 0-0, c4-c5, Ifc1 and b2-b4, etc. ±.

7 ©xd4 cxd4

Or 7...&xd4 8 &e2 &g7 (8...©f6 9 0-0, when the threats are ©b5

and &h6) 9 0-0 ©f6 10 &e3 and then ♕d2, &h6, &xg7 and f2-f4.

8 ©b5 ♕b6 9 c5! dxc5

9...♕xc5? 10 &d2 ♕b6 11 ♕a4 wins, since besides the discovered check Black is also threatening 12 &a5 ♕a6 13 ©c7+.

10 &f4 ♔f8 11 Ic1!

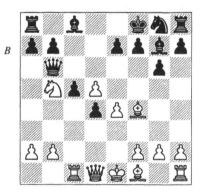

Plans and Counterplans:
Black's position is already quite gruesome:

a) 11...a6 12 &c7 ♕f6 13 ©a3 b6 14 ©c4 ±.

b) 11...©f6 12 &c7 ♕a6 13 ©a3 +−.

c) 11...&d7 12 &c7 ♕a6 13 ©a3 ♕f6 14 Ixc5 ±.

d) 11...♕a5+ 12 b4 cxb4 (or 12...♕xb4+ 13 &d2 ♕xb2 14 Ic2 +−) 13 ©c7 Ib8 14 ♕d2! with 15 ©e6+ to follow ±.

Benoni Defence

1 d4 ♘f6 2 c4 c5 3 d5 e6 4 ♘c3

White cannot give up the centre with 4 dxe6? because after 4...fxe6 followed by the advance ...d7-d5 Black smoothly takes over the initiative.

4...exd5 5 cxd5

It is wrong to place a piece on d5, as after 5 ♘xd5 ♘xd5 6 ♕xd5 Black can easily chase the white queen and gain a lead in development after 6...♘c6 with ...♘b4 or ...d7-d6 and ...♗e6.

5...d6

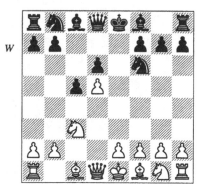

This is the basic position of the Benoni or, to be exact, the Modern Benoni (in the old Benoni Black plays 3...e5 instead of 3...e6). Black, practically regardless of White's plan, intends to play ...g7-g6, ...♗g7 and ...0-0 and exercise strong pressure on the a1-h8 diagonal. White can choose between a fianchetto of his own

light-squared bishop or, after e2-e4, he can put his bishop to e2 or d3. These two basic ideas and other 'eccentricities' are summed up by the following sections:

I. Fianchetto variation
II. f2-f4 variation;
III. Main Line viz. set-up with ♘f3, e2-e4 and ♗e2;
IV. Fashion of the nineties viz. White develops via ♘f3, e2-e4, h2-h3 and ♗d3;
V. Eccentricities in short viz. ♘f3 followed by ♗f4 or ♗g5 and a 'Sämisch-like' set-up with f2-f3.
VI. Old Benoni

There are several useful things that one should know about the Modern Benoni:

a) Black usually tries for ...a7-a6 and ...b7-b5, which threatens to dislodge the knight from c3, thus weakening White's control over the e4-square. White can hardly allow this and therefore on ...a7-a6 he usually plays a2-a4, which often threatens a4-a5, freezing Black's queenside exertions.

b) The Benoni can be reached instead of a Nimzo-Indian with 1 d4 ♘f6 2 c4 e6 3 ♘c3 c5 4 d5 exd5 5 cxd5 or instead of a Queen's Indian after 1 d4 ♘f6 2 c4 e6 3 ♘f3 c5 4 d5 exd5 5 cxd5 d6 6 ♘c3, or from a King's Indian, e.g., 1 d4 ♘f6

2 c4 g6 3 ⁇c3 ⁇g7 4 e4 d6 5 ⁇f3
0-0 6 ⁇e2 c5 7 d5 e6 8 0-0 exd5 9
cxd5.

c) 'Benoni' in Arabic means
'Son of Sorrow' but as we shall
see neither White nor Black has
any particular reason to grieve in
this opening.

I. Fianchetto Variation

**1 d4 ⁇f6 2 c4 c5 3 d5 e6 4 ⁇c3
exd5 5 cxd5 d6 6 g3 g6 7 ⁇g2
⁇g7 8 ⁇f3**
The best place for this knight is
c4! Hence the route is f3-d2-c4
from where it can attack the
pawn on d6 and help White's central action e2-e4, f2-f4 and e4-e5.
8...0-0 9 0-0 ⁇bd7
In this way the knight goes to
e5 or perhaps to b6 to counter its
opponent on c4. The other popular move is 9...⁇a6, when one
possibility is 10 e4?! ⁇e8! 11 ⁇d2
⁇c7 12 a4 b6 13 ⁇e1 ⁇g4! 14 ⁇f3
⁇e5 15 ⁇xe5 ⁇xe5 with an unclear game in which after f2-f4
White can play for e4-e5, even at
the cost of a pawn while Black
can attempt ...⁇b8, ...a7-a6 and
...b7-b5 or 10 ⁇d2 ⁇c7 11 ⁇c4 (after 11 a4 b6 12 ⁇c4 ⁇a6 13 ⁇b3
Black gladly gives up his problem
light-squared bishop for the terrific knight on c4: 13...⁇xc4 14 ⁇xc4
a6 =) 11...⁇fe8 (not 11...b5?! 12
⁇xd6 ⁇xd6 13 ⁇f4 followed by 14
d6, when the knight on c7 and
rook on a8 are simultaneously
hanging, while 11...⁇h5 12 a4 f5

13 e3 is not quite good enough for
Black ±) 12 a4 b6 13 ⁇d2!? ⁇b8 14
⁇b1 ⁇d7 15 b3 a6 16 ⁇e4! and
White exchanges the bishop on g7
with ⁇b2 (±).
10 ⁇d2 a6 11 a4 ⁇e8

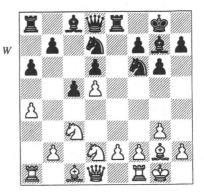

Plans and Counterplans:
Black is planning ...⁇e5, ...⁇h5
and ...f7-f5, but what can White
do about it? For example:

a) 12 a5 b5 (it is now or never,
as 12...⁇b8? 13 ⁇c4 is awkward
to meet) **13 axb6 ⁇xb6 14 ⁇b3
⁇c4 =.**

b) 12 e4 ⁇e5 13 ⁇c2 (or 13
⁇e2 ⁇h5 with ...f7-f5 to follow)
13...⁇h5 14 f4 (on 14 h3, taking
away the g4-square from the
knight, good is 14...g5!! and after
the continuation 15 f4 gxf4 16
gxf4 ⁇g6 White's king position
has been considerably weakened,
especially the h4-square!) **14...⁇g4
15 ⁇f3 f5! 16 ⁇g5 ⁇d4+ 17 ⁇h1
⁇f6** with active counterplay for
Black.

**c) 12 h3 ⁇h5!? 13 ⁇h2 f5 14
f4 ⁇df6 15 e4 fxe4 16 ⁇dxe4 ⁇xe4**

17 ♘xe4 ♘f6 (17...h6!?) 18 ♘g5 h6 19 ♘e6 ♗xe6 20 dxe6 d5!? ∞.

d) 12 ♘c4!? ♘e5!? 13 ♘a3 (White cannot achieve an advantage after 13 ♘xe5 ♖xe5 14 e4 ♖e8 as the exchange of knights allows Black to hold a firm grip on square e5 and the bishop on c8 can step out to the vacated d7-square) 13...♘h5 14 ♖b1 (on 14 f4 ♘g4 Black threatens 15...♗d4+, while on 14 e4 b5! 15 axb5 axb5 16 ♘cxb5 ♗a6 ∓) 14...♗f5!? 15 e4 ♗d7 16 b4!? cxb4 17 ♖xb4 ♕a5 18 ♘a2 b5! 19 ♗e3! ♖ac8 (19...bxa4?? 20 ♗b6 +−) 20 ♗d4 f5 with a helter-skelter position. In this line Black provoked the move e2-e4 to eclipse the bishop on g2 and to weaken the 'inner squares' in White's position (d3, f3).

II. f2-f4 Variation

---

1 d4 ♘f6 2 c4 c5 3 d5 e6 4 ♘c3 cxd5 5 cxd5 d6 6 e4 g6 7 f4

White – knowing that his plan will be the thrust e4-e5 – does not block his f-pawn with the knight. Instead he enables the immediate progress of his e-pawn. Of course with this move he also makes a sacrifice in time: the development of his pieces and safety of his king is delayed.

7...♗g7

Now White's possible continuations are:

A. 8 ♗b5+ and
B. 8 ♘f3

Nothing is gained by the aggressive **8 e5**: 8...♘fd7 (opening the position with 8...dxe5?! would only favour White: 9 fxe5 ♘fd7 10 e6! with a strong attack) 9 ♘b5 (alternatively: 9 e6 fxe6 10 dxe6 ♘b6 and Black is safeguarded against attacks; or 9 exd6 0-0 10 ♘f3 ♘f6 11 ♗e2 a6! 12 a4 ♕xd6 =) 9...dxe5 10 ♘d6+ ♔e7 11 ♘xc8+ ♕xc8 and although the king in the middle looks a little suspicious, White's pieces are still on the baseline so Black should not get into trouble: 12 d6+ ♔f8 13 ♘f3 ♘c6 14 ♗e2 h6 15 fxe5 ♘dxe5 16 0-0 ♘xf3+ 17 ♗xf3 ♗d4+ 18 ♔h1 ♔g7 and White has no real compensation for the pawn (∓); or 12 ♘f3 ♖e8 and Black castles 'artificially' after 13 ♗c4 ♔f8 14 0-0 and now the threats looming on f7 can be reduced by playing 14...♘b6 or 14...e4.

A. 1 d4 ♘f6 2 c4 c5 3 d5 e6 4 ♘c3 exd5 5 cxd5 d6 6 e4 g6 7 f4 ♗g7 8 ♗b5+

A similar check, designed to disturb the natural development of Black's pieces, can also be found in the Main Line of the Grünfeld Defence.

8...♘fd7

On 8...♘bd7?, 9 e5, followed by e5-e6, is good while on 8...♗d7? 9 e5 ♘h5 10 ♘f3, besides the powerful white centre pawns, Black also has problems with his knight on h5 (±).

9 ♗e2

White would now like to continue with ♘f3 and 0-0, in similar fashion to section B, but having forced Black's knight from f6 to d7. Other tries are:

a) 9 a4 a6 10 ♗d3 0-0 11 ♘f3 ♕c7 12 0-0 c4 13 ♗c2 ♘c5 ∞.

b) 9 ♘f3 a6 10 ♗d3 b5 11 0-0 0-0 12 ♔h1!? ♖e8!? (it is better to restrain ...c5-c4 as White would then get hold of the d4-square for his manoeuvres ♗c1-e3-d4 or ♘f3-d4-c6) ∞.

9...♕h4+!?

The only way to draw profit from the move ...♘fd7. After 9...0-0 10 ♘f3 ♖e8 11 0-0 ♘a6 12 ♔h1 ♘c7 13 a4 b6 14 f5! White can launch a promising attack, utilizing the fact that the knight is on d7, so that the pawn on e4 is not hanging and Black's king position is less well protected.

10 g3 ♕e7

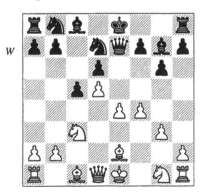

Plans and Counterplans:
White should not waste time worrying about the pawn-grabbing

...♗xc3, ...♕xe4, as for example after **11 ♕c2** 0-0 12 ♘f3 ♖e8 Black's threats are still the same, plus ...♘f6 or ...f7-f5. So **11 ♘f3!?** 0-0 (11...♗xc3+ 12 bxc3 ♕xe4 is inadvisable in view of 13 0-0 0-0 14 ♘g5! and White has tremendous play: c3-c4, ♗b2, ♗d3, f4-f5, etc.) 12 0-0 a6 13 a4 ♖e8 and Black can threaten to take on e4 after ...♗xc3 or complete his development after ...♘f6 or ...♘f8 and make use of the weakening of White's king position to play ...♗g4 or ...♗h3. For example 14 ♗d3 ♘f8 15 ♔g2! ♗g4 16 h3 ♗xf3+ 17 ♕xf3 ♘bd7 =.

B. 1 d4 ♘f6 2 c4 c5 3 d5 e6 4 ♘c3 exd5 5 cxd5 d6 6 e4 g6 7 f4 ♗g7 8 ♘f3 0-0 9 ♗e2

The bishop does not go to d3 because when White plays e4-e5, the pawn on d5 needs to be defended.

9...♖e8

Other lines are:

a) 9...b5!? 10 e5 (not 10 ♗xb5 ♘xe4 11 ♘xe4 ♕a5+ 12 ♘c3?! ♗xc3+ 13 bxc3 ♕xb5 winning back the pawn with an excellent game. It is worth remembering this pseudo-sacrifice!) 10...dxe5 11 fxe5 ♘g4 12 ♗g5 f6 (12...♕b6 13 0-0 c4+ 14 ♔h1 ♘f2+ 15 ♖xf2 ♕xf2 16 ♘e4 with a kingside attack is too risky) 13 exf6 ♗xf6 14 ♕d2! ± and Black's b-pawn is hanging while the threat is 15 ♘e4.

b) 9...♗g4 10 e5 (10 0-0 ♘bd7 followed by ...♖e8 with equality) 10...♗xf3 11 ♗xf3 dxe5 12 fxe5 ♘fd7 13 e6 ♘e5!? with an unclear game.

10 e5

The best chance because on 10 ♕c2 ♘xe4! 11 ♘xe4 ♗f5 12 ♗d3 ♕e7 13 ♘fd2 ♗xe4 14 ♗xe4 f5 Black wins. Alternatively, 10 ♘d2 c4!? 11 a4 (11 0-0 b5?!) 11...♘bd7 12 0-0 and now not 12...a6?! 13 ♔h1 ♘c5 14 e5! dxe5 15 fxe5 ♖xe5 16 ♘xc4, when Black has trouble getting his pieces coordinated, though after 16...♖f5!? his position is not hopeless, but the immediate 12...♘c5 13 e5!? (13 ♗f3 ♗h6!? 14 ♕c2 ♘d3 15 ♘xc4 ♘xc1 16 ♕xc1 ♗g4! 17 ♗xg4 ♘xg4 18 ♕d1 f5! is unclear) 13...dxe5 14 ♘xc4 exf4 15 ♗xf4 ♘fe4 16 ♘xe4 ♘xe4 ∞ and Black is threatening 17...♗xb2 followed by ...♕b6+ or ...♘c3.

10...dxe5

10...♘fd7 11 exd6 a6 comes into consideration with ...♘f6 and ...♕xd6 to follow.

11 fxe5 ♘g4 12 ♗g5!? ♕b6

After 12...f6 13 exf6 ♗xf6 14 ♕d2! Black is doomed to defend.

Plans and Counterplans:

White will now give away his e5-pawn for which he is compensated by a d5-pawn in an open position, the lack of development of the black queenside and the vulnerable black monarch. White can castle either side:

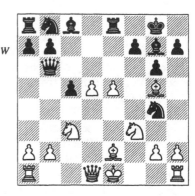

a) 13 0-0 ♘xe5 (13...c4+? 14 ♔h1 ♘f2+ 15 ♖xf2 ♕xf2 16 ♘e4 ♕b6 17 ♘d6 ♖f8 18 ♗e7 ±) 14 ♘xe5 ♗xe5 15 ♗c4 ♕xb2 16 d6 ♖f8 (16...♗f5 17 ♖xf5! gxf5 18 ♗xf7+! ♔xf7? 19 ♕h5+ ♔f8 20 ♗h6+ ♗g7 21 ♖f1! +−, but Black can play 18...♔f8! 19 ♗xe8 ♕xc3 ∞) 17 ♗xf7+ ♔g7 18 ♗d5!? ♕xc3 19 ♖xf8 ♔xf8 20 ♕f1+ ♗f5 21 ♖d1 ♘d7 22 g4 ♔g7 23 gxf5 h6! and Black holds on.

b) 13 ♕d2!? ♘d7!? (after 13...♘xe5 14 0-0-0 ♗f5 15 ♘xe5 ♗xe5 16 ♖he1 followed by g2-g4 White has the initiative) 14 d6 (14 e6 ♘de5 ∞) 14...♘dxe5 15 ♘d5 ♕xb2! 16 ♕xb2 ♘d3+ 17 ♔f1 ♘xb2 18 ♗b5! ♗e6 19 ♘c7 ♖ed8 20 ♘xa8 ♖xa8 21 ♖e1 a6 22 ♖xe6 fxe6 23 ♗d7 ♔f7 24 ♔e2 ♗f6 25 ♖f1 ♔g7 and Black has escaped to a situation in which he is actually better. Maybe these lines show that in the Benoni with f2-f4 the objective truth is as important as the players' tactical ingenuity, their ability to calculate variations precisely and their intuition.

III. Main Line

1 d4 ♘f6 2 c4 c5 3 d5 e6 4 ♘c3 exd5 5 cxd5 d6 6 e4 g6 7 ♘f3 ♗g7 8 ♗e2

For 8 h3 0-0 9 ♗d3 see section IV.

8...0-0 9 0-0

It is useless to rush in with 9 ♗g5!? as after 9...h6 10 ♗h4 g5 11 ♗g3 ♘h5 the bishop is exchanged, leaving its counterpart on g7 unopposed.

9...♘a6!?

Black plays for ...♘c7 and ...b7-b5 and if White holds him up with a2-a4 then after ...b7-b6 the bishop on c8 rears its head on a6. Practice does not favour the other two lines after 9...a6 10 a4:

a) 10...♗g4 11 ♗f4 ♗xf3 (or 11...♖e8 12 ♘d2 ♗xe2 13 ♕xe2 ♘h5 14 ♗e3 ♘d7 15 a5!? ♕h4 16 ♖a4! ♘e5 17 f3 ♘f4 18 ♗xf4 ♕xf4 19 g3 ♕f6 20 f4 ♘d7 21 e5! dxe5 22 ♘de4 ♕d8 23 f5! ±. This pawn sacrifice, releasing the d-pawn and creating an outpost for the knight on e4 is most instructive!) 12 ♗xf3 ♕e7 13 ♖e1 ♘bd7 14 a5! ♘e8 15 ♘a4 ♘c7 16 ♗g4! and after 17 ♗xd7 White is threatening a knight fork on b6. Although White achieves a small plus after ...♗g4, he can if he wishes instead prevent his opponent from getting rid of his perhaps most troublesome piece with the move-order 1 d4 ♘f6 2 c4 c5 3 d5 e6 4 ♘c3 exd5 5 cxd5 d6 6 ♘f3 g6 7 ♘d2!? ♗g7 8

e4 0-0 9 ♗e2. White then castles and the move ♘d2 will fit well into his future plans.

b) 10...♘bd7 11 ♘d2 ♖e8 12 ♕c2 ♘e5!? (trying to lure White into 13 f4?! ♘eg4 14 ♘f3 ♘h5 15 h3 f5! 16 hxg4? fxe4 17 gxh5 exf3 18 ♖xf3 ♗d4+ 19 ♔f1 ♕h4 with mate to follow!) 13 ♖a3! and after strengthening his centre White will threaten f2-f4: 14 f4 ♘g4 15 ♘d1 or first 14 h3!? is also playable. Black can prevent f2-f4 with 13...g5 but then with ♘c3-d1-e3 White can occupy the c4-square (particularly combined with the strangling move a4-a5) or after ♘d2-f1-g3 take aim at the f5-square.

10 ♘d2 ♘c7 11 a4

The b5-square must be secured for a future ♘c4.

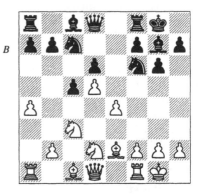

Plans and Counterplans:

Black must prepare himself for an assault on the d6-pawn with ♘c4 and ♗f4. After 11...b6 12 ♘c4 ♗a6 13 ♗f4?! he can play 13...♘h5!, when after 14 ♗xh5

♗xc4 15 ♗e2 ♗xe2 16 ♕xe2 f5! he is already better. White should postpone concrete action in order to retard Black's counterplay, e.g. after 11...b6 12 ♘c4 ♗a6 White can go 13 f3 and ♗d2, ♖b1 with b2-b4 to follow or 13 ♗g5 and ♕d2, when it is more difficult for Black to generate counterplay.

IV. Fashion of the Nineties

---

1 d4 ♘f6 2 c4 c5 3 d5 e6 4 ♘c3 exd5 5 cxd5 d6 6 e4 g6 7 h3!?

White plans to continue with ♗d3 and ♘f3, so he first prevents the pin ...♗g4.

7...♗g7 8 ♗d3 0-0 9 ♘f3

The knight can also go to e2: 9 ♘ge2 ♖e8 10 0-0 ♘bd7 11 ♘g3 a6 12 a4 ♖b8 13 a5 h5!? 14 ♗g5 b5! 15 axb6 ♕xb6 16 ♖a2 ♘e5 ∞. An interesting alternative is 9 ♗g5: 9...h6 10 ♗e3 ♘a6!? 11 ♕d2 ♔h7 12 ♘ge2! ♘c7 13 a4 b6 14 0-0 ♗d7 15 ♖b1 a6 16 b4 cxb4 17 ♖xb4 b5! ∞ and White cannot capture on b5 as his e-pawn would be hanging.

9...a6

9...b5!? leads to fierce complications: 10 ♗xb5 ♘xe4 11 ♘xe4 ♕a5+ 12 ♘fd2 ♕xb5 13 ♘xd6 ♕d3 14 ♘2c4 ♕xd1+ 15 ♔xd1 ♗a6 16 ♔c2 ♘d7 17 ♗g5! ♖fb8 18 ♖ad1 ♘e5 with sufficient counterplay for the pawn. White should therefore capture the other way: 10 ♘xb5 ♘xe4 (or 10...♖e8 11 0-0 ♘xe4 12 ♖e1 a6 13 ♘a3 ♘f6 14 ♖xe8+ ♘xe8 15 ♗g5 ♗f6 16 ♕d2 with an initiative for White) 11

♗xe4 ♖e8 12 ♘g5!? ♗a6 13 ♘c3 h6 14 ♘e6! fxe6 15 dxe6! and White is threatening with ♕d5, ♕a4 and ♗e3.

A more solid alternative for Black is 9...♖e8. Then play might continue 10 0-0 c4 11 ♗c2!? (11 ♗xc4 ♘xe4 12 ♘xe4 ♖xe4 13 ♗g5 ♗f6 14 ♗d3 ♖e8 15 ♕a4! is also better for White) 11...♗d7 12 ♗f4 ♕b6 13 ♖b1 ♘a6 14 b4! ±.

10 a4

White may instead allow ...b7-b5, hoping that he can undermine the black queenside later with a2-a4, for example 10 0-0!? b5 11 ♖e1 ♘bd7 (an unusual alternative is 11...♖e8 followed by the manoeuvre ...♖a8-a7-e7) 12 a4! b4 13 ♘b1 a5 14 ♘bd2 ♘b6 15 ♖a2 with b2-b3 and ♗b2 to follow (∞).

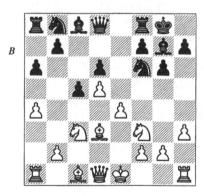

Plans and Counterplans:
Black can try for ...c5-c4: 10...♕c7 11 0-0 c4?! 12 ♗c2 ♘bd7, but then White seizes the initiative on the queenside with 13 ♗e3 followed by ♘d4, ♖c1 and b2-b4. And if the black queen does not move then

White would gladly play ♗g5, ♕d2. This can be prevented by 10...♘h5!? 11 0-0 ♘d7 and if now 12 ♗g5!? then 12...♗f6 13 ♗e3 ♖e8 14 ♕d2, but Black's position is far from harmonious. For example, 14...♘e5 15 ♗e2 ♘xf3+ 16 ♗xf3 ♗g7 17 a5! ±.

These days the Benoni is starting to go out of fashion and this line is the main reason why! White has been very successful in this fashionable variation that at the moment has superseded the popularity of the Main Line.

V. Eccentricities in short

A. 1 d4 ♘f6 2 c4 c5 3 d5 e6 4 ♘c3 exd5 5 cxd5 d6 6 ♘f3 g6 7 ♗f4 ♗g7

7...a6 8 a4 ♗g7 9 e4 ♗g4 10 ♗e2 ♗xf3 11 ♗xf3 0-0 12 0-0 leads to the note concerning ...♗g4 in the Main Line (section III).

8 ♕a4+!?
This check is the point of the whole variation as now on 8...♕d7 White has 9 ♗xd6.

8...♗d7 9 ♕b3 ♕c7 10 e4
10 ♗xd6? ♕xd6 11 ♕xb7 ♕b6 12 ♕xa8 ♕xb2 −+.

10...0-0 11 ♘d2 ♘h5 12 ♗e3 f5!? 13 exf5 gxf5 14 ♘f3 a6 15 a4 h6
Stopping the manoeuvre ♘g5-e6.

16 ♗e2 ♖e8
Black will follow up with the plan ...♘b8-d7 and then in this

unclear situation he can aim for either ...♘e5 or ...♘f6-e4.

B. 1 d4 ♘f6 2 c4 c5 3 d5 e6 4 ♘c3 cxd5 5 exd5 d6 6 ♘f3 g6 7 ♗g5 h6!?

After 7...♗g7 8 ♘d2 0-0 9 e3! White for the time being keeps his e-pawn away from vulnerable squares, and if Black should catch his bishop with ...h7-h6, ...g6-g5 and ...♘h5 then White will take possession of the weakened b1-h7 diagonal with ♕c2 and ♗d3.

8 ♗h4 ♗g7!?
The correct move-order. The question is: how far will the white e-pawn go? If 9 e4 then 9...g5 10 ♗g3 ♘h5 and White is unable to get at the weakened f5-square. Black can later even think of ...f7-f5 himself after a possible ...♘xg3 and ...0-0. And if 9 e3 then 9...0-0 10 ♘d2 ♘a6! 11 ♘c4 ♘c7 12 a4 b6 13 ♗e2 ♗a6 14 ♘a3 ♗xe2 15 ♕xe2 ♕d7 16 ♖d1 ♖fe8 and ...♘e4, with play against White's weak a-pawn.

C. 1 d4 ♘f6 2 c4 c5 3 d5 e6 4 ♘c3 exd5 5 cxd5 d6 6 e4 g6 7 f3 ♗g7

White adopts a Sämisch-like set-up.

8 ♗g5!?
On 8 ♗e3 0-0 9 ♕d2?! a6 10 a4 ♖e8!? (it is important not to prematurely block the diagonal of the c8-bishop with 10...♘bd7 as then the regrouping 11 ♘h3 and ♘f2 would protect all the critical

squares: d3, e4 and g4) 11 ♘ge2 ♘bd7 12 ♘g3 h5! 13 ♗g5 ♕a5! threatening 14...b5! and 14...♘h7.

8...h6

The tricky 8...0-0 9 ♕d2 h6?! is refuted by 10 ♗xh6! ♘xe4 11 ♘xe4 ♕h4+ 12 g3 ♕xh6 13 ♕xh6 ♗xh6 14 ♘xd6 and f2-f4, 0-0-0 ±.

9 ♗e3 0-0 10 ♘ge2

10 ♕d2 ♖e8 11 ♗xh6? ♘xe4 12 ♘xe4 ♕h4+ 13 g3 ♕xh6 and the pawn on d6 is protected by the pin along the e-file.

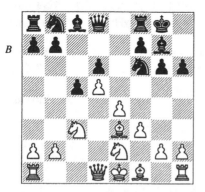

10...a6 11 a4 ♘bd7 12 ♘g3 h5!?

12...♕a5? 13 ♖a3! stops 13...b5.
13 ♗e2 h4 14 ♘f1 ♘h7 15 ♘d2 f5 ∞.

VI. 'Old Benoni' viz. Black plays ...c7-c5 and ...e7-e5

1 d4 ♘f6

It is also possible to play the immediate 1...c5 2 d5 e5, but now White can withhold his c-pawn: 3 e4 d6 4 ♘c3 ♘f6 5 ♗e2 (5 ♘f3 ♗g4) 5...a6 6 a4 (on ...a7-a6 the correct 'reflex action' is nearly always a2-a4, due to the threat of ...b7-b5) 6...♗e7 7 ♘f3 0-0 8 0-0 and White can use the vacant square c4 to regroup with ♘d2-c4 when he has good prospects both on the queenside (a4-a5, ♖b1 and b2-b4) and in the centre with f2-f4. On 2 d5 Black can also play 2...d6 3 e4 ♘f6 4 ♘c3 g6 5 ♘f3 ♗g7 6 ♗b5+!? ♗d7 (after 6...♘bd7 7 a4 0-0 8 0-0 a6 9 ♗e2 White prepares e4-e5 with ♗f4, ♖e1, ♗f1 and h3, and stops ...b7-b5 with a4-a5) 7 a4 0-0 8 h3! and Black's queenside pieces have trouble finding good squares while White, after 0-0, once again aims for e4-e5. This line can also be reached with a different move-order via 1 d4 ♘f6 2 ♘f3 c5 3 d5.

2 c4 c5 3 d5 e5 4 ♘c3

Of course it is bad to play 4 dxe6 fxe6, as after 5...d5 Black takes over the centre.

4...d6 5 e4 ♗e7

After 5...g6 the set-up h2-h3, g2-g4, ♘f3, ♗d3, ♗e3, ♕d2 with strong kingside pressure is also possible. 5...♗e7 involves a peculiar strategical plan: after ...0-0 and ...♘e8 Black opts for not only ...f7-f5 but also for ...♗g5: he would gladly exchange his locked-in bishop.

6 h3!? 0-0 7 ♘f3 ♘e8 8 ♗d3

Plans and Counterplans:
Black can try for ...f7-f5 after ...g7-g6 and ...♘g7 but he will not achieve it: 8...g6 9 ♗h6 ♘g7 10 g4! and 10...f5? is impossible in view of 11 gxf5 gxf5 12 ♖g1 ♖f7

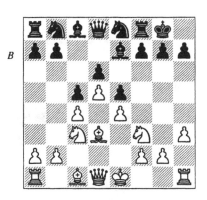

13 exf5 ±. Otherwise after ♕d2 (♕e2), 0-0-0 and ♖dg1 White has a promising attack.

Dutch Defence

1 d4 f5

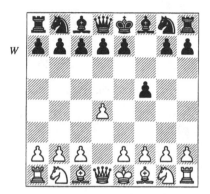

The Dutch Defence is one of the most popular openings nowadays. It can be recommended for those who prefer the unusual, something beyond the orbit of standard chess theory and naturally for those who desire a complicated game, even with Black. With White a good set-up against practically all of Black's plans is d2-d4, c2-c4, ♘f3, g2-g3, ♗g2 and 0-0. In answer to this Black has two major reactions: the Stonewall Variation where the meandering pawn chain a7, b7, c6, d5, e6, f5, g7 and h7 resembles the Great Wall of China (section I.). The other possibility is the Leningrad Variation, in which Black develops his bishop to g7 and plays for ...e7-e5 (section II.). The revival of the latter system has made the Dutch Defence fashionable again.

Besides the above mentioned customary set-up White has several other interesting and dangerous continuations. For example:

a) 2 ♗g5 c6!? (2...h6 is no go due to 3 ♗h4 g5 4 ♗g3 f4 5 e3! fxg3?? 6 ♕h5 mate, but playable is 2...♘f6 3 ♗xf6 exf6 4 e3 d5 5 c4 c6 6 ♘c3 ♗e6, although Black's game is less comfortable in view of his inflexible, immobile pawn structure) 3 ♘d2 ♕b6 (attacking the abandoned pawn on b2 is a logical idea and at the same time Black steps out of the pin) 4 e3 ♕xb2 5 ♖b1 ♕a3!? (otherwise the white pieces would develop by shooting at the enemy queen) 6 g4!? fxg4 7 ♕xg4 ♕xa2 8 ♗d3 ♘f6 9 ♕h4 ♕f7 with a very messy position. White's huge advantage in development is counterbalanced by Black's two extra pawns.

b) 2 ♘c3 d5 (talking White out of e2-e4) 3 ♗g5 (on 3 e4 not 3...fxe4 4 ♕h5+ but 3...dxe4, corresponding to line c, is playable) 3...♘f6 (there is no need to fear the doubled pawn here as White can no longer undermine the important central d5-square with c2-c4) 4 ♗xf6 exf6 5 e3 ♗e6 6 ♗d3 ♘c6 7 ♕f3 ♕d7 8 a3 0-0-0 with an equal position.

c) 2 e4 (the Staunton Gambit) 2...fxe4 3 ♘c3 (3 f3 d5 4 ♘c3 ♘f6 is only a different move-order, but very risky is 3...exf3 4 ♘xf3 as later White gets an immense attack with ♗d3 and 0-0) 3...♘f6 4 ♗g5 (or 4 f3 d5 5 fxe4 dxe4 6 ♗g5 ♗f5 7 ♗c4 ♘c6 8 ♘ge2 ♕d7 =) 4...e6 5 ♘xe4 ♗e7 6 ♗xf6 ♗xf6 7 ♘f3 ♕e7 followed by ...♘c6, ...b7-b6, ...♗b7 and ...0-0-0.

d) 2 g4. Here Black needs to know that after on 2...fxg4 3 h3, it is wrong to play 3...gxh3 as after 4 ♘xh3 White has a strong attack on the open g-file (♘g5 and e2-e4 or ♘f4, e2-e3 and ♗d3). Instead he should play 3...g3! stopping the white kingside play. If he wishes to avoid this, White can try to prepare 4 h3 with 3 ♗f4.

2 c4 ♘f6

The knight definitely belongs here and definite moves should be played first so that we have a choice of the 'indefinite' ones according to the opponent's plan. An object lesson is 2...g6?! 3 h4! ♘f6 4 h5 ♘xh5 5 ♖xh5 gxh5 6 e4! with terrific play for White.

3 ♘f3

This (or 3 g3) is the correct way to begin as according to Black's plan knight b1 will develop to c3 (Leningrad Dutch) or to d2 (Stonewall). Now Black has to choose between:

I. 3...e6 and
II. 3...g6.

I. Stonewall Variation

---

1 d4 f5 2 c4 ♘f6 3 ♘f3 e6 4 g3

The Stonewall is less effective after 4 ♘c3 d5 (4...♗b4!?) 5 ♗f4 c6 6 e3 ♗e7 (an instructive example is 6...♗d6 when 7 ♗d3 is correct, because there is no need to worry about 7...♗xf4 8 exf4 when White's advantage is guaranteed by the e5-square and his possession of the open e-file) 7 ♗d3 0-0 8 0-0 ♘e4 9 ♗xe4 dxe4 10 ♘e5 ♘d7 11 f3! and White is somewhat better as he has mopped up Black's outpost on e4. This line can also be reached via the Queen's Gambit: 1 d4 d5 2 c4 e6 3 ♘f3 c6 4 ♘c3 f5 5 ♗f4 ♘f6.

4...d5

Slightly more passive for Black is 4...♗e7 5 ♗g2 0-0 6 0-0 d6 7 ♘c3 ♕e8 8 b3 ♕h5 9 ♗a3!? with the unusual positional threat of 10 d5! e5? 11 ♘xe5.

5 ♗g2 c6 6 0-0

6...dxc4 is not yet threatened as 7 ♘e5 wins back the pawn with ease.

6...♗d6

This is a more active move than 6...♗e7 in view of both the battle for the e5-square and control over the a3-f8 diagonal. On 6...♗e7 White can play 7 b3 and then ♗a3 to exchange the dark-squared bishops, after which he will try to exchange his bishop and knight for the black cavalry. Then – if all goes well – he would be left with a knight on e5 against the sad black bishop, locked behind its own pawns. Instead of 7 b3, White can also play more slowly with 7

♘bd2, ready to support its colleague's foray to the e5-square from f3. After the continuation 7 ♘bd2 0-0 8 ♕c2 ♕e8 9 ♘e5 ♕h5 10 ♘df3 ♘e4 11 ♘d3! g5 12 ♘fe5 ♘d7 13 f3 ± White dominates the e5-square and controls e4. Later he can prepare e2-e4 with b2-b3, ♗b2, ♖ae1. The routes of the white knights should be memorized: ♘g1-f3, ♘b1-d2, ♘f3-e5(e1), ♘d2-f3, ♘e5(e1)-d3, ♘f3-e5 followed by f2-f3. The best option for Black is perhaps to set off his light-squared bishop on the long journey c8-d7-e8-h5 (g6).

7 b3

The pawn on c4 is defended and the route for ♗a3 has also opened. A brave alternative is 7 ♗f4!? ♗xf4 8 gxf4. Although White controls e5 and with the exchange of the dark-squared bishops other dark squares in Black's position have also weakened, the white king position has become airy.

7...♕e7

Black develops and prevents 8 ♗a3.

8 ♘bd2 0-0 9 ♗b2

9 ♘e1 also comes into consideration with the follow-up ♘d3, ♘f3 and ♗f4.

Plans and Counterplans:
Black's position is not easy to handle. If he regroups with ♗c8-d7-e8-h5 then White can play his plan of ♘f3-e5-d3, ♘d2-f3-e5 without being disturbed, and after f2-f3, ♕d2, ♘f2 and ♖ae1 opt for

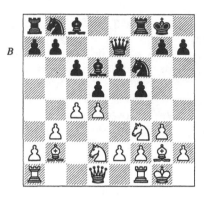

e2-e4. And if Black develops via ...b7-b6 and ...♗b7 White bides his time with ♕c2, ♖ac1 (♖fc1), ♘e5 to open up with c4xd5. A premature ...♘e4 will be answered by ♘xe4 fxe4, when after the jump of the f3-knight White can play f2-f3. Overall, White has the better chances in the Stonewall.

II. Leningrad Variation

1 d4 f5 2 c4 ♘f6 3 ♘f3 g6 4 g3

Again the bishop is well placed on g2 since it controls the squares e4 and d5 while the diagonal of the c1-bishop stays open.

4...♗g7 5 ♗g2 0-0 6 0-0 d6

6...c6 is met by 7 d5! followed by ♘c3 and e2-e4.

7 ♘c3

On the immediate 7 b3 Black can play 7...e5!? 8 dxe5 ♘g4 ∞, while 7...♕e8 8 ♗b2 h6 9 ♘bd2 g5 is also unclear. 7 d5 is also good since it fits well in nearly all future positions. But back to 7 ♘c3.

Black's main intention is to play ...e7-e5, after which both

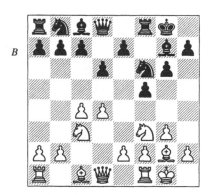

...e5-e4 and ...f6-f4 are threatened. He can also create a kingside attack with ...h7-h6, ...g6-g5, ...♕e8-♕h5, ...f5-f4, ...♗h3 and ...♘g4. White normally thwarts Black's ...e7-e5 with d4-d5 and the 'en passant' capture. In principle White would like to play e2-e4, after which he can deliver an attack on the e7-pawn and perhaps hope to place his f3-knight on e6, via g5. Black's three main continuations are:

A. 7...c6
B. 7...♘c6 and
C. 7...♕e8!?

A. 1 d4 f5 2 c4 ♘f6 3 ♘f3 g6 4 g3 ♗g7 5 ♗g2 0-0 6 0-0 d6 7 ♘c3 c6

8 d5

White vacates the d4-square for his knight on f3 while pinning Black's e-pawn. After 8 b3 ♘a6 9 ♗b2 ♕e8 10 d5 ♗d7 11 ♘d4 ♘c7 12 ♕d2 c5 13 ♘e6 ♗xe6 14 dxe6 ♖b8 15 ♘d5 ♘fxd5 16 ♗xg7 ♔xg7 17 cxd5 b5 Black is threatening to

get the advantage by means of ...b5-b4 followed by ...♘c7-b5-c3. Although the pawn-spike d5-e6 looks frightening, Black can live with it.

8...e5

For 8...♕e8!? see section C.

9 dxe6

White must remove the pawn on e5, otherwise it would keep threatening to advance.

9...♗xe6 10 b3!?

10 ♗f4 gives White nothing: 10...♗xc4 11 ♗xd6 ♖e8 12 ♕d4 ♗d5! 13 ♗xb8 ♗xf3 =. But c4 can be defended by 10 ♕d3, for example 10...♘a6 11 ♘g5 ♕e7 12 ♗f4 ♖ad8 13 ♖ad1 ♘g4 14 ♘xe6 ♕xe6 15 e4 ♘c5 16 exf5 and in the open position – having achieved e2-e4 – White stands better with his bishop pair, regardless of how Black recaptures on f5.

10...♘a6

It is strange, but in the Leningrad Dutch the knight on b8 often develops to the side since from there it has plenty of squares to chose from (b4, c5, c7). But why cannot Black exploit the pin on the long-diagonal with 10...♘e4? Because of 11 ♘xe4 ♗xa1 (11...fxe4 12 ♘d4) 12 ♕xd6! ♕xd6 13 ♘xd6 ♗c8 (13...b6 14 ♗g5 ♗f6 15 ♗xf6 ♖xf6 16 ♘e8 ♖f7 17 ♘g5 ♖e7 18 ♘xe6 wins as one of the knights will fork on c7) 14 ♗g5 ♗f6 (to avoid the loss of an exchange on e7) 15 ♗xf6 ♖xf6 16 ♘xc8 ♘a6 17 ♘e7+ ♔f8 18 ♘xc6 bxc6 19 ♘e5 ±.

11 ♗b2 ♕e7 12 ♘g5!

A multi-purpose move, stopping the menacing 12...d5 (as then White would capture e6 after which d5 is hanging and e2-e4 is in the air), while the bishop on e6 cannot retreat to c8 as it would block the rook on a8.

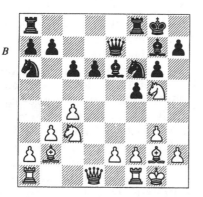

Plans and Counterplans:
After ...♘c5 and ...♖ad8 Black would like to plant his knight on e4. White in turn will capture the bishop on e6 and, after ♕d2 and ♖ad1, opt for either ♖fe1 and e2-e4 or b2-b4, exchanging the light artillery to achieve a better endgame in view of Black's vulnerable pawn on d6 and loose king position.

B. 1 d4 f5 2 c4 ♘f6 3 ♘f3 g6 4 g3 ♗g7 5 ♗g2 0-0 6 0-0 d6 7 ♘c3 ♘c6

8 d5

Again this is the only way to stop ...e7-e5.

  8...♘e5

By analogy to the Fianchetto Variation of the King's Indian Defence, also playable is 8...♘a5. Now 9 ♘d2 c5 10 ♕c2 (10 dxc6 ♘xc6 =) 10...e5 11 dxe6 ♗xe6 12 ♖d1 ♕e7 13 b3 ♘c6 14 ♗b2 ♘d4 promises good activity for Black, while 9 ♕a4 c5 10 dxc6 bxc6!? 11 ♘d4 ♗d7 12 ♘xc6 ♘xc6 13 ♗xc6 ♗xc6 14 ♕xc6 ♖c8 15 ♕a4 ♕d7! offers excellent play for the pawn. On 9 ♕d3, Black can play 9...c5 with the plan of ...a7-a6, ...♗d7, ...♖b8 and ...b7-b5 or 9...e5!? 10 dxe6 ♗xe6 11 b3 ♘c6 with equal chances.

  9 ♘xe5

  9 ♕b3 ♘xf3+ 10 exf3 e5 11 dxe6 ♗xe6 12 ♖e1 ♕d7 13 f4 c6 14 ♗e3 ♕f7 15 ♕a3 ♗xc4 16 ♕xd6 =. If instead of 10 exf3 White plays 10 ♗xf3, then Black has 10...♘d7 followed by 11...♘c5 or 11...♘e5.

  9...dxe5

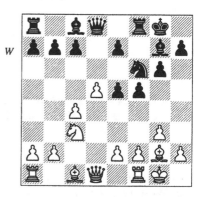

Plans and Counterplans:
White will either play ♕b3 and c4-c5 and open the d-file or play e2-e4. In both cases Black has

counter-chances on the kingside since this is where his forces are strongest. More specifically:

a) 10 ♕b3 h6 (10...e6!? helps White: 11 ♖d1 exd5 12 ♘xd5 ±) 11 ♖d1 ♔h8 12 c5 g5 13 ♗d2 e4!? ∞.

b) 10 e4 f4! 11 gxf4 (otherwise Black can play ...g5-g4-f3) 11...♘h5 12 fxe5 ♗xe5 13 ♘e2 ♕d6 with good play for Black.

C. 1 d4 f5 2 c4 ♘f6 3 ♘f3 g6 4 g3 ♗g7 5 ♗g2 0-0 6 0-0 d6 7 ♘c3 ♕e8!?

This move was developed around ten years ago and it is still the most popular and successful line for Black in the Dutch Defence. The threat is again ...e7-e5.

8 d5

Other moves are:

a) 8 ♘d5 ♘xd5 9 cxd5 ♕b5!? 10 ♘g5 h6 11 a4 ♕c4 12 ♘e6 ♗xe6 13 dxe6 d5 14 ♗e3 c6 ∞.

b) 8 e4 ♘xe4 9 ♘xe4 fxe4 10 ♘g5 ♘c6 11 ♗e3 e5 12 d5 ♘d4 13 ♘xe4 ♗f5 ∞.

c) 8 ♖e1 ♕f7! 9 ♕d3 h6 10 d5 e5 11 dxe6 ♗xe6 12 c5 ♘c6 13 cxd6 ♖ad8 =.

d) 8 b3 e5!? 9 dxe5 dxe5 10 e4 ♘c6 11 ♗a3 ♖f7 ∞. Black is threatening 12...f4 followed by ...♗g4.

8...c6

Black will complete queenside development by means of ...♗d7 and ...♘a6. The knight on b8 cannot head for d7 as then White plays ♘d4 and meets ...♘d7-c5 (to protect the e6-square) by chasing

the knight away with b2-b4. The unusual ...♕e8 fits in well the set-up ...♗d7 and ...♘a6 as it keeps an eye on the important squares c6 and b5, while the knight on a6 can aim at the e4-square via c5 or can go to c7 to activate queenside play with ...b7-b5.

Instead of 8...c6, Black can also play 8...a5 aiming for ...♘a6-c5 and obstructing b2-b4, e.g. 9 ♘d4 ♘a6 10 e4 fxe4 11 ♘xe4 ♘xe4 12 ♗xe4 ♗h3 13 ♖e1 ♘c5 ∓. Instead of 9 ♘d4 White can play 9 ♘e1!? ♘a6 10 ♘d3, when Black's knight cannot go to c5.

Black can also try 8...♘a6 at once, and after 9 ♖b1 c5 10 b3 ♘c7 strive for ...b7-b5.

9 ♖b1

White would like to develop his queenside and at the same time stop ...♘a6-c5 with b2-b4. Fewer chances are offered by 9 ♘d4 ♗d7 10 ♖e1 ♘a6 11 e4 fxe4 12 ♘xe4 ♘xe4 13 ♗xe4 ♘c7 14 ♖b1 c5!? 15 ♘e2 b5 ∞.

9...♘a6 10 b4 ♗d7

Plans and Counterplans:

Against **11 ♘d4** Black has the interesting 11...♘xb4!? 12 ♖xb4 c5 13 ♖xb7 cxd4 14 ♘b5 (14 ♕xd4?? ♘e4 −+) 14...♕c8! 15 ♖c7 ♕b8, so White should instead take on c6 to create a queenside pawn majority. Therefore **11 dxc6** bxc6 (11...♗xc6 12 b5! ♗xf3 13 ♗xf3 ♘c5 14 ♗e3 ♖c8!? 15 b6! axb6 16 ♘d5! promises White good play due to his strong initiative on the

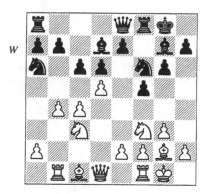

b-file) 12 b5 (12 ♘d4 ♘xb4!? 13
♖xb4 c5 14 ♖b1 cxd4 15 ♗xa8
dxc3 is slightly better for Black)

12...cxb5 13 cxb5 ♘c5 14 a4 (14
♘d4 ♘fe4) 14...♖c8!? and now on
15 a5 ♘fe4 16 ♘xe4 fxe4 17 ♘d4
e5! 18 ♘b3 ♘a4! Black seizes the
initiative (∓), while on 15 ♗b2 a6!
16 ♘d4 (White could not push as
the pawn on a4 would be hanging) 16...axb5 17 axb5 ♘fe4 18
♘xe4 fxe4 it is White who has to
opt for simplifications with 19
♘b3! (=).

In conclusion, if you want an
unclear game with tactical chances
for both sides, the Dutch Defence
is a good choice!

Old Indian Defence

1 d4 ♘f6 2 c4 d6 3 ♘c3 e5 4 ♘f3

Instead, 4 dxe5 dxe5 5 ♕xd8+ ♚xd8 'comes to mind', preventing Black from castling. However, after 6 ♘f3 ♘fd7 followed by ...c7-c6 and ...♚c7 Black shelters his king or perhaps plays ...f7-f6 and develops via ...♘a6 and ...♝c5 or ...♝b4. If he can carry this out then the control over the d5-square offered by his c6 pawn becomes important because White is weak on d4, and the black king may stand well in the centre on account of the forthcoming endgame.

4...♘bd7

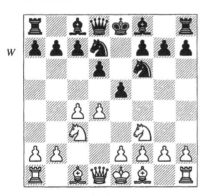

On 4...e4 5 ♘g5 ♝f5, an attractive line is 6 g4! ♝xg4 (6...♝g6 7 ♝g2 ♕e7 8 ♕b3 b6 9 h4 h6 10 h5 hxg5 11 hxg6 is clearly better for White) 7 ♝g2 and White regains the pawn on e4, castles queenside

and then advances his central pawns.

5 e4

Another interesting set-up is 5 ♝g5 and then e2-e3, ♕c2, ♝d3 and perhaps 0-0-0.

5...♝e7 6 ♝e2

White often closes the centre and at the same time the diagonal h1-a8 with d4-d5, so it seems more sensible not to fianchetto the bishop to g2.

6...0-0 7 0-0 c6

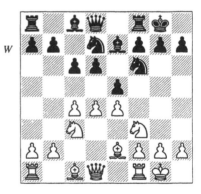

Plans and Counterplans:

White can expect a slight plus due to his spatial advantage. He can opt for a set-up with h2-h3, ♝e3, ♕c2, ♖fd1 and ♖ac1; or ♖fe1, ♝f1 and ♝g5 or he can play d4-d5. Black's most common counter is ...♕c7, ...♖e8, ...a7-a6 and ...b7-b5. White can meet ...b7-b5 with a2-a3 or c4xb5 and then b2-b4. Here are a few specific examples:

a) **8 d5** a6 9 ♗e3 cxd5 (9...c5 10 ♘e1 with ♘d3 and f2-f4 to follow ±) 10 cxd5 ♘g4 11 ♗d2 b5 12 ♘e1!? ♘gf6 13 ♘c2 ♘c5 14 f3 ♗d7 15 b4 ♘a4 16 ♘xa4 bxa4 17 ♘a3! and White is on top. The threat is ♗d3-c2.

b) **8 ♖e1** ♕c7 9 ♗f1 a6 10 a3 b5 11 ♗g5 ♗b7 12 ♖c1 ♕b8 13 ♖c2!? h6 14 ♗c1! ♖e8 15 dxe5 dxe5 16 ♘h4! ♘f8 17 ♘f5 ±.

c) **8 ♕c2** ♕c7 9 ♖d1 ♖e8 10 h3 a6 11 ♗e3 b5 12 a3 exd4?! (it is better to maintain the tension in the centre by means of ...♗b7, ...♖ac8 and ...♕b8) 13 ♘xd4 ♗b7 14 ♘f5 ♗f8 15 ♗f4! ♘e5 16 ♗g5! ±.

Gambits after 1 d4 ♘f6 2 c4

Black has two ways to immediately attack White's central pawn pair of d4 and c4. He can either play ...e7-e5 or first he may 'force' the move d4-d5 with ...c7-c5 and then sacrifice a pawn with ...b7-b5 for which he gets good play on the queenside.

I. Gambits with ...e7-e5
II. 1 d4 ♘f6 2 c4 e6 3 ♘f3 c5 4 d5 b5 (Blumenfeld Gambit)
III. 1 d4 ♘f6 2 c4 c5 3 d5 b5 (Benko Gambit)

I. Gambits with ...e7-e5

1...e5? at once is very weak: 2 dxe5 ♘c6 3 ♘f3 ♕e7 4 ♗f4 (also good is 4 ♕d5 f6 5 exf6 ♘xf6 6 ♕b3! – by attacking the pawn on b7 White ties down the bishop on c8 – 6...d5 7 ♘c3 d4 8 ♘b5 ±) 4...♕b4+ 5 ♗d2 ♕xb2 6 ♘c3! (White would fall into a trap with 6 ♗c3? ♗b4!, e.g. 7 ♕d2? ♗xc3 8 ♕xc3 ♕c1 mate!) 6...♗b4 (6...♘b4 7 ♘d4 ♗c5 8 ♖b1 ♕a3 9 ♘cb5 ♕a5 10 a3 +−) 7 ♖b1 ♕a3 8 ♖b3 (also not bad is 8 ♘d5!? ♗xd2+ 9 ♕xd2 ♕xa2 10 ♖d1) 8...♕a5 9 a3!? ♗xc3 10 ♗xc3 ♕c5 11 e4 with a large development advantage for White (±).
2 c4 e5
The Budapest Gambit.
3 dxe5

3 d5? is a lemon in view of 3...♗c5 4 ♘c3 d6 5 e4 c6 and Black is already better, e.g. 6 ♘f3 ♘g4 or 6 ♗e2 ♕b6 or 6 ♗g5 h6 7 ♗h4 g5 8 ♗g3 ♕a5 threatening ...♘xe4, ...♗b4, etc. White cannot push d4-d5 if the bishop on f8 can rush out to c5 or b4 as then suddenly all of White's dark central squares become weak. Such advances in the centre can only work if they restrict the opponent's pieces.

3...♘g4
After 3...♘e4 White has to watch that Black does not get counterplay with ...♗b4+, ...♗c5, ...♕h4, ...d7-d6 or ...f7-f5. It is best to give the pawn back for a development advantage by means of 4 a3!? (preventing 4...♗b4+ and making possible a future b2-b4) 4...♕h4 (4...♗c5 5 e3 ♘c6 6 ♘f3 ♕e7 7 b4 +−) 5 g3 ♕h5 6 ♗g2 ♕xe5 7 ♘f3 ♕c5 8 ♘d4 ♘f6 9 b3 with a small but tangible plus for White. Those who want to try for more can play 4 ♘f3!? ♘c6 5 a3 d6 6 ♕c2!? d5 (or 6...♗f5 7 ♘c3 ♘xf2 8 ♕xf5 ♘xh1 9 e6 and later White will win the knight on h1 with g2-g3 and ♗g2: +−) 7 e3 ♗g4 8 cxd5 ♕xd5 9 ♗c4 ♕a5+ 10 b4 ♗xb4+ 11 axb4 ♕xa1 12 ♕xe4 and White should emerge on top from this complicated position.
4 ♘f3

More violent continuations are:

a) 4 f4 ♗c5 5 ♘h3 d6 6 exd6 0-0 7 dxc7 ♕xc7 and Black gets good counterplay with ...♘c6 and ...♖e8 ∞.

b) 4 e4 ♘xe5 5 f4 ♘ec6 (or 5...♘g6 6 ♘f3 ♗b4+ 7 ♘c3 ♕f6 8 e5 ♕b6 ∞) 6 ♗e3 ♗b4+ 7 ♘c3 ♕h4+ 8 g3 ♗xc3+ 9 bxc3 ♕e7 ∞.

c) 4 ♗f4!? ♘c6 5 ♘f3 ♗b4+ 6 ♘c3 (6 ♘bd2!? ♕e7 7 e3 ♘gxe5 8 ♘xe5 ♘xe5 9 ♗e2 d6 10 0-0 ♗d7 – 10...0-0 11 ♘b3 and 12 a3 ± – 11 a3 ♗xd2 12 ♕xd2 and White's plan is b2-b4, ♕c3 and c4-c5) 6...♗xc3+ 7 bxc3 ♕e7 8 ♕d5 f6!? 9 exf6 ♘xf6 10 ♕d3 d6 11 e3 ♘e4 12 ♗e2 0-0 13 0-0 ♗f5 and for the pawn Black has a central initiative and has managed to shatter White's queenside.

4...♗c5

Black forces the enclosure of the bishop on c1.

5 e3 ♘c6 6 ♗e2 ♘gxe5 7 ♘xe5 ♘xe5 8 0-0 0-0 9 ♘c3 a5

On 9...d6 10 ♘a4 ♗b6 11 b3 ± White will sooner or later capture on b6 and then get going with ♗b2, f2-f4 and e2-e4.

10 b3 ♖e8

Plans and Counterplans:

On the naive **11 ♗b2?**, 11...♖a6! is extremely effective, threatening ...♕h4 followed by ...♖h6 or ...♖g6 with a mating attack! So for the time being the bishop on c1 should stay put to keep an eye on the b6-square. Therefore White plays **11 a3** and now on 11...♖a6

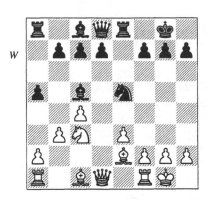

12 ♘d5! ♖h6 13 e4! ± or 11...d6 12 ♗b2 (now that the sixth rank is closed!) White is better since he has ♘d5, ♕d2 and b3-b4. Black can hardly stop this with ...c7-c6 as this would weaken the squares d6 and b6.

In these gambit variations Black stands worse because even if he gets the pawn back, the d5 square is weakened for good and may prove to be a base for the knight on c3 in the middlegame. White's best tactic against a gambit is to accept the sacrifice and then give it back for positional gains (e.g. bishop pair, spatial advantage, better endgame).

II. Blumenfeld Gambit

1 d4 ♘f6 2 c4 e6 3 ♘f3

Now 3...b6 is a Queen's Indian but here we look at a pawn sacrifice for Black instead.

3...c5 4 d5 b5!?

Black blows up the white pawn centre with a sacrifice.

5 ♗g5!

Black would be delighted with 5 dxe6 fxe6 6 cxb5, as after 6...d5 he takes over the centre and achieves an excellent game with ...♗d6, ...0-0, ...♗b7 and ...a7-a6. 5 ♘c3 b4 6 ♘a4 is also of no avail in view of 6...exd5 7 cxd5 d6 and the pawn on d5 is vulnerable to attack by ...♗b7 and ...♘bd7-b6. On 5 a4 bxc4 6 ♘c3 exd5 7 ♘xd5 ♗b7 White loses the outpost on d5 for the knight.

5...♕a5+!?

The only good continuation, or else White tightens his grip on d5, e.g. 5...bxc4 6 ♘c3 threatening e2-e4 and ♗xc4 or 5...b4 6 e4 with a later ♗d3, ♘d2 and 0-0 or 5...h6 6 ♗xf6! ♕xf6 7 ♘c3 b4 8 ♘b5 and now both 8...♘a6 9 e4 ♕xb2 10 ♗d3 d6 11 0-0 ♗d7 12 ♕a4 ± and 8...♔d8 9 e4 g5 10 e5 ♕g7 11 g4!, when White is ahead due to his plan of ♕a4 (threatening ♕a5+) and 0-0-0, are bad for Black. Another false idea is 5...exd5 6 cxd5 ♕a5+ 7 ♘c3 ♘e4 8 ♗d2 ♘xd2 9 ♕xd2 d6 10 e4 b4 as after 11 ♘d1 White plays ♗e2, 0-0 and ♘e3. The vacant c4-square will be a perfect place for the knight to pressurise the black queenside.

6 ♘c3

White can also play:

a) 6 ♗d2 ♕b6 7 ♘c3 bxc4 8 e4 ♗a6 ∞.

b) 6 ♘bd2 ♘e4 7 ♕c2 ♘xg5 8 ♘xg5 ♗e7 =.

c) 6 ♕d2 ♕xd2+ 7 ♘bxd2 bxc4 8 ♗xf6 gxf6 9 e4 ♘a6 10 ♗xc4 ♘c7 =.

6...♘e4 7 ♗d2

Or 7 cxb5 ♘xg5!? (7...♘xc3 8 bxc3 ♕xc3+ 9 ♗d2 with a slight advantage for White) 8 ♘xg5 ♗e7, followed by ...♗b7, ...0-0 and ...a6, which is unclear.

7...♘xd2 8 ♕xd2

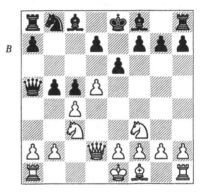

B

Plans and Counterplans:

This line used to be considered inferior for Black on account of the variation **8...bxc4?** 9 e4 ♗e7 10 ♗xc4 ♗a6 11 ♘b5! ♕b6 12 a4! But the queenside should be kept closed with **8...b4!?**: 9 ♘e4 ♗e7 10 ♘g3! (making room for e2-e4. 10 d6 is a bad mistake, because after 10...♗d8 the black queenside springs to life quickly with ...♘c6 and ...♗b7) 10...d6 11 e4 ♘d7 12 dxe6 fxe6 13 e5!? ♘xe5 14 ♘xe5 dxe5 15 ♗d3 0-0 16 0-0 g6 with interesting play and mutual chances.

In the final position White is a pawn down but this is well compensated Black's damaged pawn structure and White's control over the e4-square.

III. Benko Gambit

1 d4 ♘f6 2 c4 c5 3 d5 b5!?

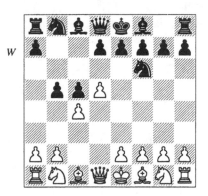

In the Benko Gambit Black gives up his a- and b-pawns for White's c-pawn to exert strong pressure on the white queenside from the open a- and b- files and often from the a1-h8 long diagonal. Meanwhile White has to safeguard his d5-pawn and watch out for Black's central blow ...e7-e6. Of course this gambit involves some risk, but with accurate play Black can obtain good play for the pawn.

4 cxb5

White captures not only for the sake of material gain but also because otherwise he cannot develop his knight to c3: 4 ♘c3 b4! 5 ♘a4 d6 followed by 6...g6 or 6...e6 and Black is better. It is no use declining the gambit with 4 ♗g5: 4...♘e4! 5 ♗f4 e6!? 6 ♘f3 ♕a5+ 7 ♘bd2 ♘d6 ∞. But the moderate 4 ♘f3!? is prudent. For example:

a) 4...bxc4?! 5 ♘c3 d6 6 e4 g6 7 ♗xc4 ♗g7 8 e5! dxe5 9 ♘xe5 0-0 10 ♕e2 ±.

b) 4...b4 5 a3 d6 6 ♘bd2 g6 7 e4 ♗g7 8 ♗d3 0-0 9 axb4 cxb4 10 0-0 ± and later White can advance with e4-e5 or use the d4-square for his knights to aim at the holes on b7 and c6.

c) 4...♗b7!? 5 ♘bd2!? d6 6 e4 b4 7 a3!? a5 8 axb4 axb4 9 ♖xa8 ♗xa8 10 ♕a4+ ♘bd7 11 e5 dxe5 12 ♘xe5 and ♘df3, ♗d3 and 0-0 ±.

d) 4...g6!? 5 ♕c2!? (White opts for e2-e4 and eventually – when the tension on the queenside has been released – envisages his knight on c3) 5...♗g7 (5...bxc4?! 6 e4 with the future plan of ♘c3, ♗xc4 and e4-e5) 6 e4 d6 7 cxb5 a6 8 ♘c3 0-0 9 bxa6 ♗xa6 10 ♗xa6 ♖xa6 11 0-0 ♘bd7 with mutual chances.

4...a6

Black could not reverse the moves ...b7-b5 and ...a7-a6, as on 3...a6? 4 a4! puts an end to his queenside expectations.

White's main lines are:

A. 5 bxa6 and
B. 5 f3

There are also some interesting sidelines:

a) 5 b6 ♕xb6 6 ♘c3 g6 7 ♘f3 ♗g7 8 e4 d6 9 ♗e2 ♘bd7 10 0-0 0-0 11 ♘d2 ♖b8 12 ♘c4 ♕c7 13 ♗f4 ♘b6 = and Black need not worry about 14 e5?! ♘e8 15 exd6 exd6 16 ♕d2 ♘xc4 17 ♗xc4 ♘f6.

b) 5 ♘c3 axb5 6 e4 b4 7 ♘b5 d6 (7...♘xe4? 8 ♕e2 ♘f6 9 ♘d6 mate!) 8 ♗f4 g5! 9 ♗xg5 ♘xe4 10 ♗f4 ♗g7 11 ♕e2 ♘f6 12 ♘xd6+ ♔f8 13 ♘xc8 ♕xc8 14 d6 exd6 15 ♗xd6+ ♔g8 16 ♕f3 ♘c6 17 ♘e2 ♕e8 18 ♗xc5 ♘e4! 19 ♗e3 b3! and combines an attack against the king in the middle with queenside threats.

c) 5 e3 axb5 (also playable is the formerly popular 5...g6 6 ♘c3 ♗g7, when instead of capturing on b5 Black can continue with ...0-0, ...d7-d6, ...♘bd7-b6 and ...♗b7 and later seek counterplay similarly to the 5 bxa6 lines) 6 ♗xb5 ♕a5+ 7 ♘c3 ♗b7 8 ♘e2 (8 e4 ♘xe4 9 ♘e2 ♘d6 10 ♗a4 g6 ∞) 8...♗xd5 (8...♘xd5 9 0-0 ♘xc3 10 ♘xc3 e6 11 e4 ♗e7 12 ♗f4 ±) 9 0-0 ♗c6 10 a4 e6 11 e4!? ♗xb5 12 ♘xb5 ♘xe4 13 ♗f4 ♘a6 14 ♘ec3! ♘xc3 15 bxc3 d5 16 c4 ♖d8 17 ♕g4 ∞ with an initiative for the pawn. Again we see White countering the gambit by sacrificing a pawn for activity.

A. 1 d4 ♘f6 2 c4 c5 3 d5 b5 4 cxb5 a6 5 bxa6

5...♗xa6
Black has 'pinned' the pawn on e2. If it moves he can stop White from castling with ...♗xf1.

6 ♘c3 d6 7 e4
White can preserve his castling options if he fianchettoes his f1-bishop: 7 ♘f3 g6 8 g3 ♗g7 9 ♗g2 0-0 10 0-0 ♘bd7 11 ♕c2 ♖a7 12 h3

♕a8 13 ♖d1 ♗c4 with an unclear game. Black can exert maximum strength on the a- and b-files with the set-up ...♖a7, ...♕a8 and ...♖b8 while at the same time threatening the d5-pawn.

7...♗xf1 8 ♔xf1 g6 9 g3
White will castle 'artificially', that is, move his king to g2 and activate the rook on h1.

9...♗g7 10 ♔g2 0-0 11 ♘f3 ♘bd7 12 h3
On 11...♘bd7 the move 12 h3 is almost a reflex action as on, for example, 12 ♖e1 Black can play 12...♘g4! 13 h3 ♘ge5 14 ♘xe5 ♘xe5, threatening 15...c4 and 16...♘d3. So 12 h3 prevents Black from occupying the e5-square with his knight!

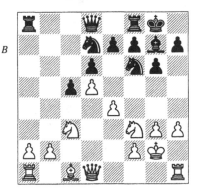

Plans and Counterplans:
Black has to proceed against the white queenside. For this he can play ...♘b6, ...♕d7, and ...♖fb8 followed by ...♘e8-c7-b5 but it seems stronger to play ...♖a6 and ...♕a8. The latter can be combined with the blow ...e7-e6, which suggests

itself due to the placement of the queen on a8 and king on g2. In the meantime White can play ♖e1 and opt for e4-e5 or first he can try to stabilize his queenside with ♖b1, b2-b3, a2-a4 and ♘b5.

B. 1 d4 ♘f6 2 c4 c5 3 d5 b5 4 cxb5 a6 5 f3

Nowadays this is the most popular line: White can easily achieve e2-e4 but he does not enjoy any material gains.

5...axb5

White is better after 5...g6 6 e4 d6 7 ♘a3! ♗g7 8 ♘e2 0-0 9 ♘c3 (±), but 5...e6!? 6 e4 exd5 7 e5 ♕e7 8 ♕e2 ♘g8 9 ♘c3 ♗b7 10 ♘h3 c4 11 ♗e3 axb5 12 0-0-0 ♕b4!? is unclear, e.g. 13 ♖xd5 ♕xc3+! 14 bxc3 ♗xd5 is a promising queen sacrifice.

6 e4 ♕a5+

On 6...b4 7 ♗c4 followed by ♘e2, 0-0 and a2-a4.

7 ♗d2 b4 8 ♘a3! d6

Or 8...g6 9 ♘c4 ♕c7 10 a3! bxa3 11 ♖xa3 ♖xa3 12 bxa3 and, after castling, White obtains a dangerous queenside initiative.

9 ♘c4 ♕a7!

Worse is 9...♕c7?! as after 10 a3 White is threatening to take on b4, while if Black captures on a3 White will achieve a passed pawn.

Plans and Counterplans:

White can insist on playing along the a-file or can just develop peacefully:

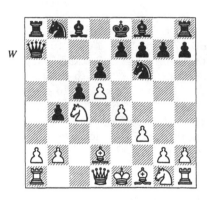

a) **10 a3** g6 11 ♗d3 ♗g7 12 ♘e2 0-0 13 0-0 bxa3 14 ♖xa3 ♕b7 ∞ and Black has no intention of taking on a3. His plan is ...♘a6 and ...♘d7-b6 or ...♖b8.

b) **10 a4** ♘bd7 11 a5 ♗a6 followed by ...g7-g6, ...♗g7 and ...0-0 is also double-edged.

c) **10 ♗d3** (the most peaceful move) 10...g6 11 ♘e2 ♗g7 12 0-0 ♘fd7!? 13 a3 (13 ♔h1 ♘e5) 13...♘e5! 14 ♘xe5 c4+ 15 ♔h1 ♗xe5 16 ♗xc4 ♗xb2 17 ♗b5+ ♘d7 (17...♗d7? 18 ♕c2 0-0 – on 18...♗xa1?? 19 ♕c8 mate! – 19 ♕xb2 ♗xb5 20 axb4 ♕b7 21 ♗h6 +–) 18 ♗c6, reaching the critical point of the whole line. Black should not allow White to sacrifice an exchange but should do so himself:

a) **18...♗b7?!** 19 ♗xb4! ♗xa1 20 ♕xa1 0-0 21 ♗xd7 ♗a6 22 ♗c6 ♗xe2 23 ♖g1 ♖ab8 24 e5 ±.

b) **18...♖b8** 19 axb4! ♗xa1 20 ♕xa1 ♕xa1 21 ♖xa1 ± threatening ♖a7, ♘d4 and b4-b5, etc.

c) **18...bxa3!** 19 ♗xa8 ♕xa8 and if the rook on a1 moves (to a2 or b1) then 20...♗a6 yields good play for Black.

Odds and ends after 1 d4

After **1 d4 ♘c6** it is best to transpose to the Nimzowitsch Defence (1 e4 ♘c6 2 d4) with 2 e4.

1 d4 b5 is also bad for Black as it hands over the centre to White:

2 e4 ♗b7 3 f3 (also good is the set-up ♗d3 and ♘f3) **3...a6 4 ♗e3 e6 5 ♘d2 d5 6 ♗d3 ♘f6 7 e5 ♘fd7 8 f4 c5 9 c3 ♘c6 10 ♘gf3,** threatening f4-f5, is slightly better for White.

1 d4 b6 2 e4 ♗b7 3 ♗d3 followed by ♘f3, c2-c3, 0-0 and ♕e2 also gives White a slight advantage.

English Opening

1 c4

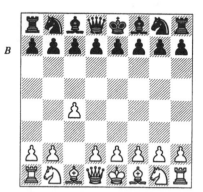

With 1 c4 White makes a claim in the centre and immediately enables the knight on b1 to develop to c3 without blocking the c2-pawn. Although White's intentions are still rather obscure, he will try to sidestep a few openings which arise after 1 d4 and 2 c4, such as the Benko Gambit or the Benoni. Black can still employ some of the openings that are played against 1 d4 (for example, the King's Indian Defence and Dutch Defence) but others may be prevented by his opponent, for example the 'Anti-Grünfeld' in section I or the 'Anti-Nimzo' in section II. The independent 'English-speaking' lines are the 'Symmetrical English', viz. 1 c4 c5 in section III and the 'Sicilian Reversed' viz. 1 c4 e5, covered in section IV.

I. Anti-Grünfeld

1 c4 ♞f6 2 ♞c3 d5

On 2...g6 White can play 3 e4!?, when Black's hopes of a Grünfeld have vanished.

3 cxd5 ♞xd5

Now after 4 d4 g6 White would really find himself in a Grünfeld. However, instead of 4 d4 he can also consider simply developing his pieces:

A. 4 ♞f3 or
B. 4 g3.

A. 1 c4 ♞f6 2 ♞c3 d5 3 cxd5 ♞xd5 4 ♞f3

4...g6

4...c5 leads to the 'Symmetrical English'.

5 ♛a4+!?

An irritating check. Whichever way Black interposes he will have to make some sort of concession.

5...♝d7

The only move since on 5...♞c6 6 ♞e5 ♞xc3 7 bxc3! ♝d7 8 ♞xd7 ♛xd7 9 ♜b1 White has a huge plus due to his bishop pair, his pawn majority in the centre and Black's vulnerable queenside. For example on 9...♜b8 White can try 10 g3 with the idea of ♝g2, ♜xb7 and ♝xc6. Also wrong is 5...c6: 6

♕d4! ♘f6 7 ♕xd8+ ♚xd8 8 e4 followed by 9 d4 ±.

6 ♕h4

Not 6 ♕d4? ♘f6 and the white queen is exposed.

6...♘xc3!?

6...♗c6 can be answered by 7 ♕d4 and 7...♘f6? 8 ♕xd8+ ♚xd8 9 ♘e5 is bad for Black, while on 7...f6 White plays the simple 8 e3 followed by ♗e2 and 0-0, when Black's pieces are out of place.

7 dxc3

7 bxc3 ♗g7, followed by ...c7-c5, ...♘c6 and ...0-0, offers good play for Black and White's queen is not very well placed on h4 either. A more exciting alternative is 7 ♕d4!? f6 8 ♕xc3 e5!? 9 ♘xe5 fxe5 10 ♕xe5+ ♕e7 11 ♕xh8 ♘c6 12 ♕c3 0-0-0 with tremendous play for Black despite his considerable material loss: ...♗g7, ...♘d4 and ...♗f5.

7...♘c6

It is important to protect the queen quickly as it will be exchanged before too long.

8 e4 e5

Plans and Counterplans:

Here White has several possibilities:

a) 9 ♕g3 f6 10 h4 ♕e7 11 h5 g5 12 ♗e2 ♘d8! 13 ♘h2! ♘e6 14 ♗g4 0-0-0 with chances for both sides.

b) Or 9 ♗g5 ♗e7 10 ♗c4 and Black must hamper the possibility of ♘g5: 10...h6 11 ♗xe7 ♕xe7 is equal.

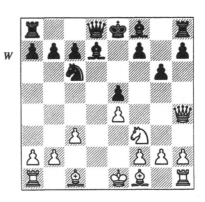

c) The most interesting is 9 ♕xd8+!? ♖xd8 10 ♗c4 (threatening 11 ♘g5) 10...f6 11 ♗e3 ♘a5! 12 ♗e2 ♗e6 13 ♘d2 b6 14 b4 ♘b7 with unclear chances. For example, 15 a4 a5 or 15 f3 h5!?, with the idea of ...♗h6, promises Black a comfortable game.

B. 1 c4 ♘f6 2 ♘c3 d5 3 cxd5 ♘xd5 4 g3

4...g6

For 4...e5 see the 'Sicilian Reversed'.

5 ♗g2 ♘b6

The other possibility is 5...♘xc3 6 bxc3 ♗g7 7 ♖b1 ♘d7 (if White captures on b7 then ...♘b6 would trap the rook on b7 in the end) 8 ♘f3 0-0 9 0-0 ♘b6 (an interesting alternative is 9...c5!?, when Black is planning to unchain the queenside with ...♕c7, ...♖b8, ...b7-b6 and ...♗b7) 10 ♘g5!, with the unusual (and powerful) plan of ♘e4-c5, when Black is worse in view of the threats to his queenside.

6 d3! ♗g7 7 ♗e3!

This is the way for White to utilize the differences between this and a normal Grünfeld. Black has no counterplay while White is planning ♕c1 and ♗h6.

7...0-0

On 7...♘c6 8 ♗xc6+! bxc6 9 ♕c1 ± and later White will compensate for the absence of the bishop with ♘f3-g5 (d4) and f2-f3 making Black suffer for his doubled c-pawns.

8 ♕c1

Plans and Counterplans:
White's threat is the 'utility attack' ♗h6, h4-h5, ♗xg7, h5xg6 and ♕h6+. After 8...♘c6 the knight would again be captured, followed by ♗h6. Black can sidestep the exchange of dark-squared bishops, but 8...♖e8 9 ♗h6 ♗h8 10 h4 ♘c6 11 h5 (the best moment to capture the knight on c6 is when it can be followed up by the exchange of the bishop on g7) 11...♘d4 12 ♘f3 ♘xf3+ 13 ♗xf3 is also slightly better for White (±).

II. Anti-Nimzo

1 c4 ♘f6 2 ♘c3 e6

With this move Black offers a Nimzo-Indian after 3 d4 ♗b4 or perhaps a Queen's Gambit with 3...d5, but White can frustrate his opponent's intentions.

3 e4!?

Threatening 4 e5. Although this can be prevented by 3...d6, this move is very passive: White plays 4 d4, and then f2-f4, ♘f3 ±. Or, for example, 3...e5 4 f4!? d6 5 ♘f3 ±. Black needs to play something else, something original and active!

3...d5!?

With this move Black does allow his knight on f6 to be removed easily. Another common move is 3...c5 4 e5 ♘g8. Now on 5 d4 cxd4 6 ♕xd4 ♘c6 7 ♕e4 d6 Black equalizes, but after 5 ♘f3 ♘c6 6 d4!? cxd4 7 ♘xd4 ♘xe5 8 ♘bd5! a6 9 ♘d6+ ♗xd6 10 ♕xd6 f6 11 ♗e3! White has good play for the pawn.

4 e5

After 4 cxd5 exd5 the diagonal of the bishop on c8 is open.

4...d4!

Instead 4...♘e4!? 5 ♘xe4 dxe4 6 ♕g4 ♘c6 7 ♕xe4 ♕d4 is an interesting sacrifice.

5 exf6 dxc3 6 bxc3

Or 6 fxg7 cxd2+ 7 ♗xd2 ♗xg7 with equality.

6...♕xf6 7 d4 e5!

Black needs to play very accurately indeed to achieve equality.

White stands better after 7...c5 8 ♘f3 cxd4 9 ♗g5! ♕f5 10 cxd4 ♗b4+ 11 ♗d2 ♗xd2+ 12 ♕xd2, followed by ♗d3 – this is the reason for White to drive the enemy queen to a light square with 9 ♗g5 – and 0-0 ±.

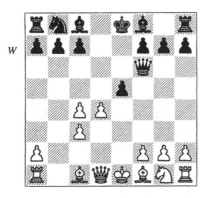

Plans and Counterplans:
White should not try to win the pawn on e5: **8 ♕e2?! ♗e7!** 9 dxe5 (9 ♕xe5 ♕xe5 10 dxe5 ♘c6 11 ♘f3 ♗g4 12 ♗e2 0-0-0 and ...♖he8 with a dangerous initiative for Black) 9...♕g6 10 ♕e3 ♗f5 11 ♘e2 0-0 12 ♘f4 ♕c6 and the threat is ...♖e8 and ...♗c5 ∓. White should therefore simply develop: **8 ♘f3! exd4 9 ♗g5!** (9 cxd4 ♗b4+ 10 ♗d2 ♗xd2+ 11 ♕xd2 0-0 followed by ...c7-c5) **9...♕e6+ 10 ♗e2 f6!?** (not 10...d3? because of 11 0-0! and the pawn on e2 is taboo due to ♕d8 mate or ♖e1 winning the queen. But the simple 10...♗e7!? comes into consideration, followed by quick queenside castling.) **11 ♘xd4 ♕f7 12 ♗f4 ♗c5 13 0-0 0-0** when White is more active but his queenside pawn structure is shattered (∞).

III. Symmetrical English

---

1 c4 c5
As 1...d5 is one of the best replies to 1 d4 and 1...e5 is one of the best replies to 1 e4, it should come as no surprise that 1...c5 is one of the best replies to 1 c4. Right from the first move it is apparent that further central actions will take place on the squares d4, d5. As to who will occupy the centre, and when, this question will be discussed in section A: 'Take it or leave it?'.

Section B deals with the 'hedgehog' set-up in which Black withdraws behind the spikes of his pawns (a6, b6, d6, e6, f7, g7, h7), but is ready to strike when the opportunity presents itself. In the 'Straight Symmetry Variation' (section C) the central battle is postponed while both sides develop their forces in tandem (section C).

A. Take it or leave it?

The main line, where we will eventually arrive, is 1 c4 c5 2 ♘f3 ♘f6 3 ♘c3 ♘c6 4 g3 g6 5 ♗g2 ♗g7 6 0-0 0-0 7 d4 cxd4 8 ♘xd4. Naturally there are many opportunities for both sides to deviate along the way. Both sides face the recurring dilemma of whether to occupy the centre or perhaps allow the opponent to do so? To put it in another way, should White play d2-d4 and Black ...d7-d5?

1 c4 c5 2 ♘f3

This move tells us that White will probably sooner or later be willing to play d2-d4, otherwise he would play 2 ♘c3 (see the 'Straight Symmetrical Variation').

2...♘f6

On 2...g6 the instant 3 d4!? cxd4 4 ♘xd4 ♗g7 5 e4 ♘c6 6 ♗e3 ♘f6 7 ♘c3 is playable with a transposition to the Maroczy Variation of the Sicilian Defence, which is very comfortable for White. However, 2...♘c6 3 ♘c3 (3 d4 transposes to the main line) 3...♘d4!? is an interesting idea, for example 4 e3 ♘xf3+ 5 ♕xf3 g6 followed by ...♗g7, ...♘f6, ...d7-d6 and ...0-0. After 2...♘f6 both players can push their d-pawns as they are now ready to recapture with the knights. Let us take a closer look, step by step!

A1. 3 d4
A2. 3 ♘c3 d5 4 cxd5 ♘xd5
A3. 3 ♘c3 ♘c6 4 d4
A4. 3 ♘c3 ♘c6 4 g3 d5 and
A5. 3 ♘c3 ♘c6 4 g3 g6 5 ♗g2 ♗g7 6 0-0 0-0 7 d4 cxd4 8 ♘xd4.

A1. 1 c4 c5 2 ♘f3 ♘f6 3 d4?!

This is premature.

3...cxd4 4 ♘xd4 e5! 5 ♘b5 d5! 6 cxd5 ♗c5

Black has the initiative, for example 7 ♘5c3 (7 ♗g5? ♗xf2+ and

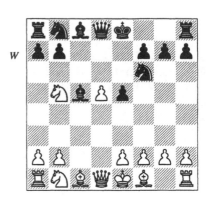

8...♘e4+ −+) 7...0-0 8 e3 e4! 9 ♘d2 ♕e7!? 10 a3 a5 11 d6!? ♗xd6 12 ♘dxe4 ♘xe4 13 ♘xe4 ♖d8 14 ♘xd6 ♖xd6 15 ♕c2 ♘c6 16 ♗e2 ♕g5! with superb play for Black.

A2. 1 c4 c5 2 ♘f3 ♘f6 3 ♘c3 d5 4 cxd5 ♘xd5

5 e4!?

Inviting Black to join an exciting battle. 5 d4 ♘xc3 6 bxc3 g6 leads to the Grünfeld.

5...♘b4

On 5...♘xc3 6 dxc3!? ♕xd1+ 7 ♔xd1, followed by ♔c2 and ♗e3, White is a little better.

6 ♗b5+ ♘8c6

Not 6...♗d7? 7 a3! ♗xb5 8 axb4 ♗d3 9 ♕a4+ ♘c6 10 b5 ♘b4 11 b6+ ♕d7 12 ♕xd7+ ♔xd7 13 ♖xa7 ±.

7 d4!

White must hurry as Black was threatening to release the pressure with ...a7-a6.

7...cxd4

Or 7...a6 8 ♗xc6+ ♘xc6 9 d5 ±.

8 a3!

Not 8 ♘xd4?? ♕xd4! –+.

8...dxc3 9 ♕xd8+ ♚xd8 10 axb4 cxb2

After 10...♘xb4? 11 bxc3 ♘c2+ 12 ♚e2 ♘xa1 13 ♖d1+ ♚c7 14 ♗f4+ ♚b6 15 ♖b1! White has a winning attack.

11 ♗xb2

White's attack should not be underestimated. For example, if **11...♘xb4**, then 12 ♚e2, followed by ♖fd1 and ♖ac1, is curtains for Black. Black has to neutralize the bishop on b2 in order to develop. But not with **11...f6?!** in view of 12 e5! ♗g4 13 ♗xc6 bxc6 14 ♘d4! and things have only got worse. Best for Black is **11...e6!** 12 0-0 f6 13 e5 f5 with mutual chances.

A3. 1 c4 c5 2 ♘f3 ♘f6 3 ♘c3 ♘c6 4 d4!? cxd4 5 ♘xd4

5...e6!?

5...g6 6 e4 ♗g7 7 ♗e3 again leads to the Maroczy Variation of the Sicilian, while White has a slight advantage after 5...d5 6

cxd5 ♘xd5 7 ♘xc6 bxc6 8 ♗d2!? ±.

6 a3!?

Nowadays this line (preventing ...♗b4) is the most fashionable. On 6 ♘db5 both 6...♗b4 7 a3 (7 ♘d6+? ♚e7) 7...♗xc3+ 8 ♘xc3 d5 and 6...d5 7 ♗f4 (7 cxd5 ♘xd5 8 ♘xd5 exd5 9 ♕xd5 ♗b4+ 10 ♗d2 ♕e7! and 0-0, ♖d8 ∓) 7...e5 8 cxd5 exf4 9 dxc6 bxc6 10 ♕xd8+ ♚xd8 come into consideration. The other major alternative is 6 g3. Now a characteristic line is 6...♕b6!? 7 ♘bd5 ♘e5! 8 ♗g2 a6 9 ♕a4 ♘ge4! 10 0-0 ♖b8 11 ♘a3 ♗c5! and 12...0-0 =.

6...♘xd4!?

Those who are not afraid of an isolated pawn might try 6...d5 7 cxd5 exd5 followed by ...♗e7 and ...0-0, but 6...♕b6?! is wrong, as after 7 ♘b3 the black queen obstructs the development of the queenside. But 6...♗c5! is tried and tested: 7 ♘b3 ♗e7 8 e4 0-0 9 ♗e2 b6 10 0-0 ♗a6 11 ♗f4 d6 12 ♖e1 ♘e5 13 ♘d2 ♖c8 14 b3 ♘g6 15 ♗g3 ♗b7 with a hedgehog-like set-up.

7 ♕xd4 b6 8 ♗f4 ♗c5 9 ♕d2 0-0 10 ♖d1 ♗b7 11 ♗d6 ♗xd6 12 ♕xd6 ♖c8 *(D)*

White offsets the troublesome bishop on b7 with e2-e3, f2-f3, ♗e2 and 0-0, while Black counterbalances White's pressure on the d-file with ...♖c6 and an attack on the pawn on c4 with ...♗a6 or by carrying out the move the ...d7-d5-break (...♕a8, ...d7-d5).

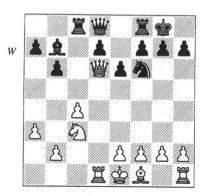

A4. 1 c4 c5 2 ♘f3 ♘f6 3 ♘c3 ♘c6 4 g3

For 4 e3 e6 5 d4 d5 see the Tarrasch Variation of the Queen's Gambit.

4...d5!

The best moment.

5 cxd5 ♘xd5 6 ♗g2 ♘c7

This prepares ...e7-e5, which is wrong at the moment on account of ♘xe5 and the knight on d5 is hanging. But a good alternative is 6...g6 7 0-0 ♗g7 8 ♘xd5 ♕xd5 9 d3 0-0 10 ♗e3 and now besides 10...♗d7, another possibility is 10...♗xb2 11 ♖b1 ♗g7 12 ♘d4 ♕xa2 13 ♘xc6 bxc6 14 ♗xc6 ♗h3 15 ♗xa8 ♖xa8 16 ♗xc5! (16 ♖e1 ♗c3 =). The latter position can also be found in section A5 with colours reversed and of course with a different move number!

7 0-0

On 7 a3, it is best to switch with 7...g6 as 7...e5? is met by 8 b4! cxb4 9 axb4 ♗xb4 10 ♘xe5 ♘xe5 11 ♕a4+ ♘c6 12 ♗xc6+ and 13 ♕xb4. The set-up of ...♘c7

and ...♗g7 might also allow the manoeuvre ...♘e6-d4.

7...e5 8 d3 ♗e7 9 ♘d2 ♗d7 10 ♘c4 0-0! 11 ♗xc6 ♗xc6 12 ♘xe5 ♗e8

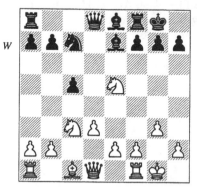

Black's bishop pair and White's loose king position offer compensation for the sacrificed pawn, but first he will have to chase away the knight from e5 to invade the light squares. White, in turn, can darn his kingside holes with f2-f3 and ♗e3.

A5. 1 c4 c5 2 ♘f3 ♘f6 3 ♘c3 ♘c6 4 g3 g6 5 ♗g2 ♗g7 6 0-0 0-0 7 d4 cxd4 8 ♘xd4

8...♘xd4

The sacrifice 8...d6?! is insufficient in view of 9 ♘xc6 bxc6 10 ♗xc6 ♗h3 (10...♖b8!? followed by 11...♕a5 deserves attention) 11 ♗xa8 ♕xa8 12 f3 ♗xf1 13 ♔xf1 ♖c8 14 ♕d3! followed by ♖b1 and b2-b3, when White is fully developed. But 8...♘g4!? is interesting: 9 e3 d6 10 b3 ♘xd4 11 exd4 ♘h6

12 ♗d2! ♘f5 13 d5 ♖b8 14 ♖c1! a6 15 ♘e4! and White is on top since 15...b5? has lost its strength in view of 16 c5!

9 ♕xd4 d6 10 ♕d3 a6!

A necessity, after which, according to White's reply, Black can choose between the plans ...♖b8-b5, ...♘d7-c5 (e5) and ...♗f5, ...♕d7.

Of course now **11 b3?** is wrong due to 11...♗f5 12 e4 ♘xe4, as the rook on a1 will be hanging after the exchanges! So the bishop on c1 must develops via the other direction. Best is **11 ♗e3!?** threatening c4-c5 or ♕d2 and ♗h6, though Black can play 11...♗f5!? 12 ♕d2 ♕d7 13 ♗d4 ♗e6! 14 b3 ♗h3 = because by forcing 14 b3 Black does not allow 15 ♗xh3 ♕xh3 16 ♗xf6 ♗xf6 17 ♘d5 ♕f5 18 ♕d3 as in the meantime the rook on a1 is hanging.

B. 'Hedgehog'

In the hedgehog Black opts for the spiky pawn formation a6, b6, d6 and e6. He can obtain this either by developing the king's bishop to e7 (B1. Simple hedgehog) or, alternatively, he can fianchetto the other bishop as well (B2. Double hedgehog).

B1. Simple hedgehog

1 c4 c5 2 ♘f3 ♘f6 3 g3 b6 4 ♗g2 ♗b7 5 0-0 e6 6 ♘c3 ♗e7

Black must watch his move-order to avoid trouble on the d6-square. Usually he should start with the moves ...d7-d6 and ...♗e7 and then, according to White's plan, play ...a7-a6, ...♘bd7 and ...0-0 in the appropriate order.

7 d4

7 ♖e1 d5 8 cxd5 exd5 (8...♘xd5!?) 9 d4 0-0 10 ♗f4 ♘a6!? leads to a Queen's Indian in which the e1-rook is not especially well placed. Black's plan might be the journey ...♘a6-c7-e6.

7...cxd4

8 d5 cannot be allowed while on 7...d5 8 ♘e5 followed by ♗f4, ♖c1, d4xc5, ♕a4 and ♖fd1 is a powerful plan for White.

8 ♕xd4

Nothing is gained by 8 ♘xd4 ♗xg2 9 ♔xg2 d6 10 b3 ♕c7 11 e4 a6 12 ♗b2 ♕b7 13 ♖e1 0-0, as after ...♘c6 and ...♖fc8 Black can aim for ...b7-b5.

8...d6

Black's almost exclusive idea used to be ...d7-d6 and ...♘bd7 but nowadays 8...♘c6!? is also popular: 9 ♕f4 0-0 10 e4 d6 11

罝d1 豐b8 12 b3 匂d7 when Black has the common manoeuvres: ...a7-a6, ...罝e8, ...奧f8 and ...匂de5, etc. 8...a6? loses to 9 奧e3! 奧c5 10 豐d3 奧xe3 11 豐xe3 d6 12 罝fd1 and d6 is weakened to a fatal degree, while on 12...豐c7 13 匂d5 wins.

9 b3!?

This neat strategy (奧a3, 罝fd1 and 匂b5) is the best way to meet the 'simple hedgehog'. After the continuation 9 e4 a6 10 豐e3 匂bd7 11 匂d4 豐c7 12 b3 0-0 13 奧b2 罝fe8 a typical slow-manoeuvring hedgehog-type position arises. White centralizes his rooks while Black regroups with ...奧f8, ...g7-g6 and ...奧g7. White's plan is a slow kingside expansion whereas Black plans to strike with ...b6-b5 or ...d6-d5.

An original alternative idea is 9 奧g5!?: 9...a6 10 奧xf6 奧xf6 11 豐d3 罝a7 12 罝ad1 奧e7 13 匂d4 奧xg2 14 含xg2 豐c8 15 f4 ∞. Instead of 10 奧xf6 the move 10 匂d2!?, followed by 匂de4 with an assault on pawn d6, deserves attention.

9...匂bd7

Or 9...a6!? 10 奧a3 匂c6 11 豐f4 d5 12 奧xe7 匂xe7 13 匂e5 0-0 14 罝fd1 ±.

10 匂b5!

White may also play 10 罝d1 a6 11 e4!? 豐c7? 12 奧a3 匂c5 13 e5 dxe5 14 豐xe5! 豐xe5 15 匂xe5 ±. Instead of 11...豐c7?, better is 11...豐c8, avoiding the exchange of queens.

10...匂c5 11 罝d1 匂fe4 12 豐xg7! 奧f6 13 豐h6 奧xa1 14 匂g5!

White has sacrificed a rook but has reached a winning position! For example:

a) 14...匂xg5 15 奧xg5 f6 16 豐g7 and 17 匂c7+ +−.

b) 14...奧f6 15 匂xe4 匂xe4 16 奧xe4 奧xe4 17 匂xd6+ 含e7 18 奧a3! +−.

c) 14...奧e5 15 匂xe4 匂xe4 16 奧xe4 奧xe4 17 f4 豐f6 18 fxe5 豐xh6 19 匂xd6+ 含e7 20 奧xh6 奧g6 21 奧g5+ 含f8 22 奧f6 +−.

B2. Double hedgehog

1 c4 c5 2 匂f3 匂f6 3 g3 b6 4 奧g2 奧b7 5 0-0 g6 6 匂c3

It is difficult to make anything out of a symmetrical set-up: 6 b3 奧g7 7 奧b2 0-0 8 匂c3 d5 9 匂xd5 匂xd5 10 奧xg7 含xg7 11 cxd5 豐xd5 12 d4 匂a6! (12...cxd4? 13 豐xd4+ 豐xd4 14 匂xd4 奧xg2 15 含xg2 and White is clearly better because of the contrast between

the knights) 13 e4 ♕d6 14 d5 e6!
is equal.

6...♗g7 7 d4 cxd4 8 ♕xd4

Or 8 ♘xd4 ♗xg2 9 ♔xg2 ♕c8
followed by ...♕b7, ...a7-a6, ...♘c6
and ...0-0 =.

Plans and Counterplans:
The tempo-gaining **8...♘c6** fails
to 9 ♕f4 (9 ♕h4 h6! threatening
10...g5!) 9...♖c8 10 ♖d1 d6 11 ♗d2
and the knight on c6 would rather
be on d7 while White, following
b2-b3 and ♖ac1, can opt for ♘d5,
while after **8...0-0!?** 9 ♕h4 d6 10
♗h6 ♘bd7 11 b3 ♖c8 12 ♗xg7
♔xg7 13 ♕d4 ♔g8 14 ♖ac1 White
is again better owing to the constant threat of ♘d5 (±). After 1 c4
c5 2 ♘f3 ♘f6 3 g3 Black should
take the centre with 3...d5 – see
section D.

C. Straight Symmetry Variation

---

1 c4 c5 2 ♘c3 ♘c6

Black can continue the symmetry for a while, at least as long as

it involves natural developing
moves.

3 g3 g6 4 ♗g2 ♗g7 5 ♘f3

White does not get rid of his
'shadow' with 5 e3 e6 6 ♘ge2
♘ge7 7 0-0 0-0 8 d4 cxd4 9 ♘xd4
d5 10 cxd5 ♘xd4 11 exd4 ♘xd5 12
♘xd5 exd5 = or 5 a3 a6 6 ♖b1
♖b8 7 b4 cxb4 8 axb4 b5 9 cxb5
axb5 =. Likewise 5 e4 e6 6 ♘ge2
♘ge7 7 d3 d6 8 0-0 0-0 9 ♖b1 a6
10 a3 b5!? 11 cxb5 axb5 12 b4
cxb4 13 axb4 is again dull equality.

After 5 ♘f3 ♘f6 6 d4 transposes to section I, but Black is not
obliged to allow this:

C1. 5...e6 and
C2. 5...e5.

Also interesting is the possibility 5...d6 6 0-0 ♗f5 followed by
...♕d7 and ...♗h3.

**C1. 1 c4 c5 2 ♘c3 ♘c6 3 g3 g6 4
♗g2 ♗g7 5 ♘f3 e6**

6 0-0

Also possible is 6 d4!? cxd4 7
♘b5 d5 8 cxd5 ♕a5+ 9 ♕d2 ♕xb5
10 dxc6 ♕xc 11 0-0 ♕d6 12 ♖d1
e5 13 e3 ♘e7 =.

**6...♘ge7 7 d3 0-0 8 ♗d2 d5 9
a3 b6**

Not 9...d4 10 ♘a4! and 11 b4
with a frightful attack against the
black queenside.

10 ♖b1 ♗b7 *(D)*

The position is equal, for example **11 cxd5 exd5** (11...♘xd5 12

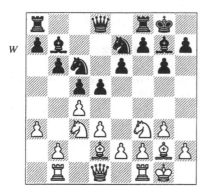

♘xd5 ♕xd5 13 ♗c3 ♖fd8 14 ♘e5
♕d6 =) 12 b4 cxb4 13 axb4 d4 14
♘a4 ♘d5 ∞ or **11 b4** cxb4 12 axb4
dxc4 13 dxc4 ♖c8 =.

**C2. 1 c4 c5 2 ♘c3 ♘c6 3 g3 g6 4
♗g2 ♗g7 5 ♘f3 e5**

**6 0-0 ♘ge7 7 a3 0-0 8 d3 d6 9
♖b1 a5**

It was again time Black that
prevented White's gain of space
with b2-b4.

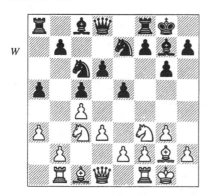

White can get moving with **10
♘e1** on the road to c2-e3-d5, but
Black can stop this just in time:

10...♗e6! 11 ♘d5 (11 ♘c2 d5)
11...♖b8 12 ♘c2 b5! 13 ♗g5 f6 14
♗d2 bxc4 15 dxc4 f5 16 ♗c3 e4 ∞.
Also fine for Black is **10 ♗d2** f5!?
11 ♕c1 ♔h8 12 ♗h6 ♗e6 13
♗xg7+ ♔xg7 14 ♘g5 ♗g8 15 f4
h6 16 ♘f3 exf4 17 gxf4 b6 18 ♕d2
d5.

IV. Sicilian Reversed

1 c4 e5

This is the mirror image – or
'reversed' position – of the Sicilian (1 e4 c5). The striking difference is that in the English the one
who plays the Sicilian is on the
move and this tempo difference
may well be significant in the
sharper variations, such as the
'Reversed Dragon'. Black therefore usually prefers rather more
peaceful systems, for example the
Closed Sicilian or a transposition
into the Scheveningen. In the 'Sicilian Reversed' Black should
only undertake sharp lines if he is
thoroughly prepared for the con-
sequences..

The material in this section is
divided into:

A. English sidelines viz. devia-
tions prior to the 'Four Knights
Variation',
B. Four Knights Variation viz.
1 c4 e5 2 ♘c3 ♘f6 3 ♘f3 ♘c6,
C. Closed Sicilian Reversed
viz. 1 c4 e5 2 ♘c3 ♘c6 3 g3 g6 4
♗g2 ♗g7.

A. English sidelines

1 c4 e5 2 ♘c3

The usual move here. Other possibilities are:

a) 2 ♘f3?! e4! 3 ♘d4 ♘c6!? 4 ♘xc6 dxc6 followed by ...♘f6, ...♗c5(d6), ...♗f5 and ...♕e7 and after castling kingside – or queenside – Black is more active.

b) 2 g3 c6!? 3 d4!? ♗b4+! 4 ♗d2 ♗xd2+ 5 ♕xd2 d6! with an equal position.

After **2 ♘c3** we come to a major cross-roads: besides the two thoroughfares

A1. 2...♘c6 and
A2. 2...♘f6.

The byways are:

a) 2...f5?! 3 d4! e4 (3...exd4 4 ♕xd4 ♘c6 5 ♕e3+!? ♕e7 6 ♘d5! ±) 4 f3! and White undermines the black outpost, e.g. 4...exf3 5 exf3!? and White's vision is ♗d3, ♘ge2, ♗f4 (♗g5), ♕c2, a2-a3 and 0-0-0.

b) 2...g6?! 3 d4! d6 4 dxe5 dxe5 5 ♕xd8+ ♔xd8 6 f4!? and Black has problems finding a safe place for his king while White can develop with a vengeance via ♘f3, ♗d2 and 0-0-0.

c) 2...♗b4!? 3 ♘d5 ♗c5!? 4 ♘f3 (4 b4!?) 4...c6 5 ♘c3 ♕e7 and Black has lost a tempo with the bishop but White has lost two with his knight! Later Black can play for ...♘f6, ...d7-d6 (...d7-d5!?) and ...0-0.

d) 2...d6!? 3 ♘f3 (3 d4 exd4 4 ♕xd4 ♘f6 5 g3 ♘c6 6 ♕d2 ♗e6 7 ♘d5 ♘e5! 8 b3 ♘e4! 9 ♕e3 ♘c5 and Black is threatening 10...c6, after which his queen can even set its sights on a5!) 3...f5!? 4 d4 e4 5 ♘g5 ♘f6 6 ♘h3 (White is planning to build a stable for the knight with ♘f4 and h2-h4) 6...♗e7 7 ♘f4 c6 8 h4 0-0 9 e3 ♘a6! with an unclear position in which Black will increase his control over the important e6-square with the unusual manoeuvre ...♘a6-c7.

A1. 1 c4 e5 2 ♘c3 ♘c6

3 ♘f3 g6

This move comes at a better moment than the previous move as after 4 d4 cxd4 the white queen cannot go to d4 to profit from the momentary weakness of Black's long-diagonal.

Also interesting is 3...f5 4 d4 e4 5 ♘e5!? (5 ♘g5 ♗b4!? 6 ♘h3 ♘f6 7 e3 ♗xc3+ 8 bxc3 d6 ∞ or 5 ♗g5!? ♗e7 6 ♗xe7 ♘cxe7 7 ♘g1!?, followed by e2-e3, h2-h4 and ♘h3) 5...♘xe5 6 dxe5 d6 7 ♗f4!? g5 8 e3 gxf4 9 ♕h5+ ♔d7 10 ♕xf5+ ♔e8 11 ♕xe4 and White's attacking chances outweigh Black's extra piece.

4 d4! exd4 5 ♘xd4 ♗g7 6 ♘xc6 bxc6 7 g3 ♘e7 8 ♗g2 d6

Another idea is 8...0-0 9 0-0 ♖b8 10 ♕c2 ♘f5 and then ...♕e7-b4.

White stands somewhat better: 9 ♗g5! f6 10 ♗d2 ♗e6 11 c5! 0-0

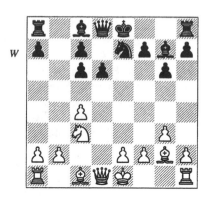

12 cxd6 cxd6 13 0-0 ± and Black still has to coordinate his pawns and pieces.

A2. 1 c4 e5 2 ♘c3 ♘f6

3 g3
The question might occur to the reader: why is White trying to play g2-g3 before all the knights are developed? There is a good reason for this. For example, on 3...♗b4 4 ♗g2 ♘c6 5 ♘d5 Black does not have 5...e4, which he could play if the knight was already standing on f3.
3...c6!?
3...g6?! is less promising: 4 d4! exd4 5 ♕xd4 ♘c6 6 ♕e3+ ♕e7 7 ♗g2 d6 8 ♘d5!? ±, but Black's best is 3...d5 4 cxd5 ♘xd5 5 ♗g2 ♘b6 6 ♘f3 ♘c6 with a transposition to section II.
4 ♘f3!?
The most critical move. Less testing are:
a) 4 ♗g2?! d5 5 cxd5 cxd5 6 ♕b3 ♘c6! 7 ♘xd5 ♘d4 and Black seizes the initiative.

b) 4 d4 exd4 5 ♕xd4 d5 6 cxd5 cxd5 7 ♗g5 ♗e7 =.
4...e4 5 ♘d4 d5 6 cxd5 cxd5
Or 6...♕b6!? 7 ♘b3 a5 8 d4 cxd5 9 ♗g2 ♗e7 10 0-0 0-0 11 ♗g5 with a slight plus for White.
7 d3! ♗c5 8 ♘b3 ♗b4 9 dxe4 ♘xe4 10 ♗d2 ♕b6 11 ♘xe4 dxe4 12 ♗xb4 ♕xb4+ 13 ♕d2 ♕e7!?
Not 13...♕xd2+ 14 ♔xd2 ± with a nearly lost endgame for Black. White might follow up with ♔e3, ♖ac1 and ♘c5.
14 ♗g2 0-0 15 0-0 ±.

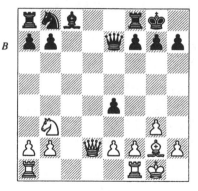

White is better as he can rapidly occupy the open files (♕e3, ♖ac1, ♖fd1, ♘c5 or ♘d4), while Black's over-extended pawn on e4 needs constant nursing (±).

B. Four Knights Variation

1 c4 e5 2 ♘c3 ♘f6 3 ♘f3 ♘c6
Here White usually opts for one of two kinds of Sicilian set-ups:

B1. Paulsenlike and
B2. Dragonlike.

Other conceptions:

a) 4 d4 exd4 5 ♘xd4 ♗b4 6 ♗g5 h6 7 ♗h4 ♗xc3+ 8 bxc3 d6 9 f3 ♘e5! 10 e4 ♘g6 11 ♗f2 0-0 12 ♕d2 c6 13 ♗e2 d5! =.

b) 4 e4 ♗b4 (4...♗c5 5 ♘xe5! ♗xf2+ 6 ♔xf2 ♘xe5 7 d4 ±) 5 d3 d6 6 g3 0-0 7 ♗g2 ♘e8 and Black will aim for ...♗xc3 and ...f7-f5.

c) 4 d3 d5!? (4...♗b4 is wrong here, as after 5 ♗d2 White will force ...♗xc3 with a2-a3 and re-capture with the bishop) 5 cxd5 ♘xd5 6 e3 ♗e7 7 ♗e2 ♗e6 8 0-0 0-0 and later Black can play a normal Scheveningen with colours reversed after ...f7-f5, ...♔h8 and ...♕e8-g6, with balanced chances. 4...d5 was made possible by the enclosure of the bishop on f1 as White did not get the chance to indirectly attack Black's centre (the pawn on e5) with ♗f1-b5.

d) 4 a3!? is a cunning move, as on 4...d5?! 5 cxd5 ♘xd5 6 ♕c2 ♗e7 7 e3! White switches to a Paulsen-like game in which he is threatening 8 ♗b5, after which serious problems arise with the pawn on e5, and d2-d4 has become possible. This is not prevented by 7...♘xc3 since after 8 ♕xc3 White again has too many threats: ♗b5 or b2-b4, ♗b2 and b4-b5. Therefore on 4 a3!?, correct is 4...g6! 5 g3 ♗g7 6 ♗g2 0-0 7 0-0 d6 (7...♖e8 8 e4! d6 9 h3! and Black has obtained neither ...e5-e4 nor ...♗g4) 8 d3 ♘d4! 9 ♘d2 c6 10 b4 ♗e6, followed by ...♕d7 and ...Black has equalized.

B1. Paulsenlike

1 c4 e5 2 ♘c3 ♘f6 3 ♘f3 ♘c6 4 e3

In this way, White prohibits 4...d5?!: 5 cxd5 ♘xd5 6 ♗b5! ♘xc3 7 bxc3 ♗d6 8 d4 ±.

4...♗b4!?

More or less the only sufficient method for Black. White cannot allow Black to capture c3 as then he would have to recapture with the pawn and his bishop on c1 would have difficulties joining the game behind the pawns on e3 and c3.

5 ♕c2

5 ♘d5 has been suffering from rough times lately: 5...e4 6 ♘g1 (or 6 ♘xb4 ♘xb4 7 ♘d4 c5 8 ♘b5 d5 9 cxd5 0-0 10 a3 ♘d3+ 11 ♗xd3 exd3, threatening 12...♕xd5 followed by ...♕g5 and ...♗h3) 6...0-0 7 a3 ♗d6 8 ♘e2 ♖e8 9 ♕c2 and 9...b6 and then ...♗b7 is strong, but even better is 9...b5! 10 ♘xf6+ ♕xf6 11 cxb5?! ♘e5 12 ♕xe4 ♗b7! and on 13 ♕xb7 ♘d3+ and ♘xf2+ while on 13 ♕c2 ♘g4! is winning. Of course White should not capture on b5 but then Black takes control with ...♗b7 and ...♘e5.

5...♗xc3!

Or 5...0-0 6 ♘d5 ♖e8 7 ♕f5!? ∞.

6 ♕xc3 ♕e7 7 a3 d5 8 cxd5 ♘xd5 9 ♕b3 ♘b6 10 d3

Plans and Counterplans:

White now completes his development with ♗e2 and 0-0 and then opts for a queenside expansion

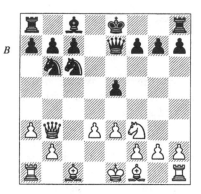

with ♛c3 and b2-b4. This must be obstructed by ...a7-a5, when Black may exert pressure on both the b3-square (...a5-a4 and ...♗e6) and the d3-pawn along the d-file.

B2. Dragonlike

1 c4 e5 2 ♘c3 ♘f6 3 ♘f3 ♘c6 4 g3
There are two common moves:

B2a. 4...♗b4 and
B2b. 4...d5.

And the sidelines are:
a) 4...♗c5 5 ♗g2 0-0 6 0-0 d6 7 d3 h6 8 a3 a5 ∞.
b) 4...♘d4!? 5 ♗g2 (but not 5 ♘xe5? ♕e7 6 ♘d3?? ♘f3 mate!) 5...♘xf3+ 6 ♗xf3 ♗b4 7 0-0 0-0 with mutual chances.
c) 4...g6?! 5 d4! exd4 6 ♘xd4 ♗g7 7 ♗g2 0-0 8 0-0 ♖e8 9 ♘xc6 bxc6 10 ♗f4 ♖b8 11 ♕d2 followed by b2-b3 and ♖ad1 ±.

B2a. 1 c4 e5 2 ♘c3 ♘f6 3 ♘f3 ♘c6 4 g3 ♗b4

5 ♗g2
Or 5 ♘d5!? e4 6 ♘h4 0-0 7 ♗g2 ♖e8 8 0-0 d6 9 d3 exd3 10 ♕xd3 ♘e5 11 ♕c2 ♘xd5 12 cxd5 ♗c5 13 b3 and White has the option of a central pawn-roller while Black's c-pawn is restrained (±).
5...0-0 6 0-0 e4
Alternatively, 6...♖e8 7 ♘d5 ♘xd5 8 cxd5 ♘d4 9 ♘xd4 exd4 10 e3! ±.
7 ♘g5!
Or 7 ♘e1 ♗xc3 8 dxc3 h6! – a provision against ♗g5 – followed by ...♖e8, ...b7-b6 and ...♗b7 =.
7...♗xc3 8 bxc3
One should always recapture towards the centre if possible!
8...♖e8 9 f3!

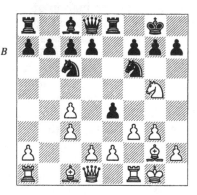

Plans and Counterplans:
White would like to open up the centre for his bishops and centre pawns. However, Black can set a positional trap with **9...e3!?**, as after 10 dxe3 b6 11 f4 h6 12 ♘f3 ♗b7 he is better as White's pawns are worthless and the bishops are inactive. Therefore correct is 10

d3! d5 11 ♕b3! ♘a5 12 ♕a3 and after 12...c6 13 cxd5 cxd5 14 f4! ♗g4 15 ♖e1 ♘c6 16 ♖b1 White's bishops offer him the better position as things open up. Later he can play ♗b2, ♘f3 and c3-c4.

After **9...exf3** 10 ♘xf3 White's strategy might be e2-e3 and ♘d4 or d2-d3 and ♗g5. On 10...d5 11 d4! dxc4 12 ♗g5 White is threatening 13 ♗xf6 ♕xf6 14 ♘e5.

B2b. 1 c4 e5 2 ♘c3 ♘f6 3 ♘f3 ♘c6 4 g3 d5!?

It is a difficult decision as to whether to undertake an Open Sicilian here. Naturally, due to the lack of tempo, Black will have to opt for a modest set-up.

5 cxd5 ♘xd5 6 ♗g2 ♘b6
Practically the only move as White was threatening 7 ♘xe5, when the knight on d5 is hanging. 6...♗e6?! is wrong due to 7 0-0 and on 7...f6 8 d4!; on 7...♗e7 also 8 d4!; while on 7...♗c5 either 8 ♘xe5 followed by 9 d4 or 8 d3 (threatening 9 ♘g5) 8...f6 9 ♕b3! (threats are 10 ♕xb7 and 10 ♘xe5) and White has a big advantage.

7 0-0 ♗e7 8 a3
White's general plan is a2-a3, b2-b4, d2-d3, ♗e3 and ♘e4-c5, harassing Black's queenside pawns. A couple of interesting alternatives are:

a) 8 d3 0-0 9 ♗e3 ♗e6 10 ♕c1 ♘d5!? 11 ♖d1 ♖e8 12 ♘e4 ♘xe3 13 fxe3 ♖b8! 14 ♘c5 ♗d5 15 e4 ♗xc5+ 16 ♕xc5 ♗e6 =.

b) 8 ♖b1 g5!? 9 d3 h5 10 a3 h4 11 b4 hxg3 12 hxg3 ♕d6! 13 ♘b5 ♕h6 14 ♘xc7+ ♔d8 15 ♘xa8 ♘xa8 and Black has a fairy-tale attack to compensate him for the loss of material but of course White is not without chances either. For example, on the aggressive ...♗h3 he might answer ♘h4!

8...0-0
8...a5? is a weakening move, as when White plays 9 d3 0-0 10 ♗e3 ♗e6 11 ♘a4 ♘xa4 12 ♕xa4 the rooks arrive on the c-file; often they will just take on c6!

9 b4

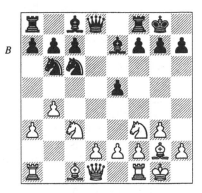

Plans and Counterplans:
On **9...♗e6** White plays 10 ♖b1 with the threat of 11 b5 ♘d4 12 ♘xe5 and at the same time protecting the b3-square. So best for Black is 10...f6 11 d3 a5! 12 b5 ♘d4, e.g. 13 ♘d2 ♗d5!? (13...♘d5? 14 ♗xd5! ♗xd5 15 e3 and 16 e4, winning a piece) 14 ♘xd5 ♘xd5 ∞. Note that here Black does well to force b4-b5 before playing ...♘d4, since this reduces the queenside

tension and means that the white pawns become somewhat more vulnerable. Black's other try is 9...♖e8 10 b5?! ♘d4 11 ♘xe5 ♗f6 12 ♘f3?? ♘xe2 −+. On 10 d3 ♗f8, Black's plan is again 11...a5 12 b5 ♘d4. Compared to the previous set-up (...♗e6, ...f7-f6) the drawback is that Black has not yet solved the problem of developing the bishop on c8 or the defending the pawn on b7. White does not capture knight on d4 but sidesteps it with ♘d2 and then chases it away with e2-e3. Then he pursues his play against the black queenside.

C. Closed Sicilian Reversed

1 c4 e5 2 ♘c3 ♘c6 3 g3 g6 4 ♗g2 ♗g7 5 d3

5 ♖b1 prepares for the advance b2-b4-b5, which also increases the scope of the bishop on g2. One interesting answer is 5...a5 6 a3 f5!? 7 d3 ♘f6 8 b4 axb4 9 axb4 ♕e7 10 b5 ♘d8 and later the knight can return via e6 and c5. White can also try 5 e3!? followed by ♘ge2, which preserves the option of d2-d3 as well as d2-d4. For his part, Black can wait with ...d7-d6, ...♘ge7 and ...0-0 and then prepare for ...♗h3 with ...♗e6 and ...♕d7 or ...♗d7 and ...♕c8.

5...d6 6 ♘f3

Also playable is 6 e4, planning ♘ge2, 0-0, ♗e3, ♕d2, ♘d5 and ♘ce3 which Black can oppose with ...f7-f5, ...♘f6, ...0-0, ...♘e7!? and ...c7-c6.

6...f5!?

Also possible is 6...♘f6 7 0-0 0-0 8 ♖b1 a5 9 a3 h6!? (to prevent 10 ♗g5, which would actually endanger d5) 10 b4 axb4 11 axb4 ♗e6 12 b5 ♘e7 followed by ...♕d7, ...♗h3 and ...♖b8 if the pawn on b7 needs protection.

7 0-0 ♘f6 8 ♖b1 h6!?

Again Black plays to thwart ♗g5.

9 b4 0-0 10 b5 ♘e7 11 a4

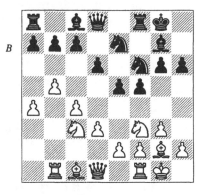

B

Plans and Counterplans:

White is planning ♘d2 and a4-a5-a6, but Black can avoid this with 11...♗e6 12 ♗a3 (12 ♘d2 d5!?) 12...♖c8 13 ♘d2 b6, and then launch an attack of his own on the kingside with ...g6-g5 and ...f5-f4. Instead of 13 ♘d2, correct is 13 c5! b6 14 cxd6 cxd6 15 ♕d2 followed by ♖fc1 with chances on the queenside.

Réti Opening

1 ♘f3 d5

Of course this move can only be played if one is ready to transpose into the Queen's Gambit after 2 d4. Non-Queen's Gambit players should start with 1...♘f6 and on 2 g3, 2...d5 as after 3 d4 c6!? White can hardly play 4 c4? in view of 4...dxc4 and then ...b7-b5.

2 g3

White may also opt for a Reversed King's Indian or Benoni with 2 c4. Then after 2...c6 3 b3 ♗g4!? 4 e3 ♘f6 5 ♗b2 e6 6 ♗e2 ♘bd7 followed by ...♗d6, ...0-0, ...a7-a5 and ...♕e7 Black can play as he would do against the Réti. Instead 2...dxc4 3 e3 c5 4 ♗xc4 e6 5 d4 leads to the Queen's Gambit Accepted. A more dynamic plan is 2...d4!? 3 e3!? c5 4 b4!? leading to a Reversed Blumenfeld Gambit.

2...c6!?

Of course Black can also play 2...♘f6, but 2...c6 distracts White from a premature c2-c4 as Black could then capture and defend with ...b7-b5.

3 ♗g2 ♘f6 4 0-0

On 4 c4 dxc4 5 ♘a3 (5 ♘e5?! ♕d4!) 5...b5 6 ♘e5 Black has the exceptional move 6...a6! (the pawn on b5 was hanging) 7 ♘xc6 ♕b6! 8 ♘xb8 (8 ♘xe7 ♗b7! −+) 8...♖xb8 and ...♗b7 =. After 4 0-0 Black would like to continue with ...e7-e6, ...♘bd7, ...♗d6 or ...♗e7 and

...0-0, but naturally he will first develop his light-squared bishop:

I. 4...♗f5 and
II. 4...♗g4.

I. 1 ♘f3 d5 2 g3 c6 3 ♗g2 ♘f6 4 0-0 ♗f5

---

5 d3

This move goes well with a future e2-e4 or c2-c4. The other line is 5 b3 e6 6 ♗b2 ♗e7 7 d3 h6 8 ♘bd2 0-0 9 ♖e1 ♗h7 10 e4 a5!? ∞.

5...e6

There is no need to fear 6 ♘h4 ♗g4 7 h3 ♗h5 8 g4 ♗g6 9 ♘d2, because after 9...♘fd7! 10 ♘xg6 hxg6 White is weak on the king's flank.

6 ♘bd2

A tricky alternative is 6 c4 h6 7 ♗e3!?, threatening 8 ♕b3 by hindering Black's protective move

8...♛b6. Should Black defend the b7-pawn with 8...♛c8 then White obtains play on the c-file with ♘c3 and ♖ac1. So on 6 c4 h6 7 ♗e3!?, best is 7...dxc4! 8 dxc4 ♛xd1 9 ♖xd1 ♘bd7 with equal chances.

6...h6

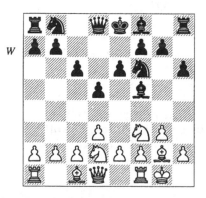

Now it becomes important to provide the bishop on f5 with sanctuary.

7 ♛e1!? ♗e7

7...♗d6? loses at once to 8 e4 followed by the fork e4-e5 and 7...♘bd7 is also a blunder: 8 e4 ♗h7 9 e5 and Black has to retreat to g8 (±). But ...♘bd7 will be playable after castling, because then the knight on f6 will have a free square on e8.

8 e4 ♗h7

Black must not swap on e4 as White could then swiftly seize the open d-file and c4-square.

9 ♛e2 0-0 (D)

Plans and Counterplans:

Black can answer **10 e5** by 10...♘fd7 with ...c6-c5 and ...♘c6

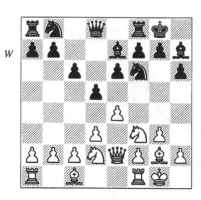

to follow. On **10 b3** the typical 'Réti' answer is 10...a5! threatening ...a5-a4. 11 a4 can be met by 11...♛b6, and then ...♛a6 with the threat of d5xe4 (there is a pin between the queens on a6 and e2!), and Black forces e4-e5. After the centre has become inflexible Black can initiate play on the queenside with ...b7-b5. On 11 a3 Black has a similar idea: ...b7-b5, ...♛b6, ...a5-a4 and ...c6-c5. It is important to withhold the b- and c-pawns until White pushes with e4-e5 as otherwise the bishop on g2 may spring to life following a possible c2-c4 and an exchange of the central pawns. White can think about ♘f3-e5 and f2-f4 or b2-b3, followed by ♗b2, c2-c4 and ♖fc1.

II. 1 ♘f3 d5 2 g3 c6 3 ♗g2 ♘f6 4 0-0 ♗g4

---

5 b3

On 5 ♘e5 Black plays 5...♗h5 and ...e7-e6, ...♗d6, ...0-0 and ...♘bd7, while 5 d3 gives Black a chance to carry out 5...♘bd7 6

♘bd2 e5 followed by ...♗d6, ...0-0 and ...♖e8 =.

5...♘bd7 6 ♗b2 e6 7 h3 ♗h5 8 d3 ♗d6

8...♗c5!? comes into consideration as well.

9 ♘bd2 0-0 *(D)*

W

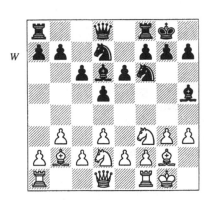

Plans and Counterplans:

One possibility now is **10 e4** e5 11 g4 ♗g6 12 ♘h4 ♖e8 13 ♘f5 ♗c7 ∞, and another interesting set-up for White is **10 c4** followed by ♖ac1-c2, ♕a1 and ♖fc1, while Black can choose from ...♕e7 and ...e6-e5 (...♗a3) or ...a7-a5 and ...b7-b5.

Rare Openings and Follies

A basic goal for White in the opening is occupation or control of the centre. Being the first to move, he can set his sights on this and right from the off he can possess a central square (1 e4, 1 d4) or control such squares (1 c4, 1 ♘f3). If White does not follow this principle he gives his opponent the chance to occupy the centre himself, and Black, though a tempo behind, can emerge as 'White'. Acceptable rare moves for White are: 1 a3, 1 b3, 1 b4, 1 d3, 1 e3, 1 c3, 1 f4, 1 g3 and 1 ♘c3.

The moves 1 a4? and 1 h4? are considered as follies, as are 1 ♘a3? or 1 ♘h3?, sidelining the knights? On these moves Black seizes the initiative and invades the centre with ...e7-e5 and ...d7-d5. Then all he has to do is develop his pieces in a natural fashion (for example with ...♘f6, ...♘c6, ...♗e7 or ...♗c5 and ...0-0) and he 'automatically' gets the advantage.

One should know that after 1 g4?!, it is dangerous to play 1...d5 2 ♗g2 ♗xg4 in view of the double attack after 3 c4 c6 4 cxd5 cxd5 5 ♕b3! and White wins back the pawn (b7 or d5). Therefore it is better to play 2...c6!? 3 h3 e5!, followed by ...♗d6 and possibly ...h7-h5!, when White's g-pawn faces an uncomfortable decision.

Among the rare openings, 1 a3, 1 ♘c3, 1 c3, 1 d3 and 1 e3 can also be answered with 1...e5 or 1...d5. Then we reach theoretical lines with colours reversed in which White's extra tempo is only sufficient for equality. Of course Black must watch that the tempo difference does not become decisive, as after 1 a3 d5 2 d4 c5?, when after 3 dxc5! e6 4 b4! Black does not regain the pawn with ...b7-b6 (as White does in the Queen's Gambit) because White has already played a2-a3. So on 1 a3 d5 2 d4, correct is 2...♘f6 and then ...c7-c6, ...♗f5, ...e7-e6, ...♗d6 and ...0-0, while 1 a3 g6!? is also not bad as it is unlikely that a2-a3 will be useful to White against Black's flank opening.

After 1 g3 d5 2 ♗g2 Black can also continue in 'Réti-style' with 2...c6!? followed by ...♘f6, ...♗f5 (or ...♗g4), ...e7-e6, ...♗d6 (or ...♗e7), ...0-0; of course 2...e5!? is also playable, and then ...♗d6, ...♘f6 and ...c7-c6; or Black can perhaps copy White's Anti-Pirc strategy with 2...e5!? and then ...♘c6, ...♘f6 and ...♗e7.

Black has to prepare more thoroughly for:

A. 1 b3
B. 1 b4 and
C. 1 f4.

These moves have interesting unique connotations and can even be recommended as an occasional weapon for White. Although the main lines (1 e4, 1 d4 and 1 c4) remain the real McCoys...

A. 1 b3

1...e5

Of course Black has many playable moves, e.g. 1...♘f6 and ...g6, ...♗g7, ...0-0 and ...d6. Or 1...c5 followed by ...d5, ...♘c6, ...e6 and ...♘f6. Besides 1...e5, the most logical move is 1...d5: 2 ♗b2 ♗g4!? 3 h3 ♗h5 4 ♘f3 (White can also play 4 d3 and then ♘bd2) 4...e6 (another good plan is 4...♗xf3 5 gxf3 e6 with ...♘f6, ...g6 and ...♗g7 = to follow) 5 e3 ♘f6 and Black can again opt for a Réti set-up with ...♗d6, ...♘bd7, ...c6, ...0-0 and ...♕e7, with equal chances.

2 ♗b2 ♘c6 3 e3

3 c4 ♘f6 4 e3 d5 5 cxd5 ♘xd5 leads to the Sicilian Reversed.

3...d5 4 ♗b5 ♗d6

Plans and Counterplans:
In accordance with his original plan, White can rely on the power of his dark-squared bishop while Black can keep the long-diagonal closed with ...f7-f6. For example 5 f4?! f6!? (also interesting is 5...♕h4+ 6 g3 ♕e7 7 ♘f3 ♗g4 8 h3 ♗xf3 9 ♕xf3 ♘f6 10 ♘c3 0-0 and now 11 ♘xd5 is wrong in view of 11...♘xd5 12 ♕xd5 ♘b4! and wins) 6 fxe5 fxe5 7 ♘f3 (7

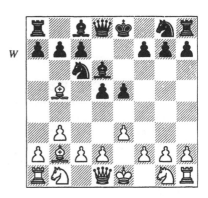

♗xe5 – based on ♕h5+ – loses to 7...♕h4+! 8 g3 ♕e4 –+) 7...♕e7 8 ♗xc6+ bxc6 9 ♘xe5 ♕h4+ 10 g3 ♕h3 11 ♕e2 ♘f6 and Black wins with the simple ...♘g4 and ...0-0. Of course White should not rip open his undeveloped kingside but should instead continue quietly with 5 ♘f3 or 5 c4!?

B. 1 b4

1...e5

The other good move is again 1...d5: 2 ♗b2 e6 3 e3 ♘f6 4 b5 c5 and Black constructs his position with ...♗e7, ...0-0, ...b7-b6, ...♗b7 and ...♘bd7.

2 ♗b2 ♗xb4

2...f6 also comes into consideration. but it is even better to maintain the f6-square for the king's knight.

3 ♗xe5 ♘f6 4 ♘f3

Or 4 c4 0-0 5 ♘f3 ♘c6 6 ♗b2 d5 7 cxd5 ♕xd5!? 8 ♗xf6 gxf6 and White's poor development is balanced by Black's scattered pawns.

4...d5 5 e3 ♗d6 6 ♗b2 c5 =.

C. 1 f4

1...e5!?

With the move f2-f4 White has weakened his vulnerable diagonal e1-h4, and From's Gambit tries to exploit this. The other line is of course 1...d5, when Black plays a Reversed Dutch with ...♘f6, ...g7-g6, ...♗g7 and ...0-0.

2 fxe5

2 e4 transposes to the King's Gambit, so the From can only be played by those who are prepared for the King's Gambit!

2...d6 3 exd6

3 e4?? is strictly prohibited owing to 3...♕h4+.

3...♗xd6

Nothing less is threatened than 4...♕h4+ 5 g3 ♗xg3+ 6 hxg3 ♕xg3 mate!

4 ♘f3 g5!?

Plans and Counterplans:
White has to do something about ...g5-g4 which, after driving the

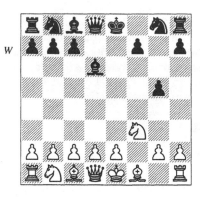

knight away, threatens ...♕h4+ and mate. White has two possibilities:

a) 5 d4 g4 6 ♘e5 (or 6 ♘g5 f5 and the threat is 7...h6) 6...♗xe5 7 dxe5 ♕xd1+ 8 ♔xd1 ♘c6 and Black can later pick from the moves ...♘xe5, ...♗e6, ...0-0-0 and ...♘e7-g6 (f5).

b) 5 g3 g4 6 ♘h4 ♘e7 (6...f5!?) 7 d4 ♘g6 8 ♘g2 (or 8 ♘xg6? hxg6 threatening 9...♗xg3+) 8...♘c6 9 c3 h5 10 e4 h4 11 e5 ♗e7 12 ♖g1 hxg3 13 hxg3 ♖h2 followed by ...♗f5 and ...♗g5, when Black has sufficient counterplay.

CPSIA information can be obtained
at www.ICGtesting.com
Printed in the USA
BVHW070113070221
599337BV00001B/93